NEW ORLEANS
IMPRESSIONIST CITYSCAPES

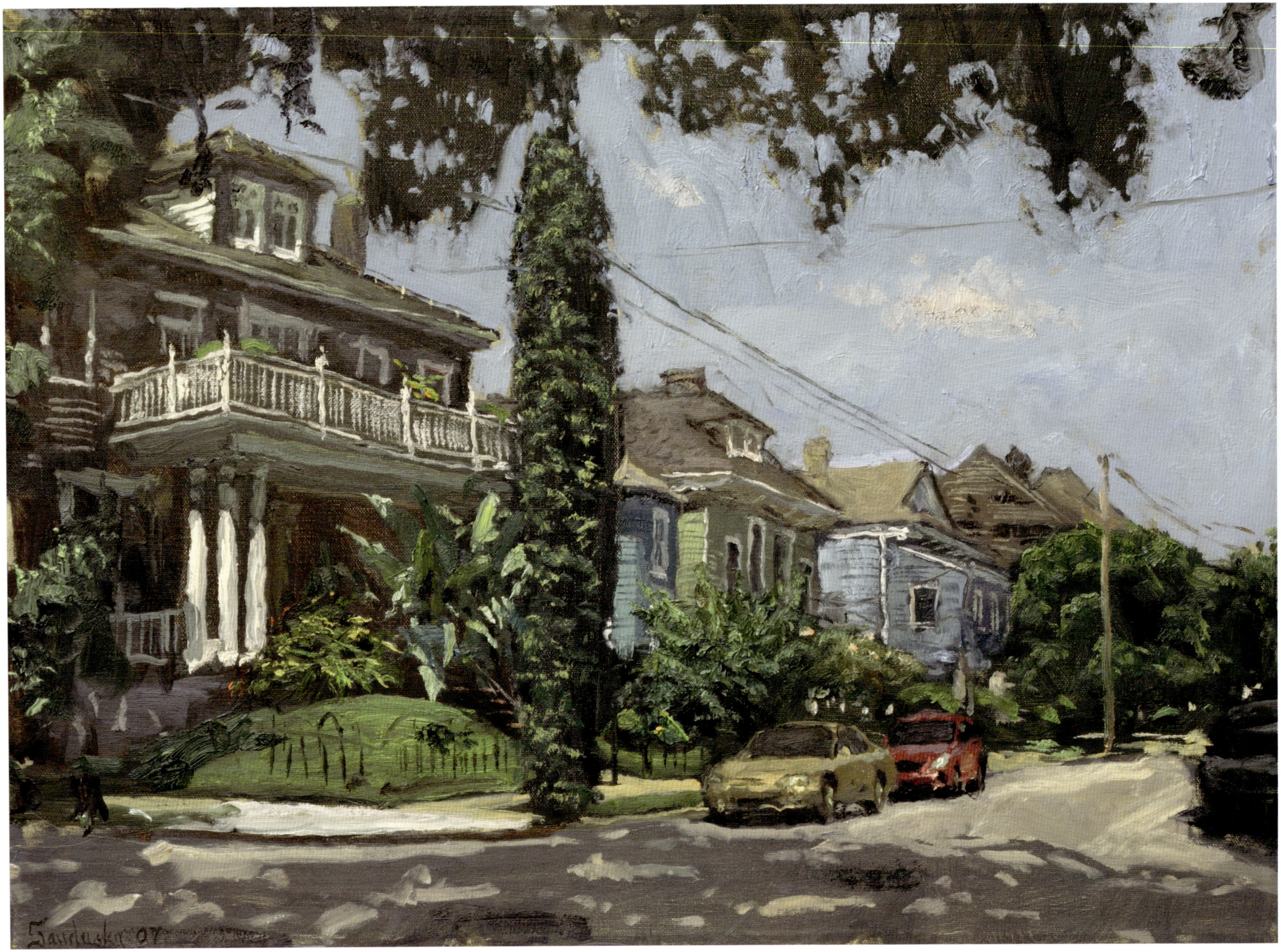

INTERSECTION OF COHN AND SHORT STREETS 18" X 24"

NEW ORLEANS
IMPRESSIONIST CITYSCAPES

PHIL SANDUSKY

PELICAN PUBLISHING COMPANY
GRETNA 2012

To my loving wife Michele and to the people who have supported my life's work by purchasing my paintings

Library of Congress Cataloging-in-Publication Data

Sandusky, Phil.
New Orleans impressionist cityscapes / Phil Sandusky.
pages cm
ISBN 978-1-4556-1680-0 (hardcover : alk. paper)—ISBN 978-1-4556-1681-7 (e-book) 1. Sandusky, Phil—Themes, motives. 2. New Orleans (La.)—In art. 3. Plein-air painting—Louisiana—New Orleans. I. Title.
ND237.S277A4 2012
759.13—dc23
2012002202

Printed in China
Published by Pelican Publishing Company, Inc.
1000 Burmaster Street, Gretna, Louisiana 70053

NEW ORLEANS
IMPRESSIONIST CITYSCAPES

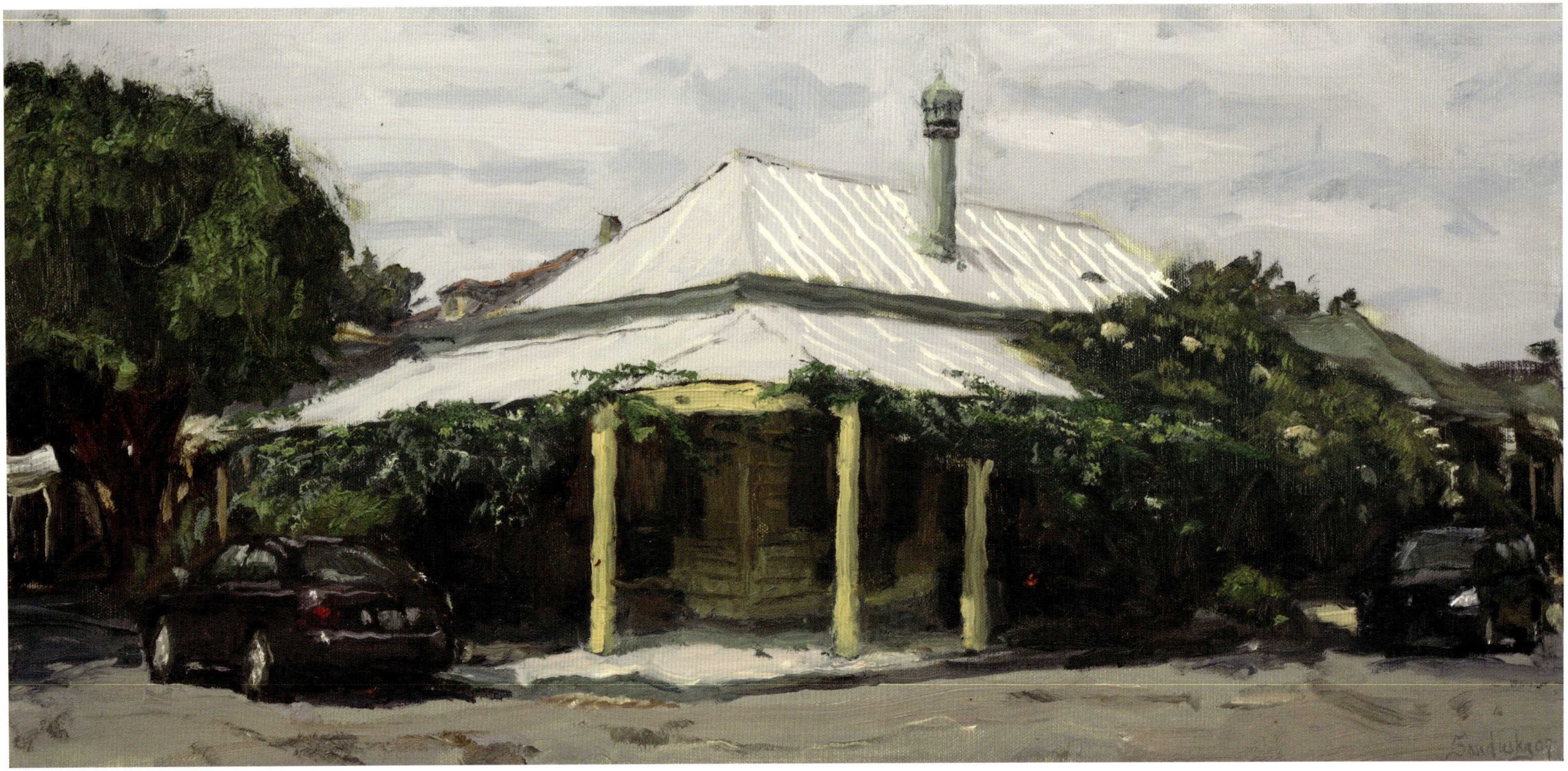

HOUSE AT THE INTERSECTION OF ARABELLA AND LAUREL STREETS 12" X 24"

Preface

When I moved to New Orleans in 1984 I was drawn to its eclectic old architecture, its lush tropical foliage, its dense atmosphere, and not least of all its rich culture. I've never since wanted to live anywhere else. As beautiful as I find New Orleans, though, I've never quibbled too much over the subject matter of my paintings. I'm more interested in the bigger issue of vision, making people appreciate what and how they see. Practically any subject is good for this. But because New Orleans is where I live and considering that I work only from life, *New Orleans* must provide my subject matter. And because I prefer to be outside like a lot of people, such as roofers and students doing their homework in the park, I am predominantly a *plein air landscape painter* by default. Furthermore, I select *where* to paint often for ancillary reasons: perhaps I have to stay close to home because of an appointment later, or maybe a vantage point from under the overhang of a corner storehouse provides convenient shelter from the rain. I might set up somewhere just because it's quiet and contemplative when I'm feeling edgy, or gravitate to busy crowded environs when I'm more sociable. I'm a little ashamed to admit that occasionally I've even chosen locations because of their proximity to little neighborhood joints where I'd like to have lunch. The steering currents that guide me to my painting destinations seem to be driven less often by subject matter, because I've come to realize that there is great potential hidden in every subject. I can't say that I'm not occasionally attracted by grand, iconic New Orleans views, but by and large, I have made an inadvertent portrait of this region with my life's work rather than one by design. I believe that such a treatment that focuses more on the ordinary can be more insightful and probing than the more common approach that emphasizes the extraordinary quintessential aspects of a subject, such as what might be shown on post cards.

In this book, as in my first book *New Orleans en Plein Air,* I have chosen a cross section of my work that makes a sweeping portrait of New Orleans as seen from out of doors. It will pick up where my last New Orleans book, *Painting Katrina* left off (about Fall 2006) and capture post-Katrina New Orleans to present. There will be a few paintings of post-Katrina rebuilding and blight, including some blight that predated Katrina, but most of the work will capture views of New Orleans that were either never significantly affected by Katrina or those that have been restored to their pre-Katrina state. Specifically, this subject matter will be different from *New Orleans en Plein Air* in the following ways: although there will be about as many paintings of Uptown and the Garden District, there will be fewer paintings of City Park and Audubon Park, none of the cemeteries, and fewer of the Mississippi River. Instead there will be more paintings of the Central Business District and many paintings of outlying areas such as Abita Springs, Fontainebleau Park, and the fishing communities of lower St. Bernard Parish—Violet, Yscloskey, and Delacroix. Instead of having quite as many paintings of the French Quarter, there will be a great many more of the Faubourg Marigny and Bywater neighborhoods. There will also be more paintings from the Esplanade Ridge, including a few of Bayou St. John, and there will be a few industrial scenes in the metropolitan area, an aspect explored only incidentally in my first book.

In *New Orleans en Plein Air* paintings were sampled over a fifteen-year period during which my style was changing. About half of the paintings in that book were executed in an earlier more fauvist style that I used to dispel a tight academic approach with which I had become fed up. The later paintings in that book are of the same academic-impressionistic style of painting that I presently employ but may *seem* different stylistically to the paintings reproduced in this and the last two books because of the way that they were photographed. Prior to converting to digital imaging in 2005, I photographed my paintings with 35mm tungsten film in warm incandescent light. Accordingly, the reproductions in the first book

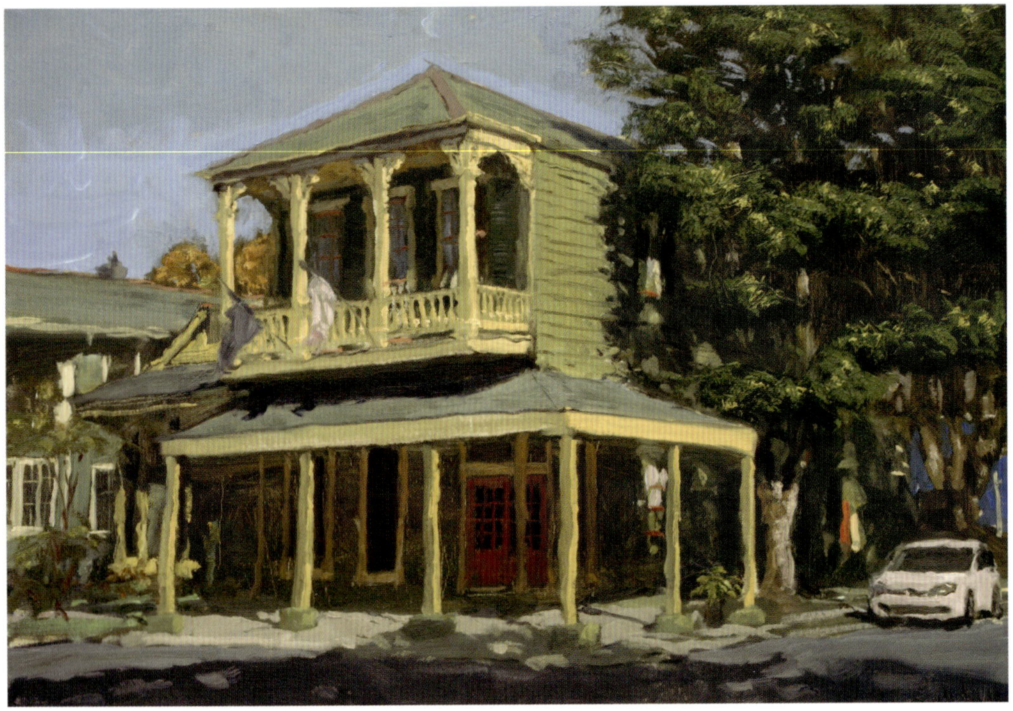

INTERSECTION OF ADAMS AND HAMPSON STREETS 18" X 24"

have a softer, warmer cast than those in my later books.

As for the text, in my books I have tried to enlighten the reader about often-overlooked aspects of art important not only to my artistic style but to representational painting in general. For the benefit of those who have collected all of my books, I have broached a unique topic each time, though the text of each book must stand alone for the benefit of those who might collect only a single book. Accordingly, there must be fibers common to each of my art book essays woven into the broader topic that bridge the text to my paintings, explaining my personal philosophy and specific style, making a succinct statement from the live subject. I hope that the quality of my paintings will lend some extra weight to my voice, where the norm seems to have always been that most people who write about art are not artists themselves.

The Allure of the Image

One of the most common art clichés is the artist with a comical Salvador Dali mustache wearing a beret and a paint-covered smock. He is holding up his thumb at arm's length in the direction of his subject, seemingly looking at it intently through one eye with the other closed, though moving it around frequently as though he is sighting a pistol at a target that is making rapid, jerky movements. This common parody of the artistic process, itself often spoofed by a large painting of a thumb, is derived from a real method that academic artists use to compare the spatial proportions of their drawings to those of the subject. Artists more often use the shaft of their pencil or the handle of their paint brush (considerably more efficient than a thumb) as an improvised measuring device called a sight stick. An artist holds the sight stick up toward the subject at arm's length and adjusts his grip such that the portion of the stick extending beyond the hand corresponds to some smaller dimension of the subject. Then he reorients the sight stick to check how many times this smaller dimension goes into some larger dimension. Next, he uses the sight stick to determine if this same proportion has been accurately rendered in the drawing. This is one of many methods that artists use to check the *accuracy* of their work.

Before photography, the primary function of representational art was documentation. It was the only way that the likenesses of deceased family members could be preserved for their descendents. On the bigger stage, in a largely illiterate world, it was the best way that societal values and historical narratives could be conveyed. The credibility and overall effectiveness of art in its documentation role was dependent not only upon how accurately narratives were conveyed, but also upon how accurately artists rendered natural forms and colors in their artwork. Although one might imagine that there were vast legions of artists who accurately documented over the centuries, the cannons of pre-photography art

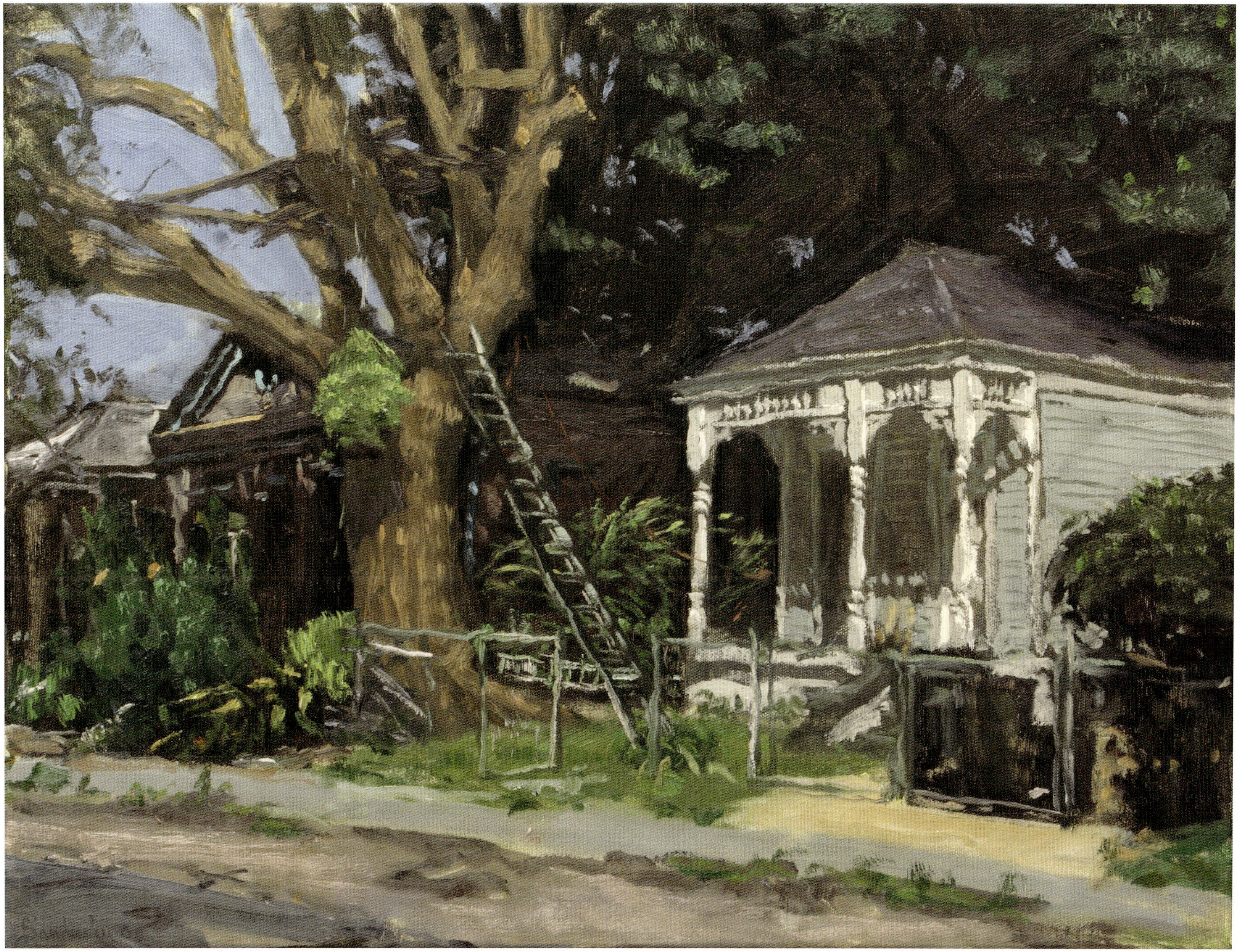

Weekend Project (Seen from Adams Street near Freret Street) 16" x 20"

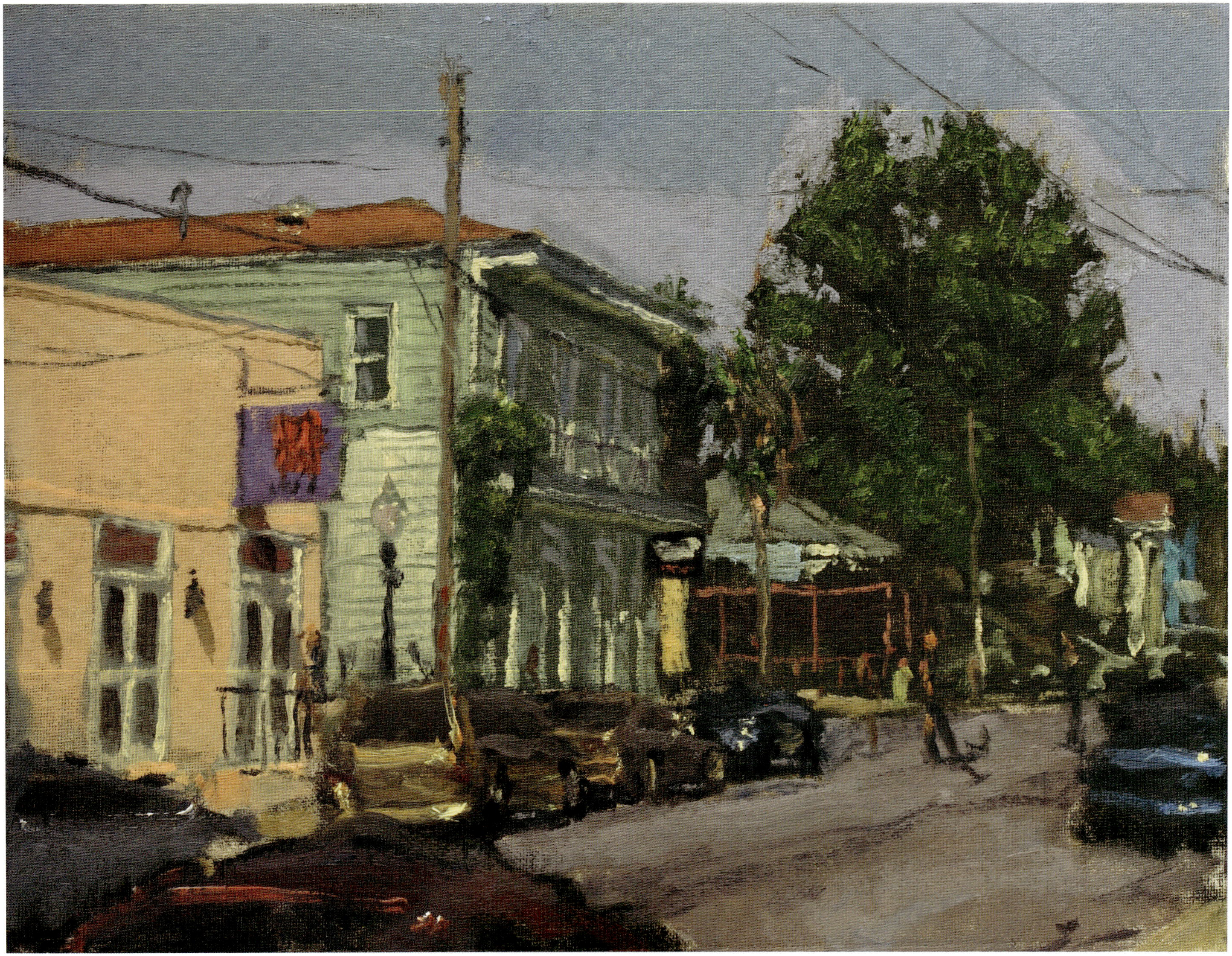

PJ's coffee shop on Maple Street between Hillary and Adams streets 11" x 14"

were formed by many hundreds to perhaps a few thousand artists such as Rafael, Rembrandt, Velázquez, Constable, Turner, and Courbet (to name but a few) whose work rose above mere accuracy to accomplish something more. These artists made paintings and drawings that seemed more alive and vibrant than most of their contemporaries. Their work communicated an individual point of view and usually seemed to have more impact as a whole when viewed from a distance, despite often having few details. This intangible high quality of the crème de la crème of representational painting we have always intuitively connected to more meaningful aspects of human vision, though we have never been able to quantify it. A mere copy of the physical image whose only purpose is correctness is boring. Dell Weller, an elder statesman of the academic painting community in New Orleans quotes Duke Ellington, "It don't mean a thing if it ain't got that swing."

This intangible higher quality of vision became a lifeboat for visual art as photography commandeered its utilitarian function of documentation. The last great movement of representational art, Impressionism, focused more upon these higher qualities of vision and provided a springboard from which entirely new art forms were launched such as Expressionism, Cubism, and Abstract Expressionism. These new movements attempted to abstract and distill the essence of human vision even further than impressionism but produced greatly generalized statements. For example, an abstraction consisting of dense, numerous streaks of red and yellow color across the canvas may evoke a general feeling of heat and crowdedness, but representational painting was still needed for the *nuance* of a specific experience or type of experience that involves heat and crowdedness. For that purpose, pared-down lineages of representational painting survived on through the twentieth century. But as the survival of representational art was becoming more dependent upon these higher qualities and less upon accuracy, accuracy still played an important role in this new era. Representational artists like Monet, Sargent, Henri, Hopper, and Freud could only deliver

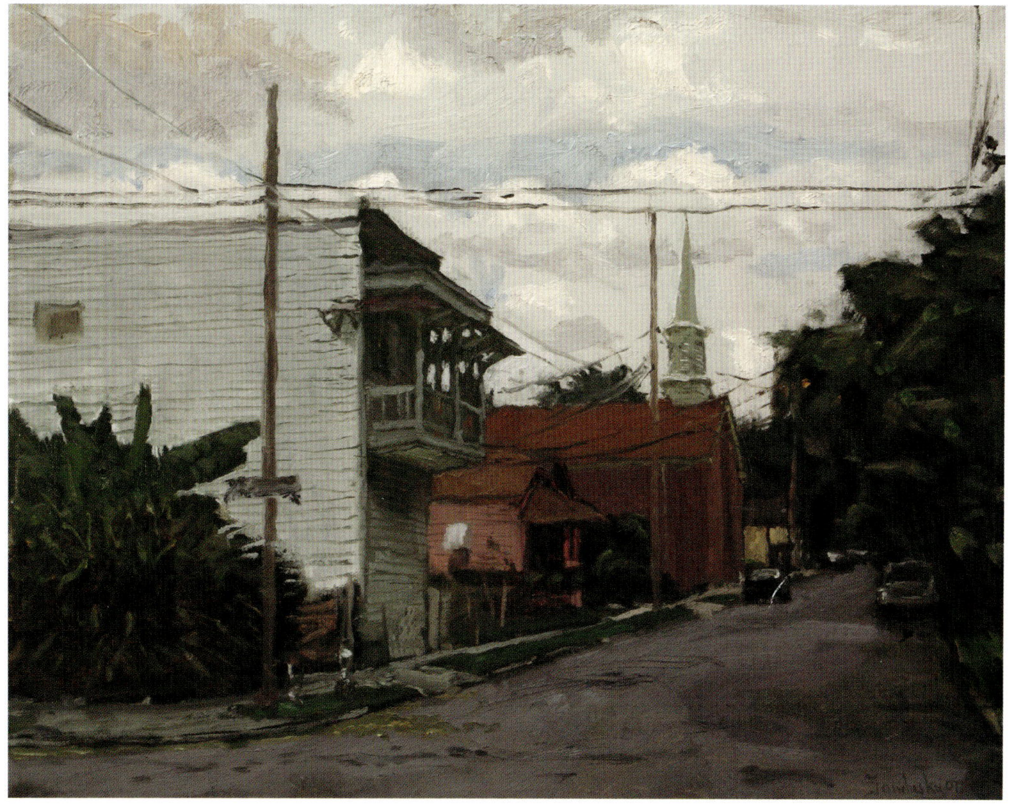

VIEW FROM THE INTERSECTION OF OAK AND BURDETTE STREETS 16" X 20"

these higher qualities with a *convincing* image. They had to learn from the objective image. They used a sight stick at certain times in their career just as did their predecessors who were more concerned with documentation. But just like the higher echelon of their predecessors, they somehow knew when to use the sight stick and when to ditch it. They knew how to walk the fine line between nuance and accuracy. They could not explain why, but they knew that what they saw was different than a photograph. Their paintings seem so accurate and real and yet every pattern, every proportion, and every color is at least a little different than that of a photographic image of the subject. We might rationalize that their paintings are just beautiful lies, but something deep within us tells us that they are the truth. No lie could be so beautiful and seem so truthful as a Lucian Freud nude or an Edward Hopper house.

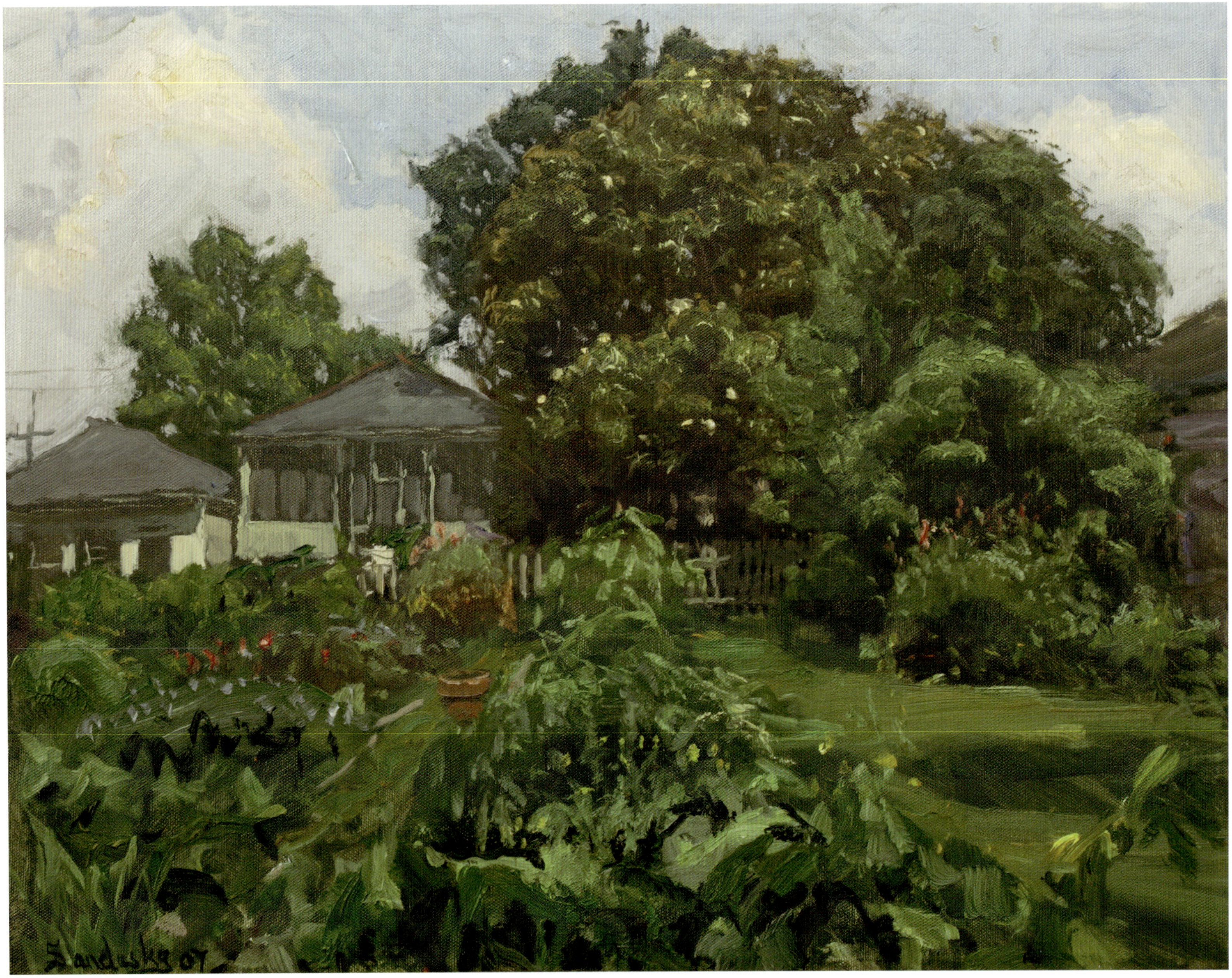

COMMUNITY GARDEN ON DANTE STREET NEAR BURTHE STREET 16" X 20"

It is clear that in this modern era representational artists are having greater difficulty jettisoning from the objective image. This has not been the case for caricaturists and cartoonists like Reginald Marsh and Dr. Seuss who blast away from objectivity with multistage rockets. But we in low earth orbit who split out the sharpest truth about what we see, we academic realists, among whom impressionists such as myself are included, are having much more difficulty than our forbearers breaking free of the objective image to make a statement that gets to the deeper truth about what we *see.* Allowing that all representational artists, in order to evoke a sense of what they see, must design an image at least somewhat similar to the objective image emanating from their subject, our predecessors were only *further* tethered to the objective image by a few little nick knacks like sight sticks, view finders, and the rare camera obscura. Unobtrusively, throughout the last century, the objective image has been gaining more allies and more gravity. Academic artists are now caught in a whirlpool of such ingredients as fine art photography, photographic references, high quality digital imaging, and less rigorous academic training. As a result there is a battle being fought in artists' minds between what they see and the cold physical image of light that focuses on the retina of the eye. The objective image, with the aid of all its new allies, is prevailing more often over vision in this era and the art world is paying a price. My goal is to make clear the measure of this price and to plot a course back to vision.

Instead of having a distinct protagonist in vision, as you might imagine, and a distinct antagonist in the image as black and white as an old fashioned Saturday afternoon matinee, in this conflict there are shades of gray more like those in the complex character developments of art films. Our first and most difficult task will be to extract and separate these two intangible combatants that are tangled up in the mind. Many academic realists understand that there is a difference between vision and the image, using terminology like "the

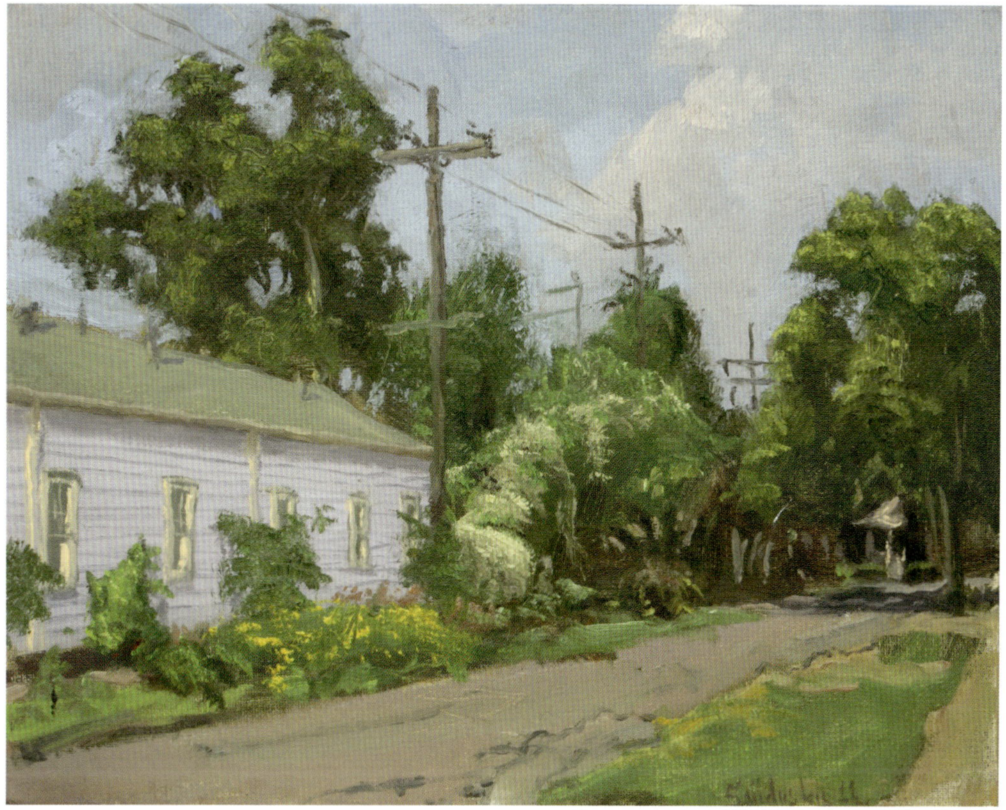

CONFEDERATE JASMINE SEEN FROM THE INTERSECTION OF FERN AND PEARL STREETS 11" X 14"

mind's eye" to make the distinction, but their understanding is only intuitive and too vague to effectively argue their point in the face of the objective image's increasing influence. A great many academic realists make no distinction between the image and what is seen, considering them in effect to be synonyms. Some hold that the image is better than vision, but as vision becomes more perfect, it converges upon the image. I heard an account of a teacher of academic realism giving a final exam consisting solely of having each student *verbally* recount everything that they saw outside of the class room in minute detail. One prominent academic realist that I know vehemently insists that what he sees is not *inside* of

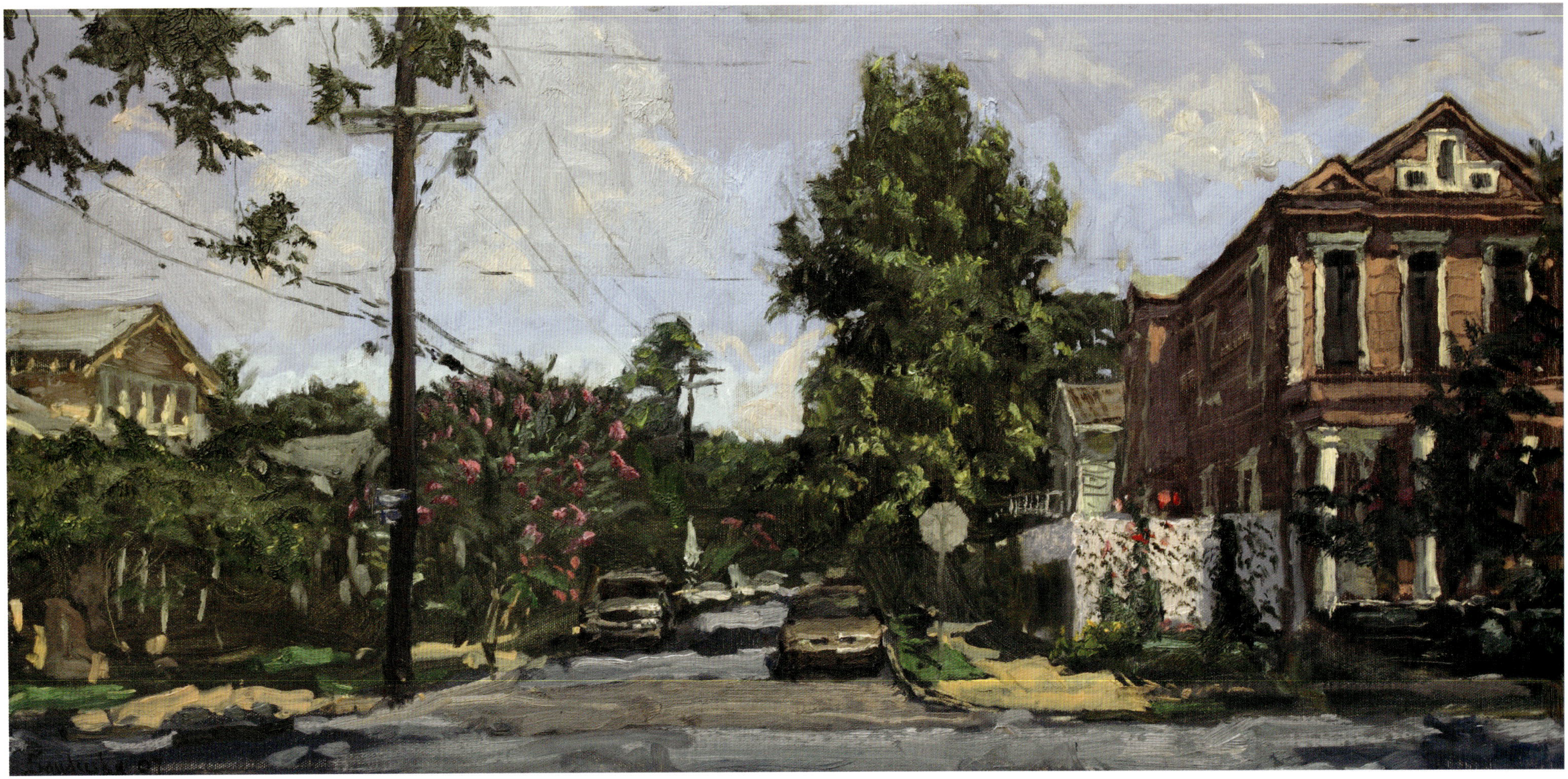

Intersection of Freret and Dublin streets 15" x 30"

his head but rather *outside* of it. Contrary to this popular misconception that vision is an imperfect image, vision is actually our response to the stimulus of the image, and some other stimuli as well, but very different from the image.

When I'm painting outdoors a compliment frequently paid to me by onlookers is that my picture looks as good as a photograph. I know that a layman means well by this, having no point of reference to understand as most artists do that a really fine painting transcends the objective physical image typically reproduced by a camera to further communicate a point of view, a poetry, a higher meaning, or in essence, *what is seen.* (This is not to demean photography as an art form. Photographers also communicate a point of view, though historically they were limited to making a statement only through composition and selection of subject matter and vantage point. Recently, with new imaging techniques, Photoshop, and Photorealist painting, the boundary between painting and photography has become a bit blurred.) In this age more than ever we are inundated with two-dimensional images in all aspects of our lives: in magazines, smartphones, TVs, the internet, signage, etc. A non-artist's favorable comparison of a painting to a photograph is understandable given that photography is by far the most common vehicle for 2D images, and that the average photograph is generally considered to be more perfect in the more common and *tangible* purpose of documentation than the average painting. Even before the industrial revolution and the advent of photography our ancestors' conceptualization of vision must have been shaped by paintings, drawings, and etchings, the primary purpose of which was also documentation. Though their experiences of 2D images were rarer than ours, the cumulative effect of images upon them was likely as great as it is with us. Then and now our visual experiences of historical events and the present world outside of our own close environs are provided more by second-hand flat images than by direct experience. In the twentieth and twenty-first centuries, photographic images have become so much a part of our life that most of us likely conceptualize what we see, our

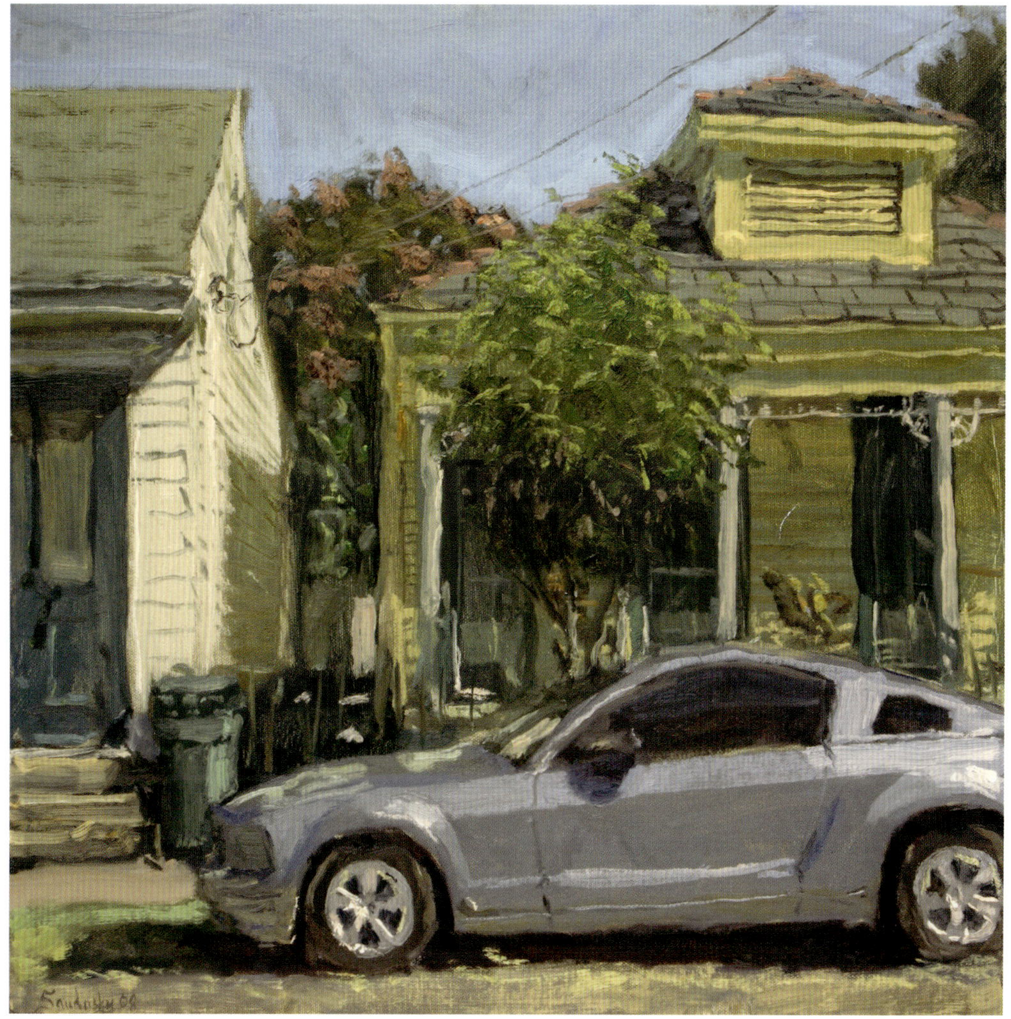

MUSTANG ON PEARL STREET BETWEEN BURDETTE AND FERN STREETS 18" X 18"

vision and visual memories, in terms of them. Because they are infinitesimally thin, we can imagine that there could be billions of them stored away in our mind.

Though we will see that this idea of vision as being like photographs is a fallacy, the photographic image has been so ingrained into our way of thinking that it must be properly contextualized as a starting point for our discussion. The image

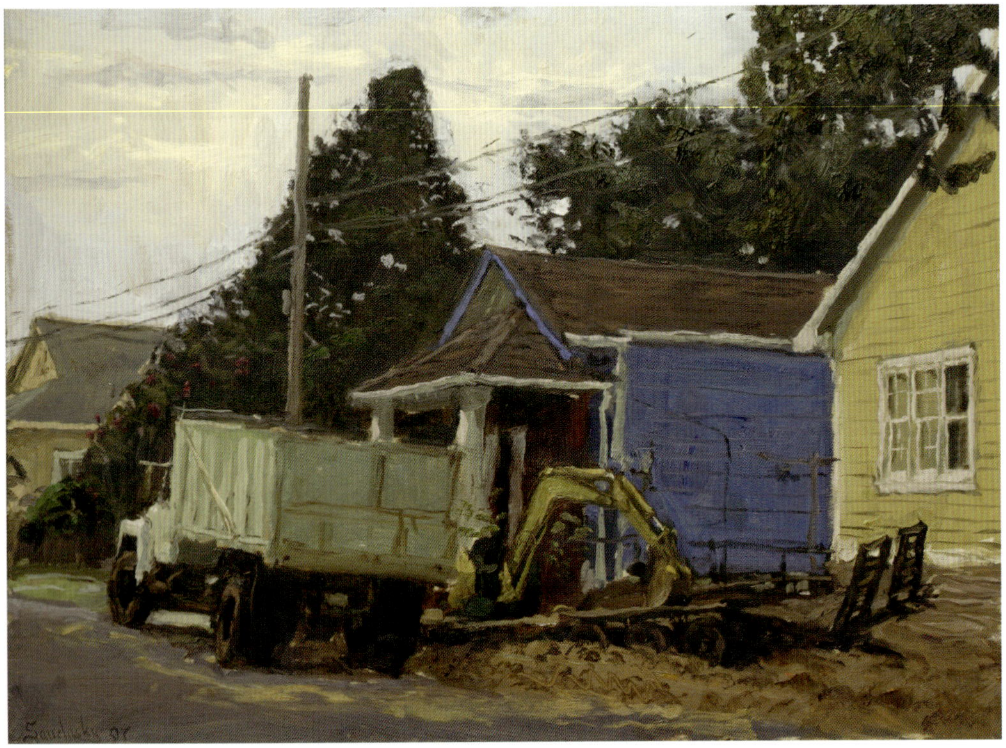

Construction at the Intersection of Burdette and Dominican Streets 16" x 20"

that enters our eye at any given time usually has much more data than a photograph, in the form of smaller details, more subtle variations in color, and *much* greater contrast. Parts of the image can be as bright as the sun causing the iris of our eye to constrict and causing us to squint or shield our eyes with our hands, and parts of it can be so dark as to be almost void of light. Conversely, the contrast within the photo has a limited range. If we were to illuminate a photograph with a very bright light both the lights and darks in the photograph would become lighter, but with no increase in contrast. A photograph usually enters our eyes as *part* of an overall image that is caused not only by light reflecting off of the photo but also off of the objects around it, such as our hands that are clasping it and objects in the background. Where a photograph has crisp edges and usually occupies only a small part of our field of vision, we are not aware of the edges of the total image that enters our eye. Every time we try to look over to see where it ends, our whole field of vision shifts. Yet, if we allow for these discrepancies, we can think of the objective image that enters our eye as being like a photograph (or perhaps two slightly different photographs if we consider our stereovision).

The Eye

Just as we have used the photograph as a familiar point of reference to conceptualize the image that enters our eye, a digital camera will provide a good starting point to discuss the function of our eye. Because light incidental to the eye or a camera comes from all directions, it does not become an image until it is focused by a lens. Instead of light being focused through the camera's lens onto a segment of film, as in old fashioned cameras, in digital cameras the image is focused onto a sensor. There are millions of small photoreceptors called photosites evenly distributed across the camera's sensor in a perfect grid. In effect, each photosite records an average color for a very small part of the overall image. The data from all photosites is captured when a photograph is taken. Later, this information is transferred as individual pixels of color onto a computer monitor or a hardcopy print arranged in exactly the same grid as the photosites were arranged on the sensor. Each photosite on the sensor directly corresponds to a pixel in the same relative location on the print or monitor. This is illustrated in the top of figure 1 (see page 18).

To a certain point, the eye is similar to a digital camera. The image from the lens of our eye is focused onto the retina, located on the inside back of the eyeball. Similar to the sensor of a digital camera, the retina contains photoreceptors called cones. Just as the density of photosites on the camera's sensor correlates to the sharpness of the print, the density of the cones on the retina correlates to our visual acuity, or

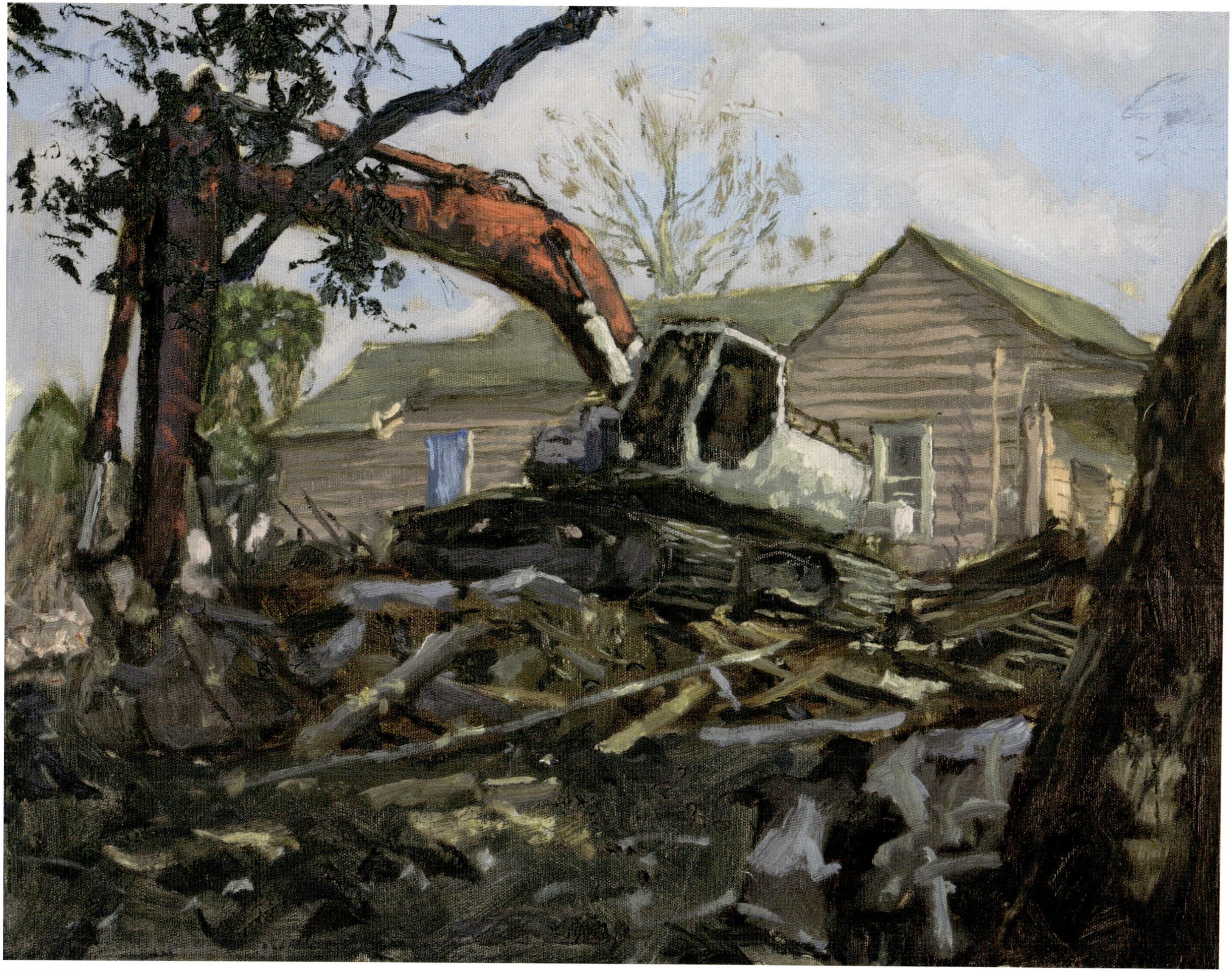

I stumbled across this amazing view of a backhoe sitting atop the wreckage of a house on Hillary Street close to Hurst Street while walking my dogs one morning. I hurried back with my gear to quickly capture it on this 16" x 20" canvas before the demolition work resumed.

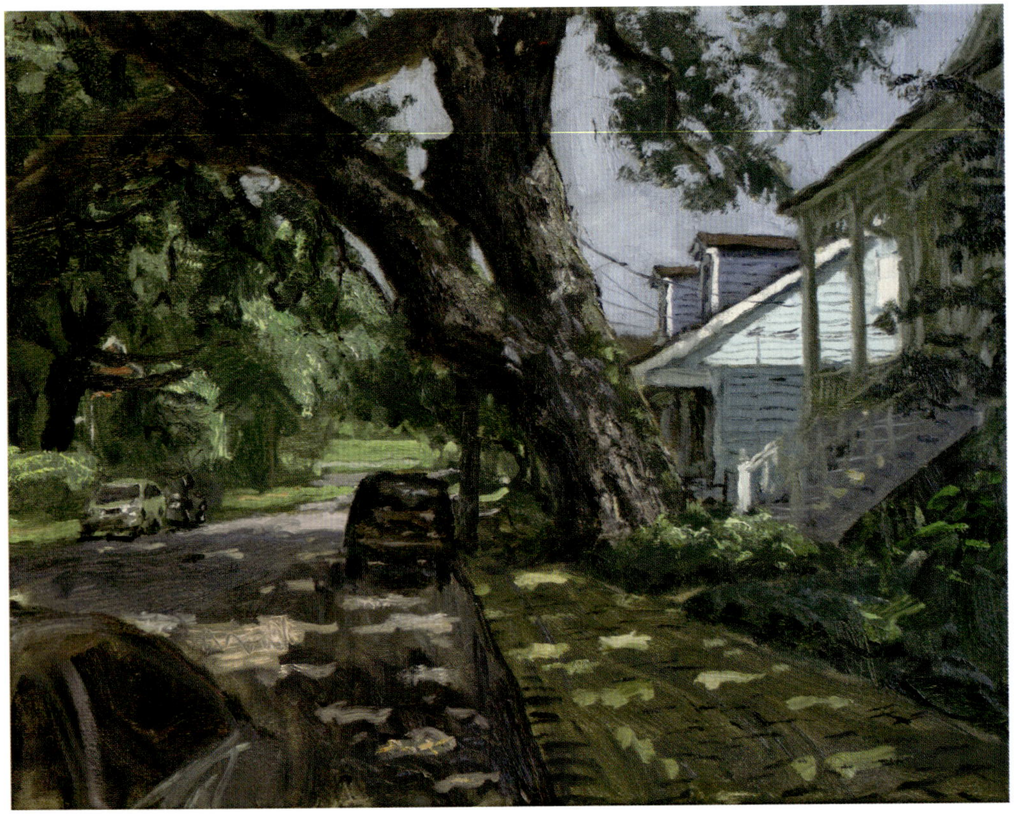

View down Dominican Street near Burdette Street looking toward the levy 16" x 20"

our ability to discern small details. The greater the density of cones, the greater is our visual acuity. It is the variation in the density of cones across the retina that provides our point of departure from the photograph-like image that has surreptitiously come to symbolize what we see.

Cones are not evenly distributed as are the photosites on the camera's sensor. Cones are densely concentrated in a small place in the center of the retina called the macula, outside of which they are more sparsely dispersed. To give you a better idea of how cone density and acuity decreases away from the macula, focus on your thumbnail when held at arm's length. The area that corresponds to your thumbnail has an average cone density that is ten times as great as the area outside of your thumbnail.

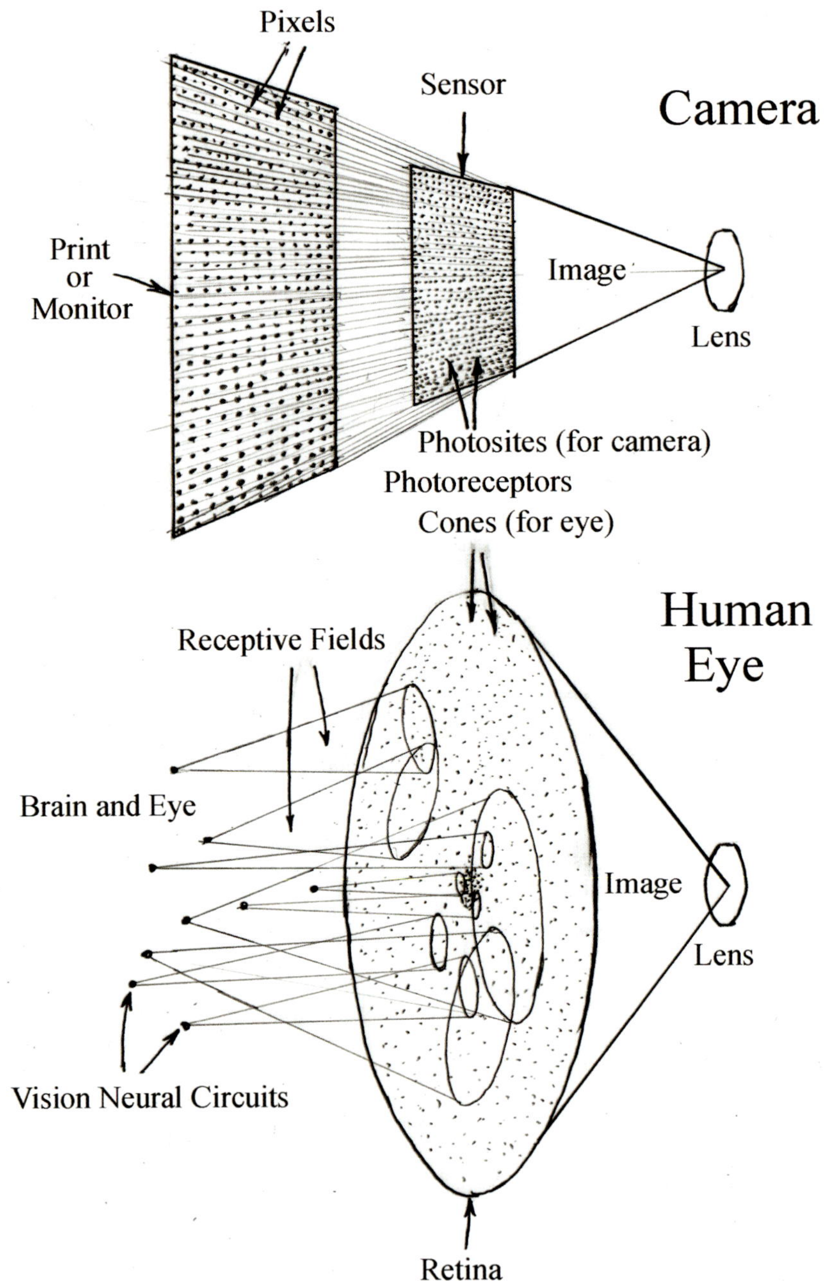

Figure 1: Camera and Eye illustration

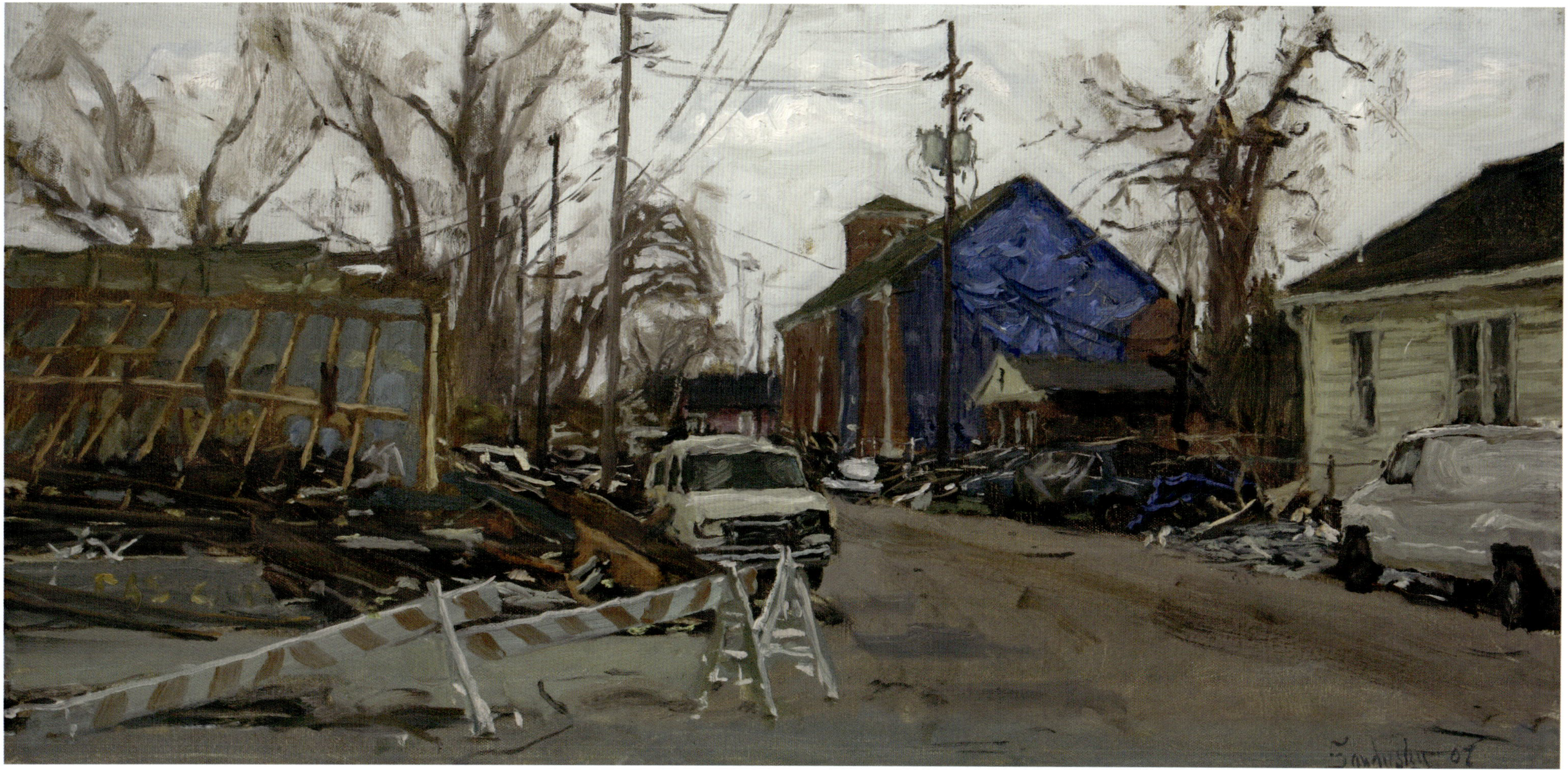

Aftermath of the great F2 tornado of 2007 seen from the intersection of Hurst and Cherokee streets 15" x 30"

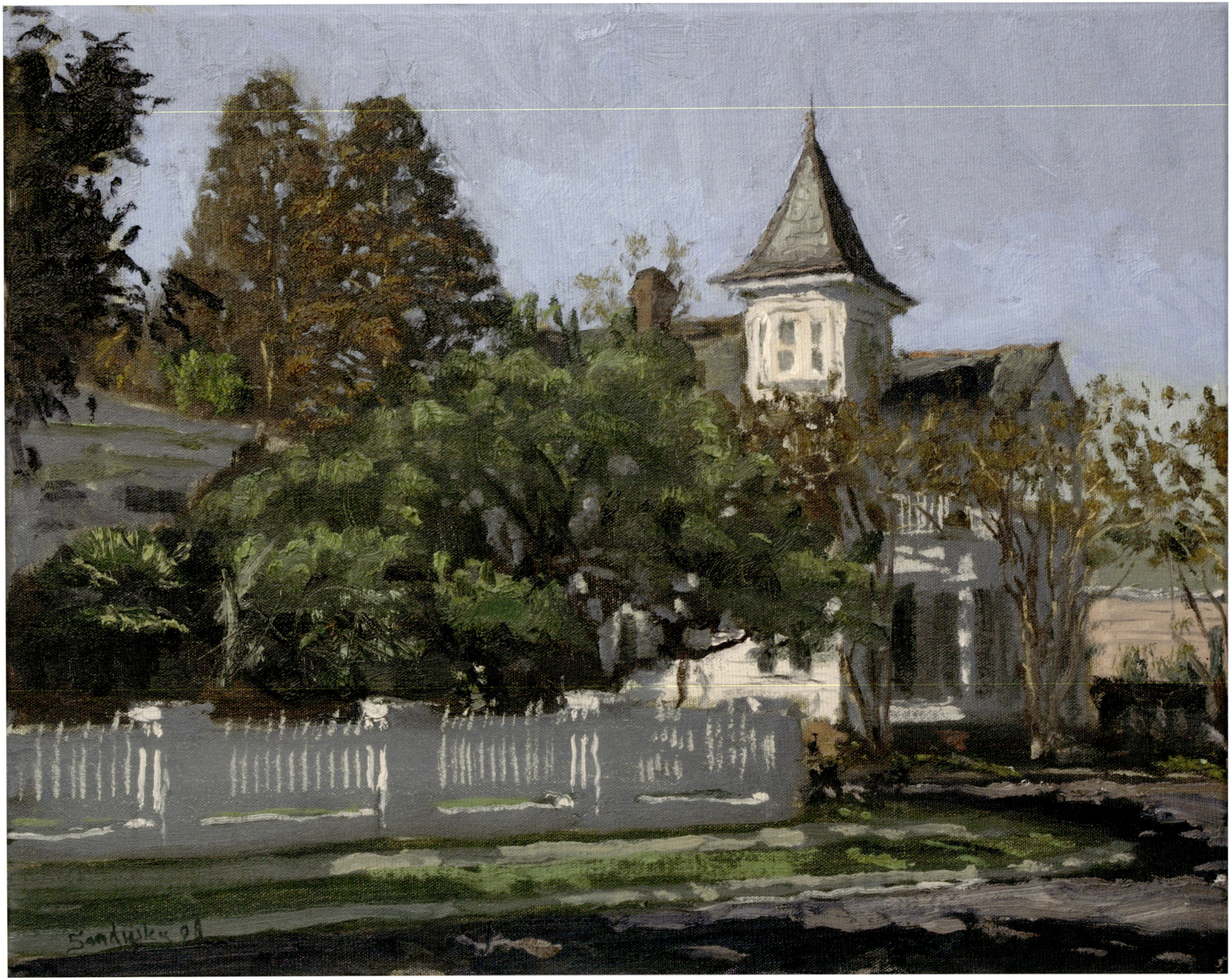

View from Hampson Street near Hillary Street 16" x 20"

When focusing on the spine of a book on the book shelf, it should not be possible to read the title of a book next to it. The visual patterns in the periphery are indistinct. It only seems that you see so much more than this in any given moment because you gather visual information over time by unconsciously glancing from one place to another so that the high acuity center of vision can move all around the view. There are two significant points that can be taken from this. First, the photograph-like image that enters our eye and focuses onto the retina has been immediately truncated by the distribution of cones. It can only have the potential to exist a few microns below the surface of the retina as an image that is highly detailed only in a small area in the middle and very indistinct everywhere else. This is in sharp contrast with the objective image, which has a close analogy in a photographic print, every part of which is equally distinct. Second, we have seen the first evidence that our vision of an unchanging scene happens in time. An unchanging image of light reflected from physical objects exists in its entirety at one instant. It exists only in space, having no time dependency. However, given that our high acuity center of vision must move around a view, as our eye moves, and sample over time, our vision of an unchanging view must have *at least* some time dependency. With these two bits of insight we have just begun a journey into a psychophysical labyrinth. Along the way we will acquire tools that we will need to understand at its center vexing-but-enlightening truths about vision.

Our eye is not only different from the camera with respect to the distribution of photoreceptors but also, and even more importantly, in how information is gathered and reported from those photoreceptors. In this respect the function of our eye is not even remotely similar to the camera. Data from the camera sensor is simply and directly transposed from the grid on the sensor to exactly the same grid on the print or monitor. For human vision, there are a huge number of little mechanisms in the eye and brain called vision neural circuits that each process information from groups of cones on the retina called receptive fields. Some receptive fields are very small with only a few cones and some are large with multitudes of cones spanning a large area of the retina. Receptive fields overlap and share cones with each other, but any given receptive field provides input to a single neural circuit that is looking for a specific feature. This is shown in the bottom section of figure 1. Vision neural circuits test not only for color but also for different forms, shapes, textures, and other visual qualities within their receptive fields. There are circuits that test for

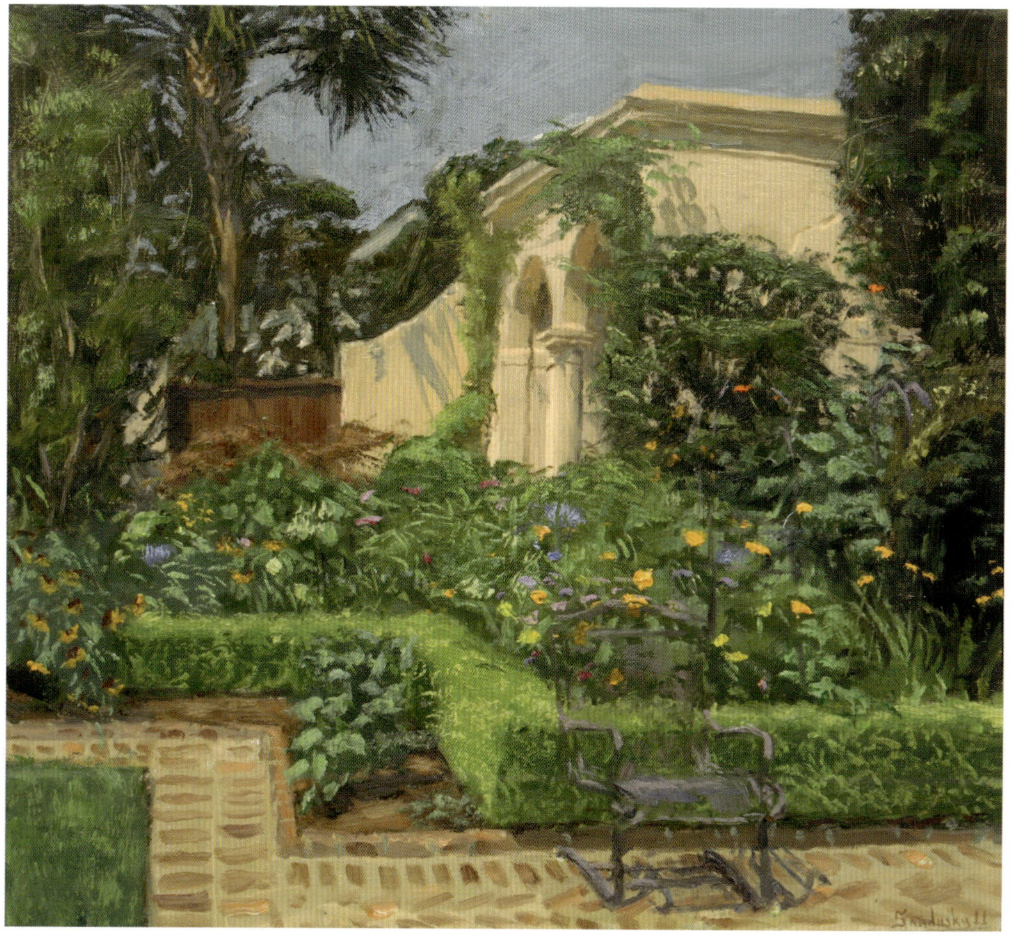

CATHY'S GARDEN 20" X 20"

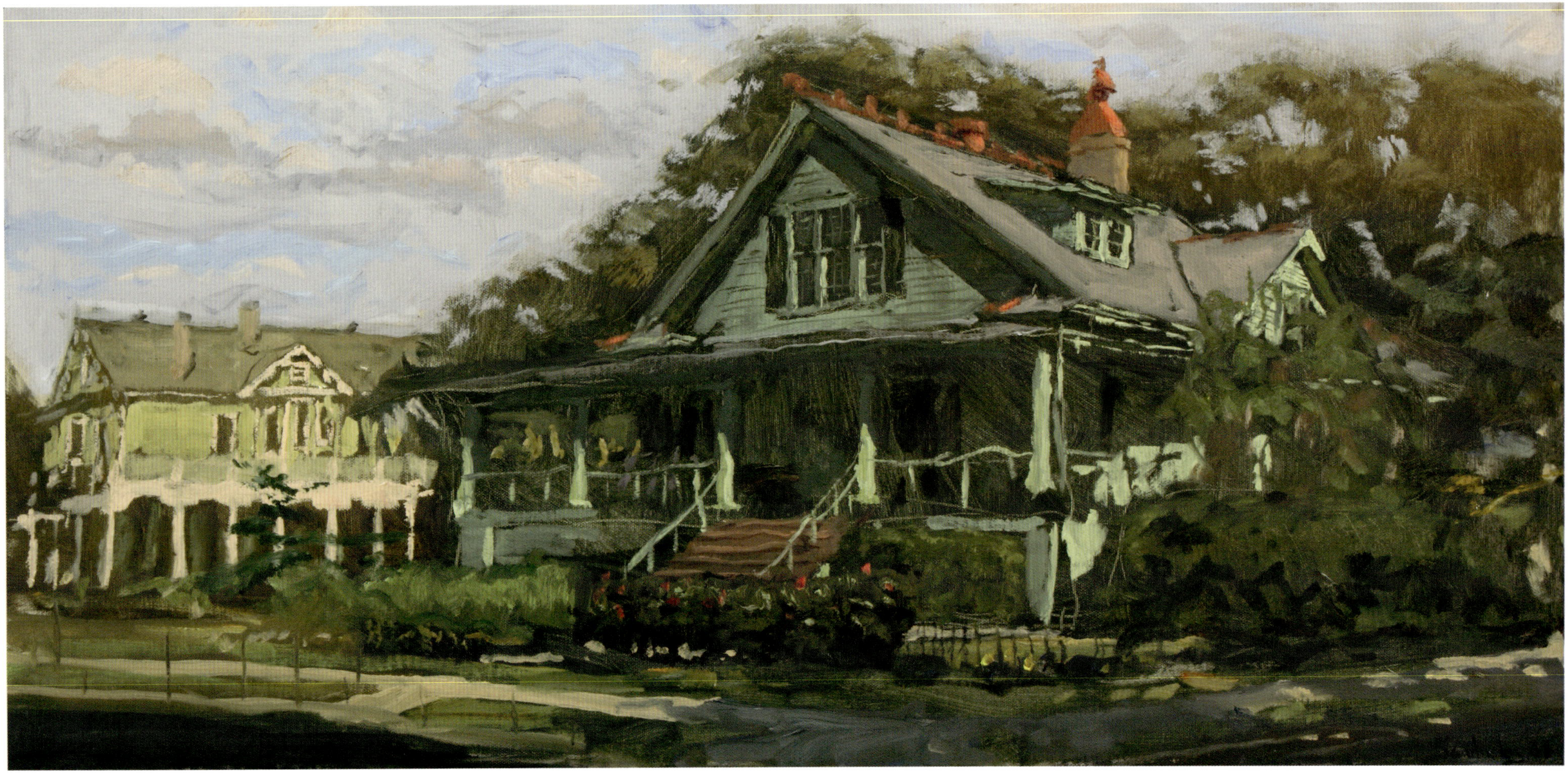

HOUSES SEEN FROM THE INTERSECTION OF HAMPSON AND PINE STREETS 15" X 30"

simple characteristics, such as diagonals, and there are complex circuits, such as one that tests for juxtapositions of forms that resonate like a human face. These circuits test for how smaller parts are different from each other, not how those parts exist absolutely. For example there are circuits that test for horizontal, vertical, and diagonal forms but they are in effect testing for specific *juxtapositions* of image characteristics within their receptive fields. A circuit that tests for color can only see differences in color, not which colors are present. If its receptive field is immersed in a solid color it finds nothing, but it responds strongly if its receptive field is oriented across the boundary between two different color patterns. There are not only circuits that test for spatial differences within their receptive fields, but there are also circuits that test for time changes of image characteristics within their receptive fields. Such temporal circuits are crucial for our perception of movement and changing light. Where the objective image is absolute, every aspect of our vision is relative.

For these vision circuits and all neural circuits that abstract data from the senses, the outputs are not nearly as interesting as the diagonals, color differences, shapes, sounds, movement, or other distinct juxtapositions for which they are testing; instead the outputs are simple electric pulse telemetry. So simple is this telemetry output by any given circuit that it does not contain any information about the properties of the juxtapositions for which it is testing, but only indicates the certainty with which it has found the juxtaposition for which it is testing. So a circuit that finds a strong positive testing for diagonals produces an output *identical* to a circuit that finds a strong positive testing for a certain color difference, which for that matter, produces an identical signal to a circuit that finds a strong positive testing for a certain sound. Only the wiring of the circuit provides the identification of the juxtaposition for which it is testing, in much the same way that when you press the door bell button at your front door you know which gizmo in the house is going to be activated. Instead of a color,

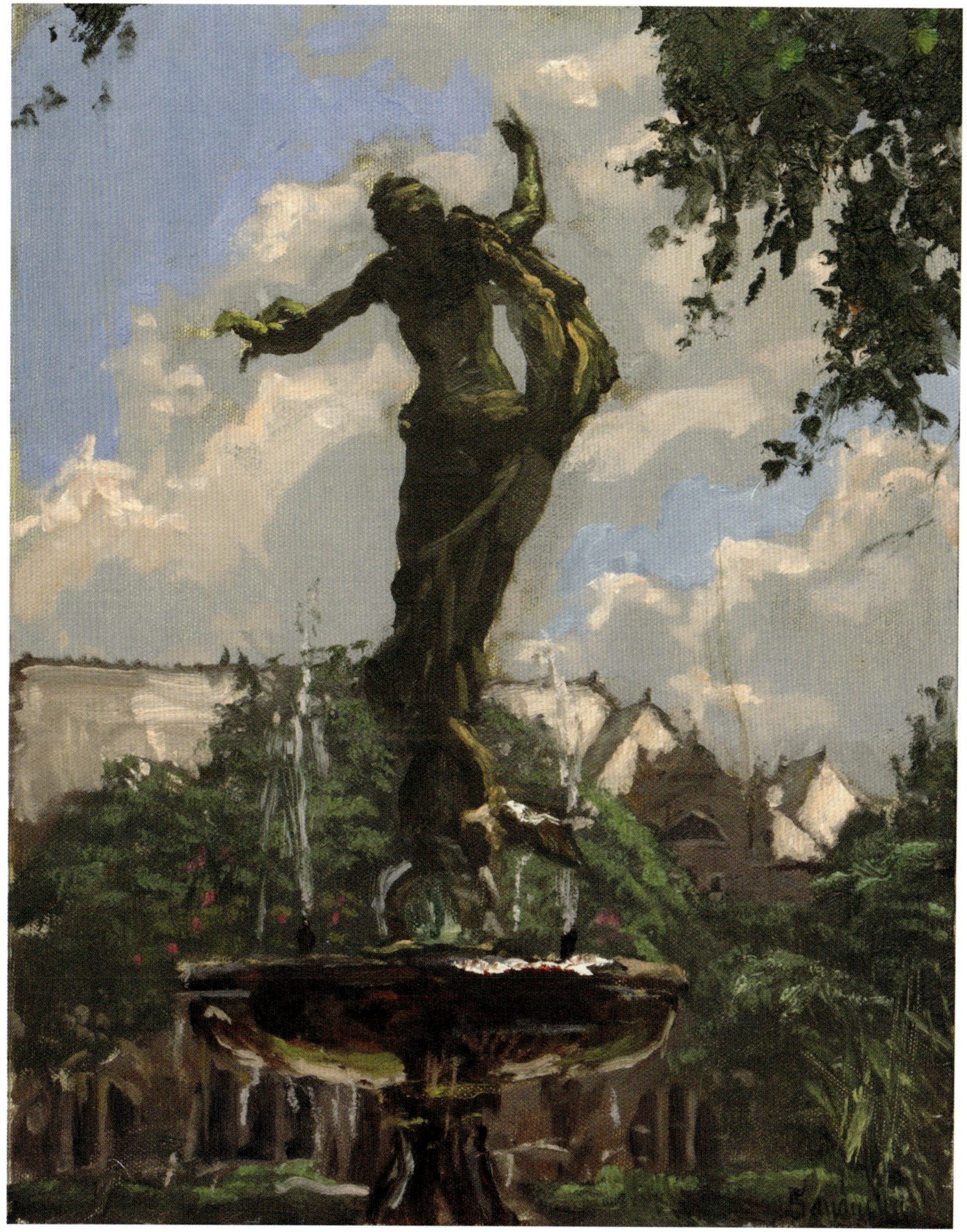

FOUNTAIN IN AUDUBON PARK 14" X 11"

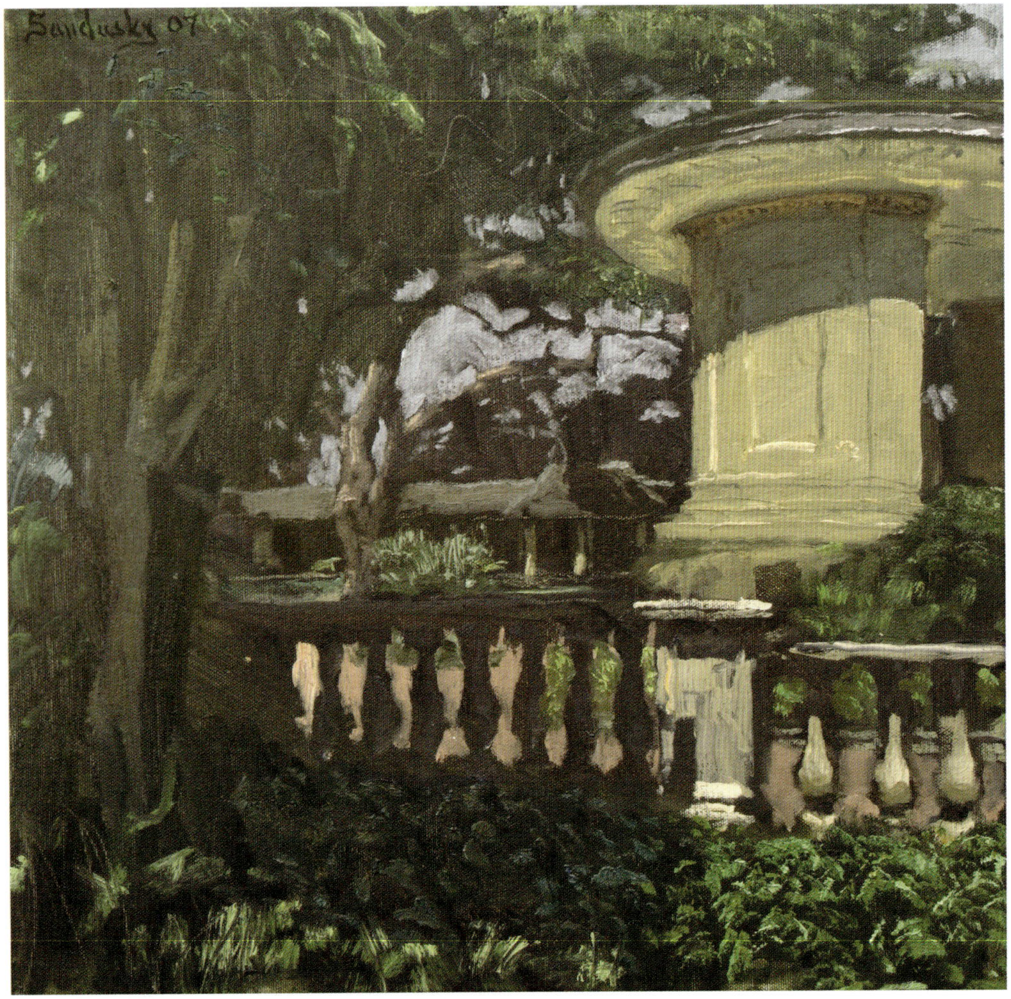

THE BANDSTAND IN AUDUBON PARK 18" X 18"

diagonal, or sound emanating from a neural circuit, imagine a monotone robotic voice saying, "strong, strong, strong, strong," or "moderate, moderate, moderate, moderate," or "very strong, very strong, very strong, very strong, " or "weak, weak, weak, weak," or "nothing, nothing, nothing, nothing." You might surmise that these uninteresting electric signals could be reassembled somewhere further along in the brain as an interesting image, much the same way that such signals coming into your TV are converted to a picture. But keep an open mind and keep looking in the direction where we've been heading, away from the image toward something very different.

The Emotional Component of Vision and the Role of Memory: Mandates and Qualifiers

We all agree that there is an all-important emotional response to what we see. But most people think of their emotions as being a property of a separate essential self that responds to a kind of projection of the senses and perceptions. However, science has shown that all aspects of our cognition are interwoven and that there is no crisp demarcation between emotion and vision or any of our other senses. To further explore vision we must examine our volitional behavior because it is the common denominator between all aspects of the mind. The pragmatic evolutionary reason for these sensory and emotional components of our mind is to produce the best possible volitional behavior that maximizes our chances of surviving and reproducing. The emotional components provide mandates for our body's behavior and the sensorial components provide much needed qualifiers.

I find it useful to model volitional behavior as being driven by a competition between elastic mandates that may be thought of as urges, drives, or emotional needs. One very simple elastic mandate would be our urge to breathe. It is *elastic* because we can hold our breath, but the urge to breathe builds like the tension of a stretching rubber band. Unconditioned responses, such as flinching at a sudden loud noise, could be conceptualized as *rigid,* inelastic mandates that produce perfectly predictable behavior like the gears in a clock. It seems reasonable that rigid mandates would have evolved to become more elastic to allow for quick behavioral adaptation using memory and learning. Elastic mandates are better suited for this because they can be delayed and prioritized. In addition to the urge

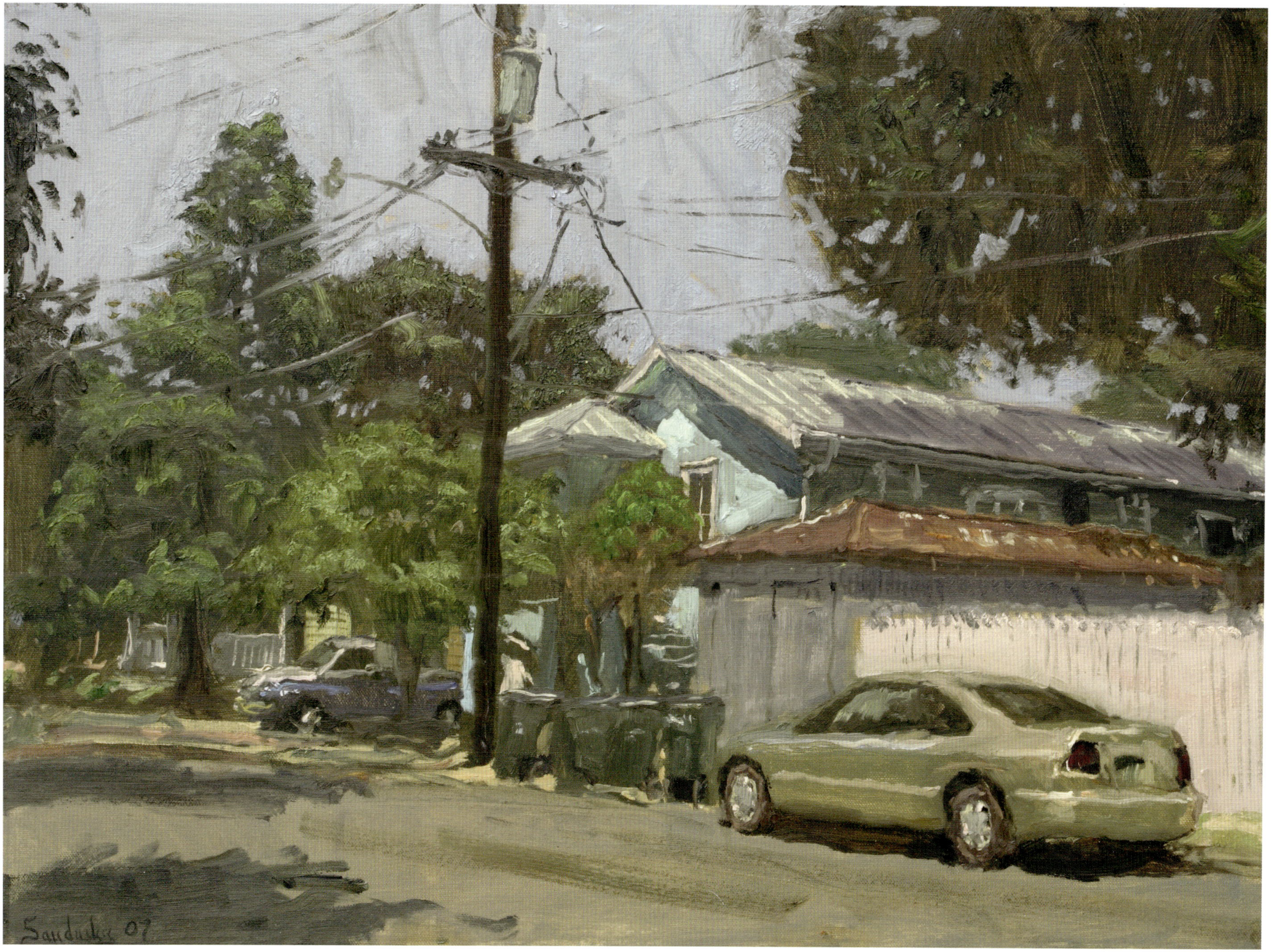

View from Dublin Street near Freret Street 18" x 24"

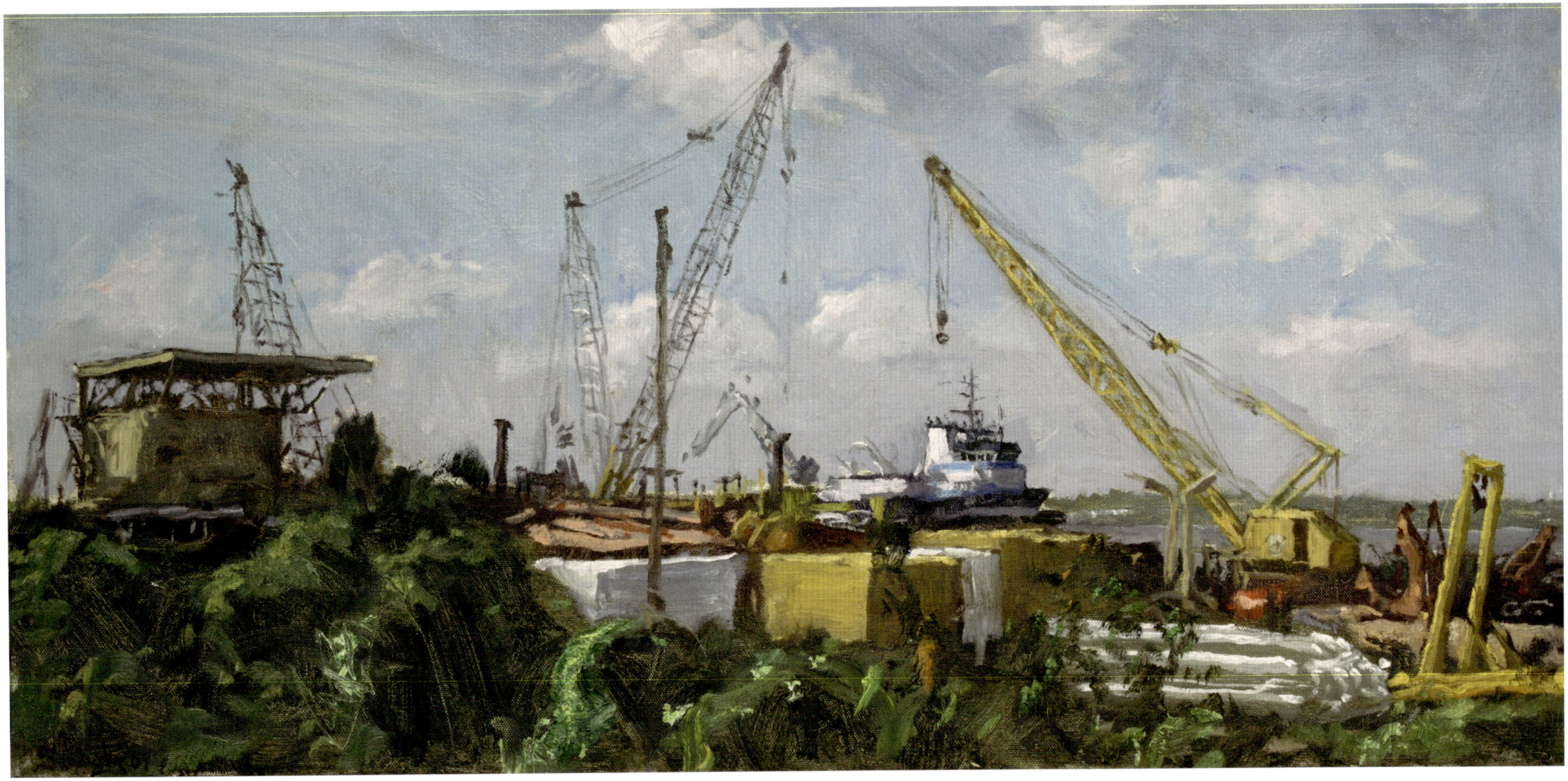

View of the Bisso Marine yards from Dog Hill 15" x 30"

to breathe, we could speculate that there are other *elastic* mandates basic for the survival of our body such as the urges to "eat" (hunger), to "drink" (thirst), to "flee" (run away), to "hoard" (save up resources), to "maintain or regain freedom of movement," "to avoid injury," and many more. We can also speculate that there are elastic mandates that stem from our having evolved to thrive in groups. Perhaps there is a drive to "maintain or strengthen our position in the group" and an urge to "gain assistance" from members of the group. There certainly must be urges or emotional needs that form our more altruistic side, such as our needs to "assist," to "teach," and to "protect." I have just used the terms "urge," "drive," and "emotional need" more or less randomly here. Perhaps for all practical purposes they are one in the same.

To show you how our volitional behavior can be driven by a competition between these elastic mandates consider this scenario: Having just witnessed a driver lose control of his vehicle and swerve off of a bridge, you stand at the edge of the bridge and see the car with its unresponsive driver sinking into the water. Two competing mandates for volitional behavior rise quickly in you—one to "assist" (the driver) the other to "avoid injury" (of your own body). Each of these mandates *alone* would procure different combinations of learned behaviors to satisfy or lower them. The lone mandate to "assist" would have you dive head first into the water right over the sinking car to get to the driver as quickly as possible. The lone mandate to "avoid injury" would have you cling to the guardrail on the bridge. But the two mandates together evoke a combination of learned behaviors that will possibly satisfy or lower *both* mandates. If you're a weak swimmer, perhaps you will cling to the guard rail and cry out for help or dial 911. If you're a strong swimmer, you might run further across the bridge away from where the car went in and where the water is likely deeper, carefully jump off of the bridge feet first (assuming the bridge is not too high), and then swim over to the car to assist the driver.

Of course there are many more than just two elastic

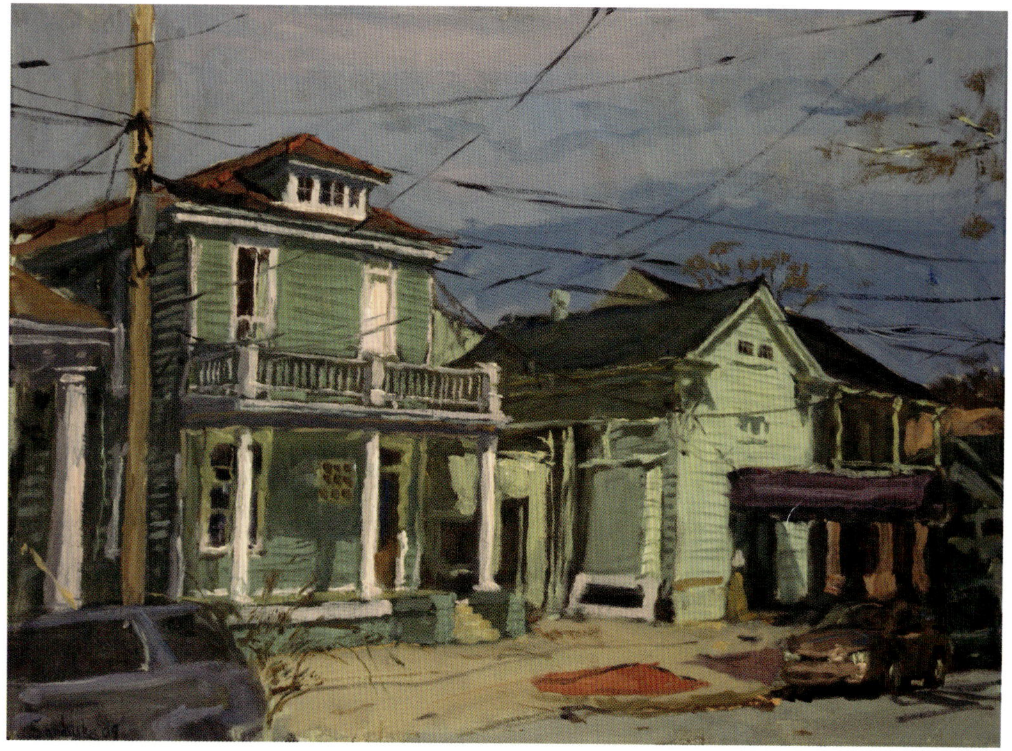

VIEW FROM LOWERLINE STREET CLOSE TO FRERET STREET 18" X 24"

mandates at any given time vying for remembered behaviors that will lower them. More often than not there are no combinations of remembered behaviors that can lower or satisfy all elastic mandates at once, so the squeakiest wheels get greased first. This is the advantage of their elasticity. They can wait to be lowered, or satisfied. Different clusters of remembered behaviors will be summoned *serially* to place greatest emphasis on first lowering the mandates that have risen the highest, followed by those that are lower. For example, "eat" (hunger) might have been the principle mandate that compelled you to drive to a restaurant, but along the way several other mandates popped up such as a mandate to "relieve epidermal irritation." Remembered behavior could be summoned that allowed both mandates to

(Continued on page 30)

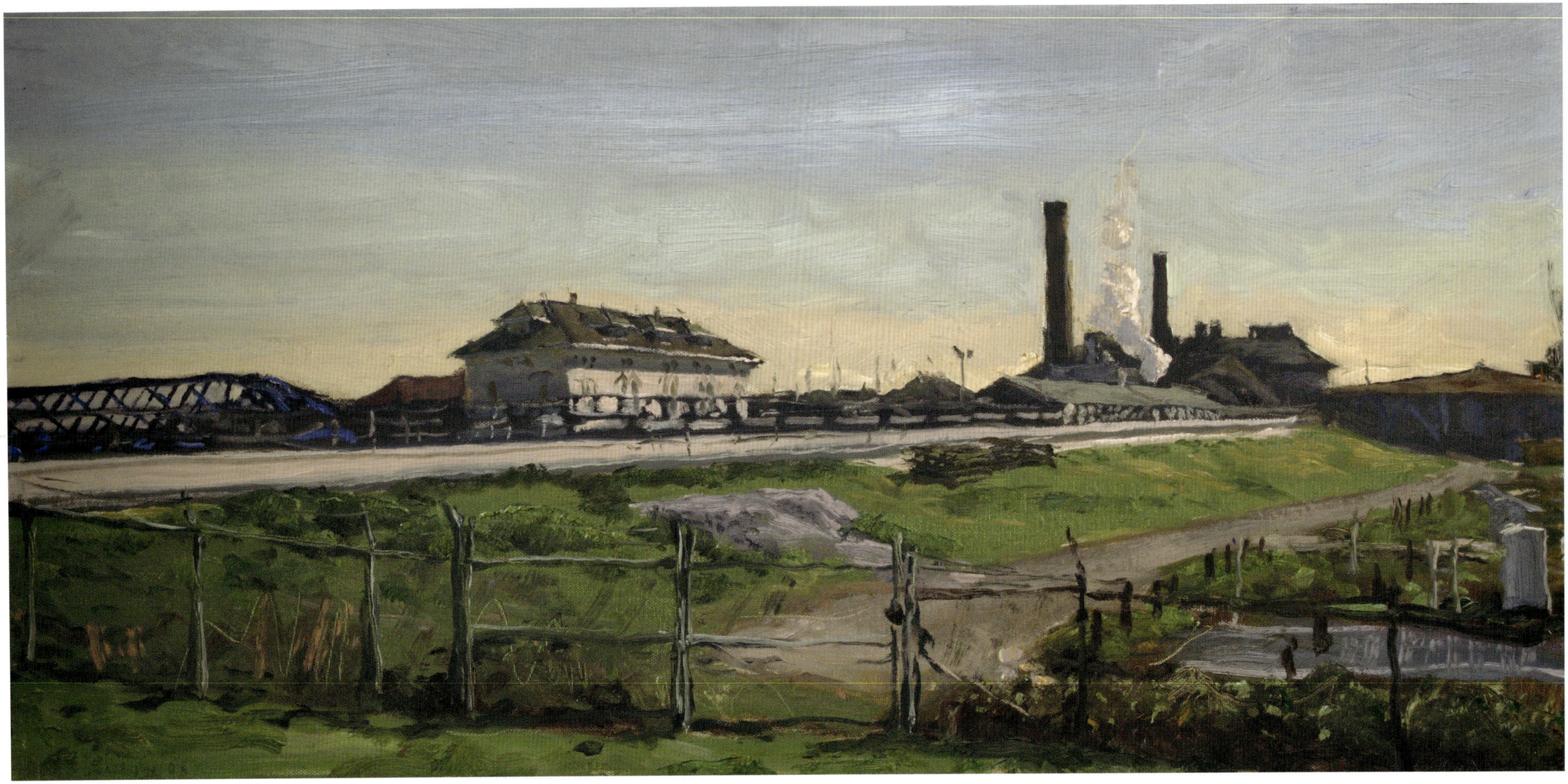

THE WATER PROCESSING PLANT SEEN FROM MONTICELLO AVENUE 15" X 30"

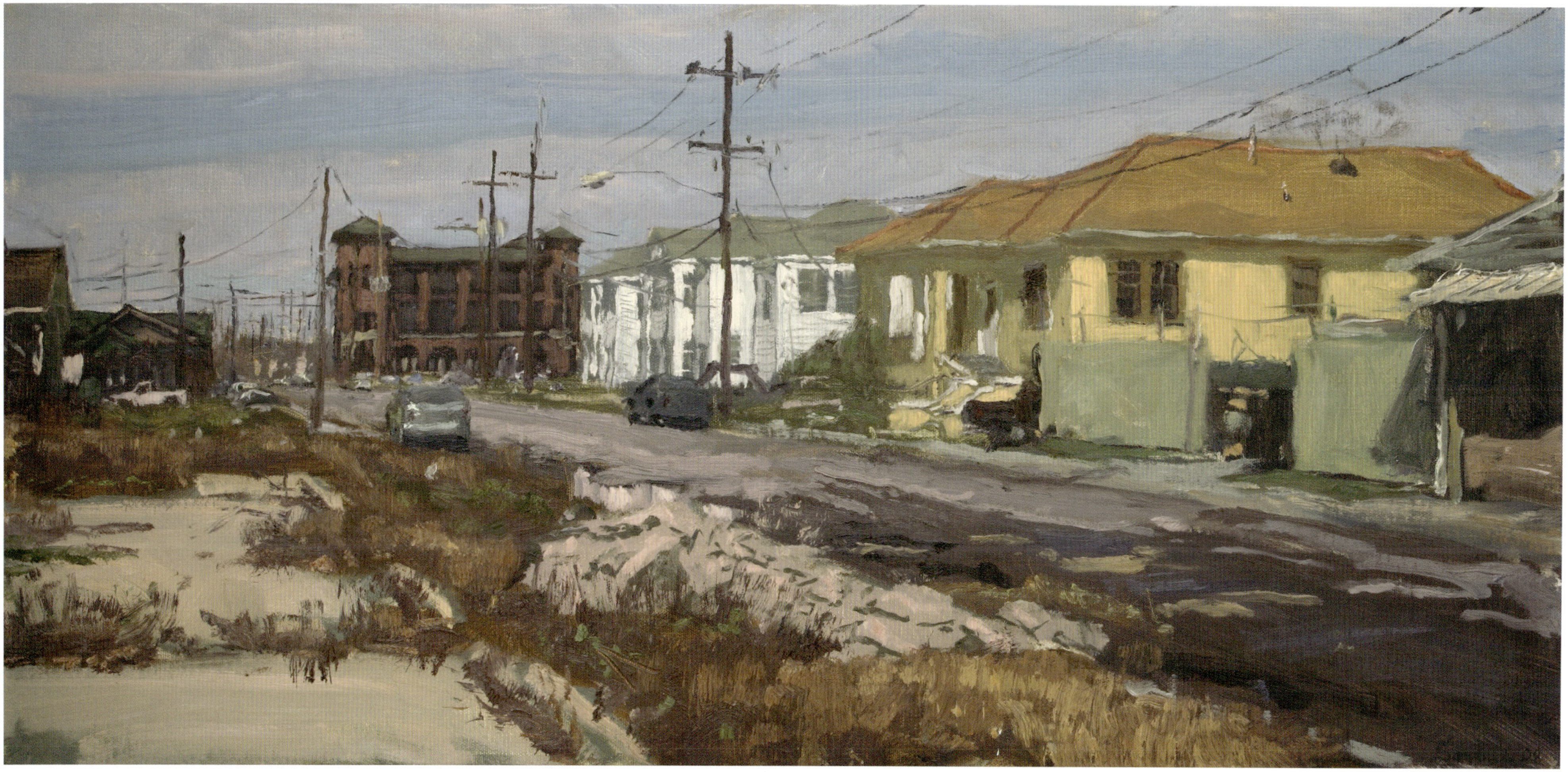

Looking down Fig Street close to South Carrollton Avenue 15" x 30"

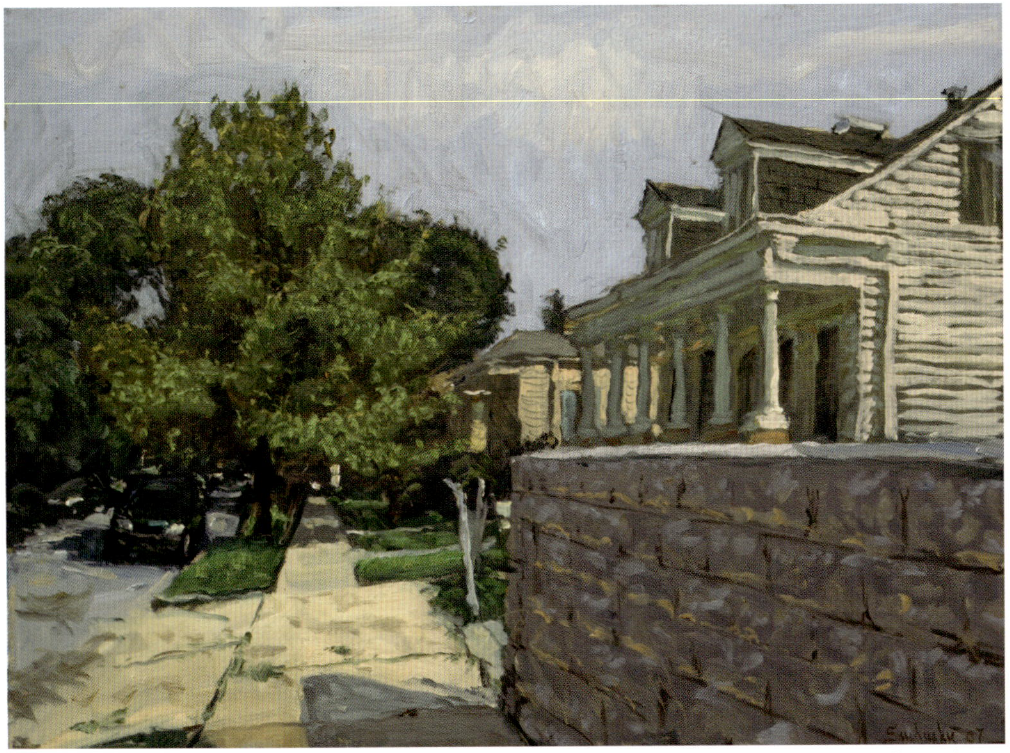

Stone wall on Freret Street near South Carrollton Avenue 18" x 24"

be lowered simultaneously, briefly using one hand to steer while the other scratched the itch on your nose. Further along though, you happened upon the incident at the bridge. Then, the mandates to "assist" and to "avoid injury" suddenly stole the show. You can think of your cognition as mediating the competition between these elastic mandates for your volitional behavior or you could consider your cognition to *be* the *unmediated* competition between these mandates.

Regardless of your philosophy, qualifiers are doubtless crucial to this competition. For our bridge example, how could you have known that you were on a bridge and that someone needed assistance without qualifiers to contextualize the mandates? We can think of the outputs of the vision neural circuits and those of the other senses as being qualifiers for our cognitive function. Without qualifiers accompanying your hunger, you could only be as Pac-Man smacking your mouth open and closed moving forward, hoping that you run into some food. A more articulated behavior to reduce hunger, such as reaching out to grab an apple, is brought about by referencing the unique set of qualifiers produced when you are in the presence of the apple to similar remembered sets of qualifiers produced by previous similar experiences, that were in turn associated to remembered behaviors that reduced your hunger in those situations.

At least the greatest majority of the qualifiers and mandates input to our volitional behavior are provided by our memories. Initially scanning a new scene with your eyes produces very many qualifiers. We can't rule out the possibility that it even produces some mandates. A certain high-pitched sound could directly evoke a mandate to "assist an infant." Any sound increasing in volume and any image pattern increasing in size on the retina is most often associated with an approaching object and therefore might *directly* evoke a mandate to "flee." But these initial qualifiers and mandates can only produce meaning and volitional behavior when they evoke memories. It is easy to overlook the lifetime of learning that was needed to interpret the initial qualifiers and mandates produced directly by eye scanning. The initial sensory evoked qualifiers and mandates are used to summon dense arrays of qualifiers and more meaningful mandates from memory that are to them as a cigarette butt is to the forest fire that it kindled.

No better evidence of the dominance of memory in our vision lies in the drawings of beginning art students. Standing close to a simple shotgun house in 3/4 view, an objective image would show edges delineated somewhat like the diagram in figure 2 (see page 33). The beginning art student's drawing of the house is shown to the right of it.

The greatest difference between the objective rendering of the house and the student's drawing is that, instead of having diagonal lines that represent the top and bottom of the

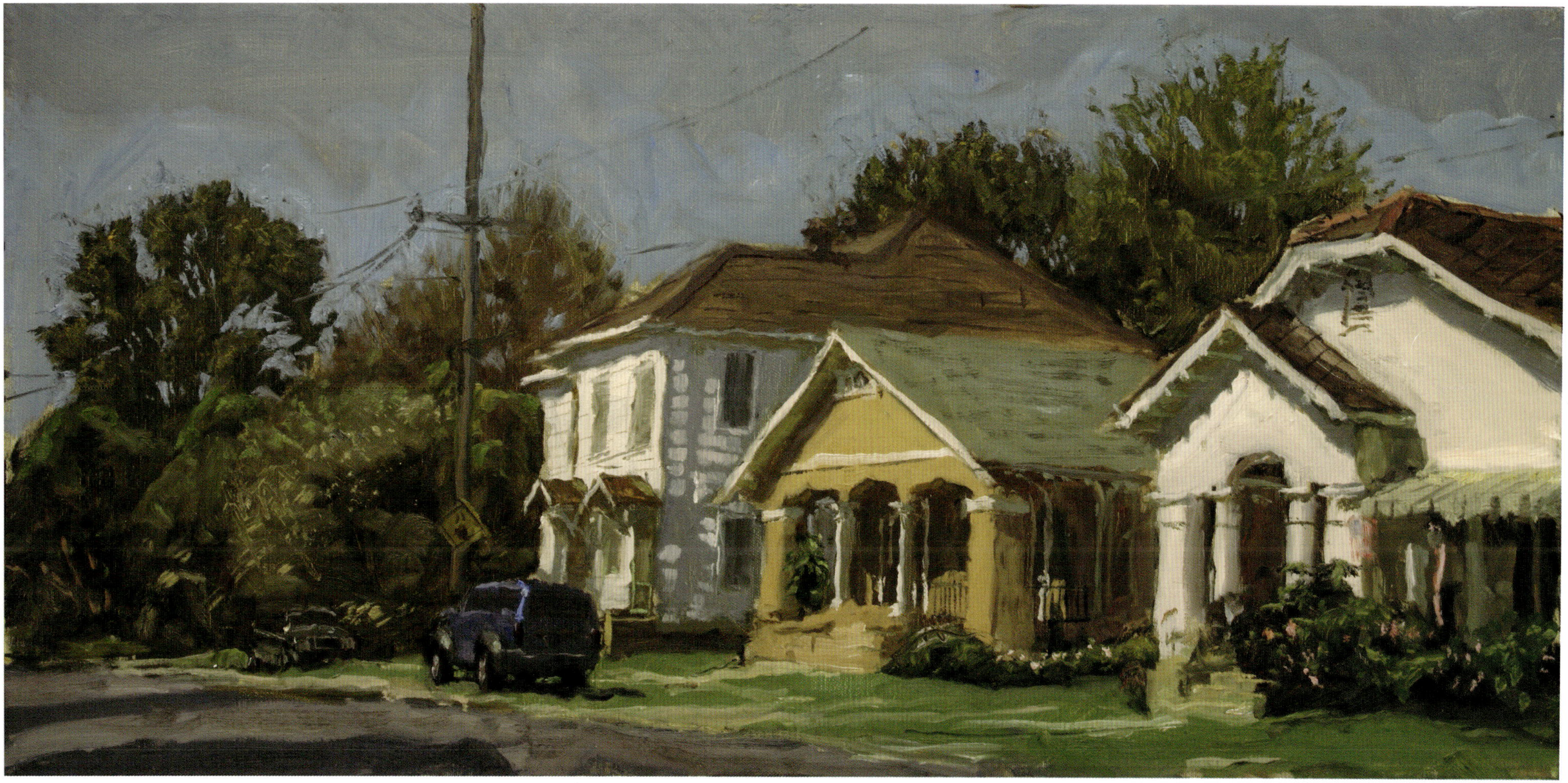

Houses along Cambronne Street near Zimpel Street 15" x 30"

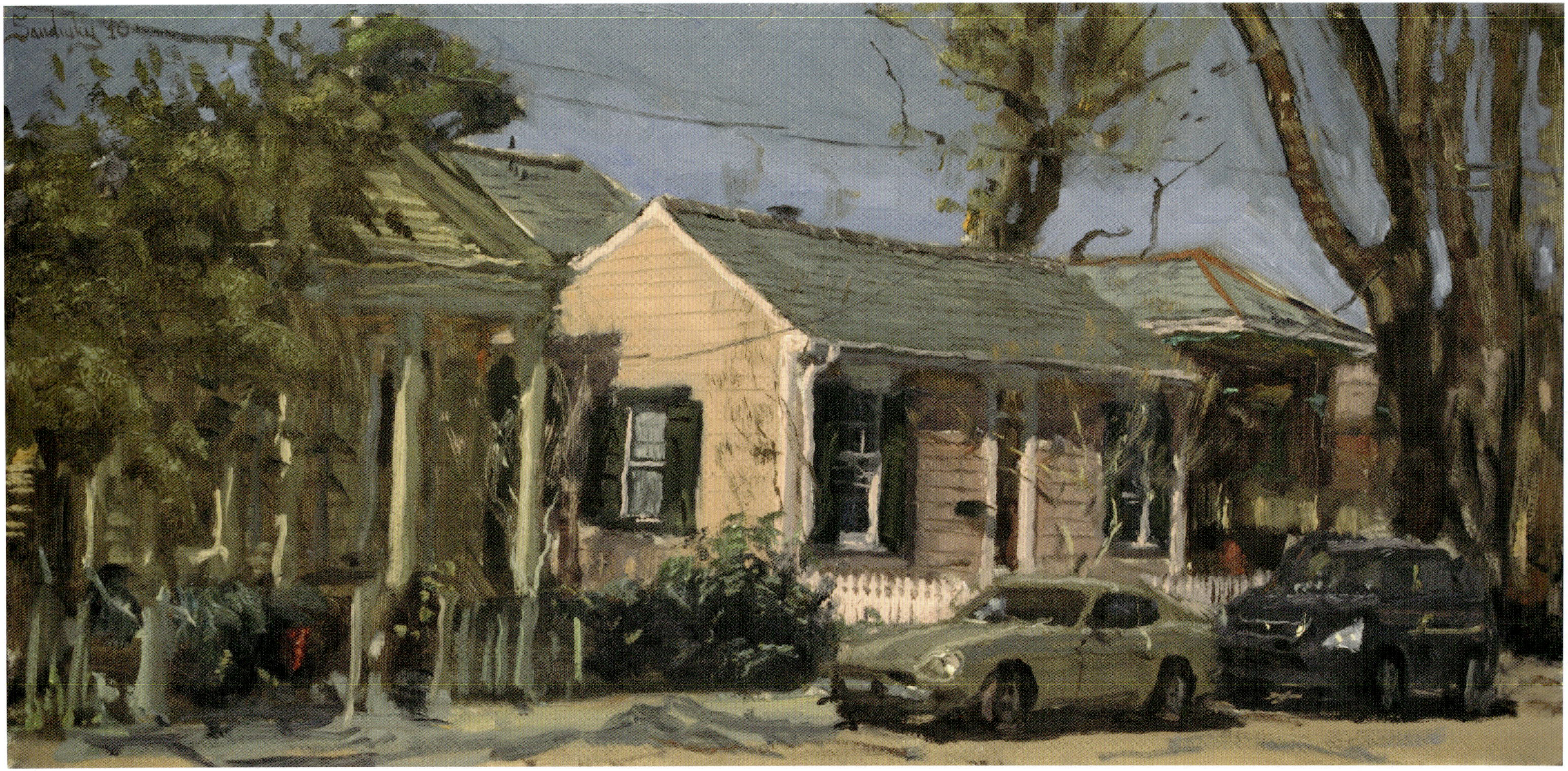

My Creole cottage and my neighbor's 280Z 15" x 30"

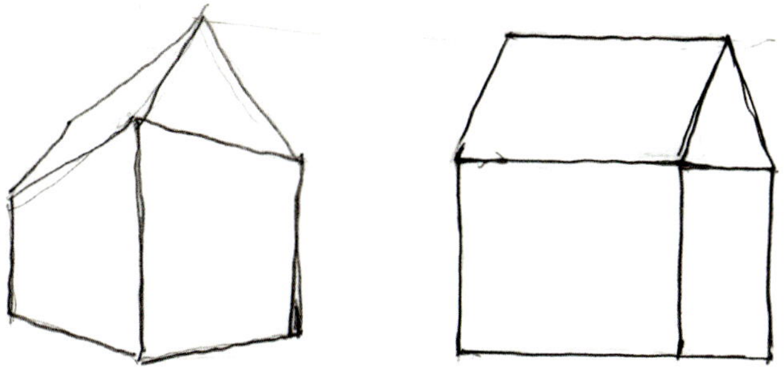

FIGURE 2: FROM LEFT TO RIGHT, OBJECTIVE HOUSE AND STUDENT'S HOUSE

house, the student uses parallel horizontal lines. Most drawing instructors would fondly say that the student is drawing what he *knows* and not what he *sees*. On the contrary, while the student's drawing is not objective, he *has* drawn what he sees because what he sees comes mostly from memory. The parallel horizontal lines representing the top and bottom of the house are produced by a simple learned behavior that provides the most effective visual stimulus to evoke the most prominent qualifiers from his memory: those that tell him that the house is level and that the top of the house is the same distance above the ground everywhere. The less prominent qualifiers initially produced by eye scanning would be best evoked by the diagonal lines in the objective illustration. If *these* qualifiers were more prominent in the student's vision there is no reason he couldn't have drawn diagonal lines instead of the parallel horizontal lines, because both are equally easy to draw. Granted, the student's drawing is unconvincing, but for now we are only discussing his vision, not the quality of his artwork.

Memory must provide the meaningful complete set of qualifiers and mandates that can be used to query for remembered behaviors that can lower or satisfy the mandates. For our bridge scenario, without memories you could not know that the gray-blue pattern indicated water that could be jumped into, although it would likely be cold (mandate to warm your body) and that you could be hurt in

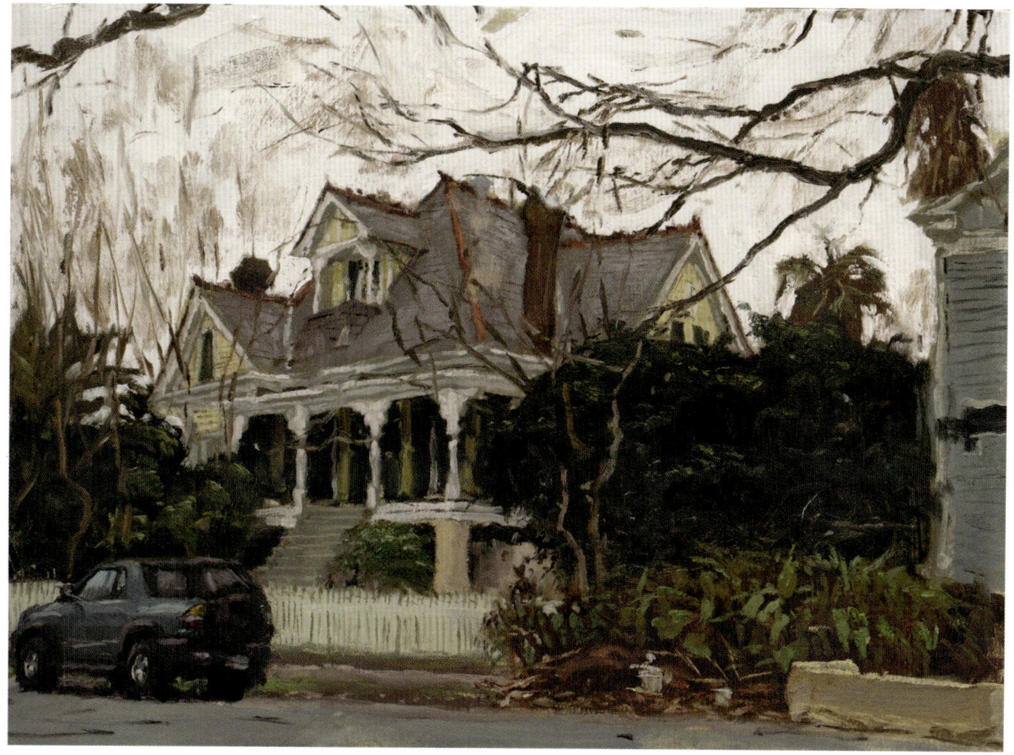

HOUSE ON CAMP STREET NEAR AUSTERLITZ STREET 18" X 24"

the jump (mandate to avoid injury). You could not know that certain intricate, changing patterns indicated a human being (multitudes of qualifiers and mandates) trapped in a sinking car (mandates to gain freedom of movement and assist). You could not even know such minute points as that the bridge is level and not inclined, despite diagonal qualifiers *initially* evoked by your eye scanning because of the perspective of your vantage point. In fact, without memory there is no meaningful experience.

Let's explore a couple of specific examples of how memory dictates what we see. Suppose you are looking at an orange in the produce section of the grocery store. Immediately, it seems to be orange in color, and yet, as we have seen, there is nothing coming from your eyes telling you that its color

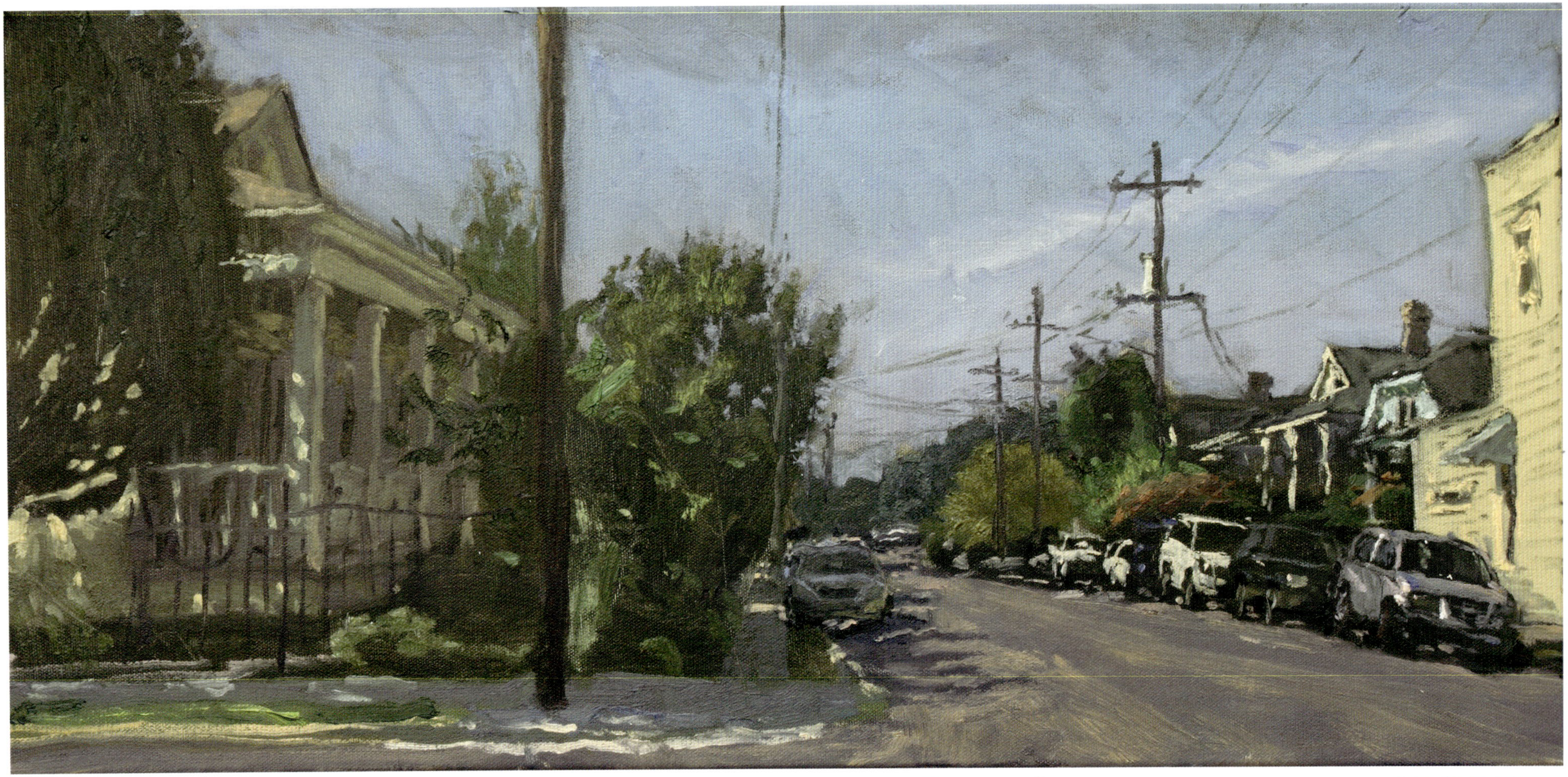

INTERESTINGLY, SINCE I PAINTED THIS VIEW (12" X 24") LOOKING UP LAUREL STREET FROM ELEONORE STREET, IT HAS BECOME COMPLETELY OVERGROWN BY TREES ON BOTH SIDES OF THE ROAD AND IS UNRECOGNIZABLE EXCEPT FOR THE SEGMENT OF THE LARGE YELLOW BUILDING ON THE FAR RIGHT.

is orange. All that is provided from your senses about color tells how a pattern's color is different from the colors that surround it and those that preceded it. And, as we have seen, this initial sensory input is not the only contribution, and in many cases will not even be a significant contribution, to what will ultimately form your perception of the color of a thing. In this case the color of the orange, as measured by a calibrated scientific instrument, is found to be yellow, not orange as you perceived it to be. It seems to have orange coloration because information from the neural circuits that test for color is only one of many inputs that will help to conjure up your perception of the orange. There are your memories of being in produce sections of grocery stores looking in the direction of the oranges. Color is only one aspect of your memories of oranges. There are many attributes that this orange has in common with other oranges, such as its roundness, the tiny pits on its skin, the fact that it is sitting in the same bin with other oranges, that it is the same approximate size, etc. This leads you to generalize all of its attributes including its color. The best fit that reconciles your raw senses to memories is the fruit named orange, most of which are orange in coloration. You where taught as a young child that oranges are orange in color. You colored them with orange crayons in your coloring books. This fruit must be named orange for a reason. All of this knowledge, which is nothing less than memories, makes you see the color *orange* even though objectively it has been determined that its actual color in this case is yellow. "Memory Color" is the term vision scientists give to this phenomenon where a person reports seeing a color for an object that is different than the actual color.

Perhaps the best example of memory color lies in ganzfeld (total field) experiments. A ganzfeld is achieved when a person's entire field of vision is filled with a uniform homogeneous color. Because there are no different color patterns to compare within the ganzfeld, the only input is from the circuits that detect *time* changes in color. You can create a ganzfeld by lying on your back on an elevated platform outside in an open field on a day with a clear blue sky. The output from the circuits that report time changes in color fatigues to the generic background signal within two minutes of the emersion of your field of vision in the blue sky. After that period of time, you will have no remnant of any raw sensation of color. Yet the sky will still *seem* blue to you, because of what you know about (or memories of) your environs.

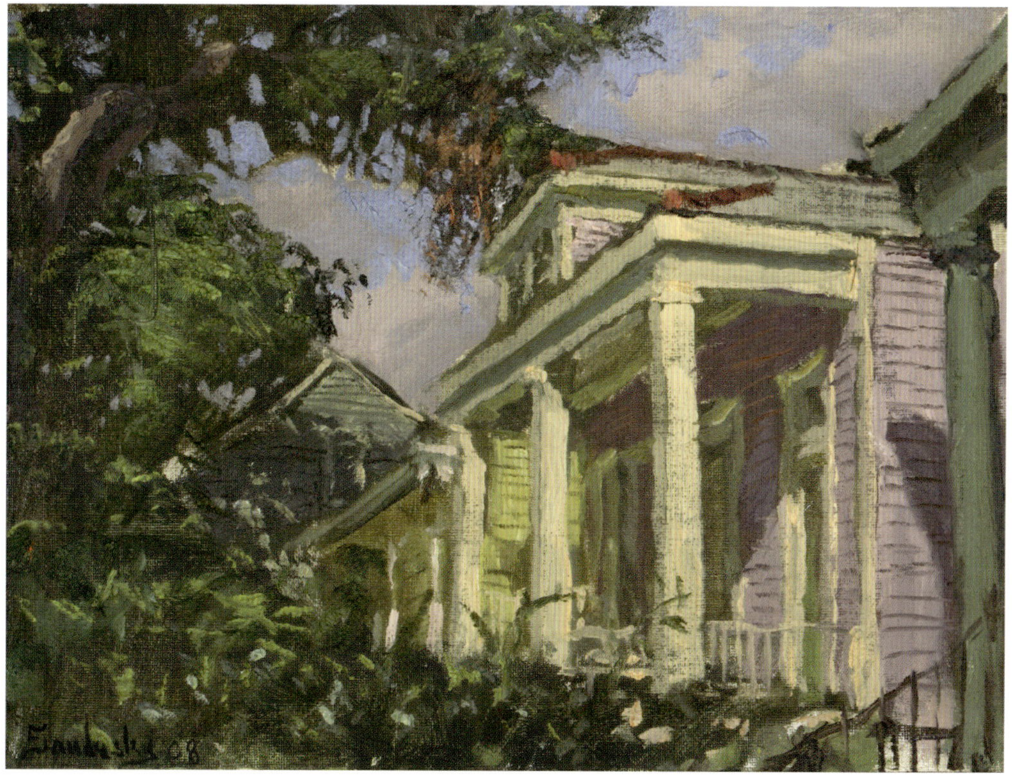

GREEK REVIVAL COTTAGE ON ANNUNCIATION STREET NEAR VALMONT STREET 11" X 14"

What a clear blue sky and an orange have in common is that they are prominent in our memories; therefore, memory provides the vast majority of qualifiers and mandates that form our perception of them. There are less meaningful experiences that have fewer references to memory. Consider a flat piece of

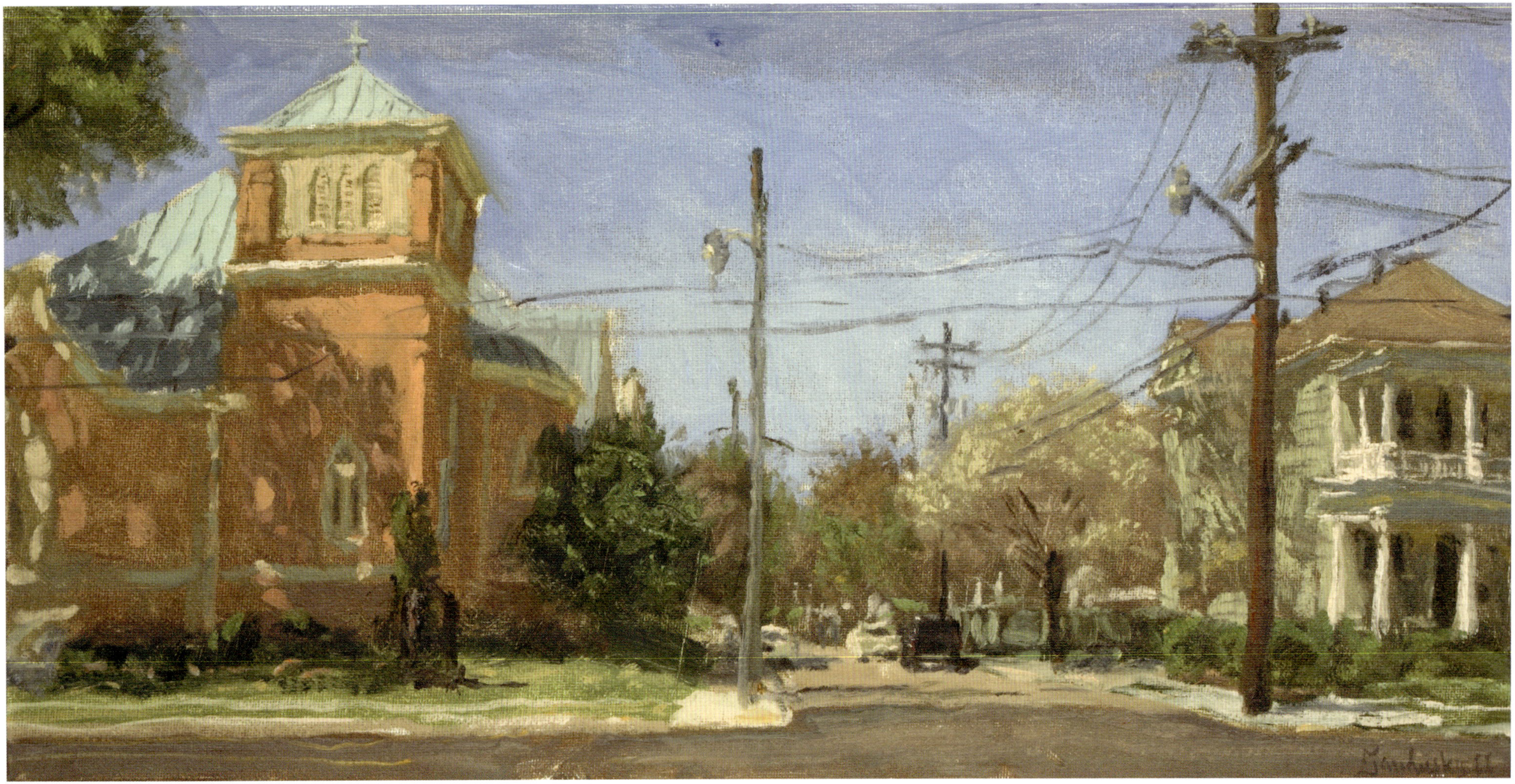

For Ally, intersection of Nashville Avenue and Perrier Street 10" x 20" This was the last painting that I did accompanied by my much-loved dog Ally. During this painting session we met a young artist passing by who coincidentally was also named Ally.

paper printed with patterns of random shape and color. If we believe that these patterns are arbitrary, much more of what we see is provided by the qualifiers and mandates produced directly by eye scanning. But even so, there will be *some* references to memory. If one of the patterns is red, memories of fire, which is also red, may evoke mandates such as "cool down." We will later explore the significance that *all* qualifiers evoke memories, though our experiences of flat arbitrary patterns are much less meaningful and would likely never be the subject of a representational painting. It has been demonstrated that beginning art students very accurately render an image of a familiar object if the image is turned upside-down, destroying the object's familiarity in the student's mind. In our previous example of the beginning drawing student and the house, had the student been asked to draw from a photograph of the house that had been turned upside-down, the diagonal qualifiers evoked directly from eye scanning would have prevailed, enabling him to render the objective image of the house more accurately. We will see that when used sparingly, such tricks can be effective learning tools, but if they become a mainstay of the artist's process, conveyance of the artist's vision is exchanged for objective accuracy.

If what we see is mostly memory, why can we not seem to pull up crisp visual memories when we close our eyes? Instead, it just seems dark. Or perhaps we are able to summon visual memories but they seem sketchy and faint, as though they are hidden from us by darkness and we might be able to see them if the lights were turned on. When we are awake, the memory-evoked qualifiers and mandates, though much greater in number, are subordinate to the sensory-evoked qualifiers and mandates. When we are awake with our eyes closed, the reality to which the sensory-evoked qualifiers and mandates keep us connected is that we have closed our eyes and therefore it is dark. Consider though how vivid are the visualizations in your dreams when you're asleep and effectively cut off from your senses. Also consider that in the

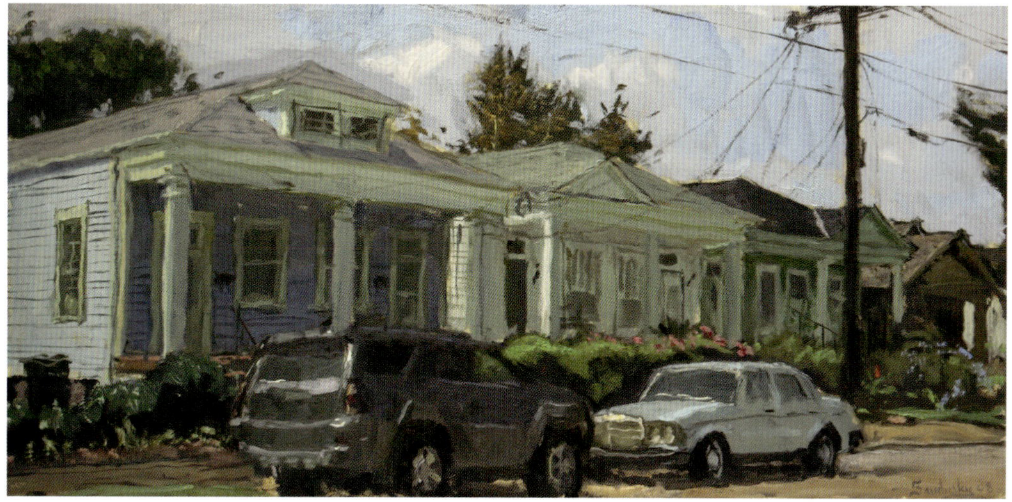

HOUSES ALONG ANNUNCIATION STREET NEAR VALMONT STREET 15" X 30"

case of certain types of mental illness, like schizophrenia, people experience imaginary sights and sounds that are mixed in with their objective reality and *seem* just as real.

We usually think of memory as manifesting after the fact—being summoned when we try to recall. Although visual memories are indeed summoned through recollection, you must now embrace this counterintuitive idea that our first hand *real-time* vision is *also* formed mostly from memory.

We got the first hint that qualifiers are not too interesting in themselves when we saw that the output from a corresponding neural circuit merely indicates the certainty that it has found the qualifier for which it is testing, nothing so interesting as a projection of a diagonal, color, or shape. While we have to be able to distinguish qualifiers from each other and, accordingly, they must be distinguished from each other in how we *feel* them, the mandates—or the emotional component of our vision—must have a greater role in our cognition. Qualifiers alone can provide no beauty or ugliness or any emotional connection to anything that you experience. It is erroneous to believe that something like a pure visual sensation of a rose void of emotion is *in itself* meaningful. Having a rose in your visual field evokes countless

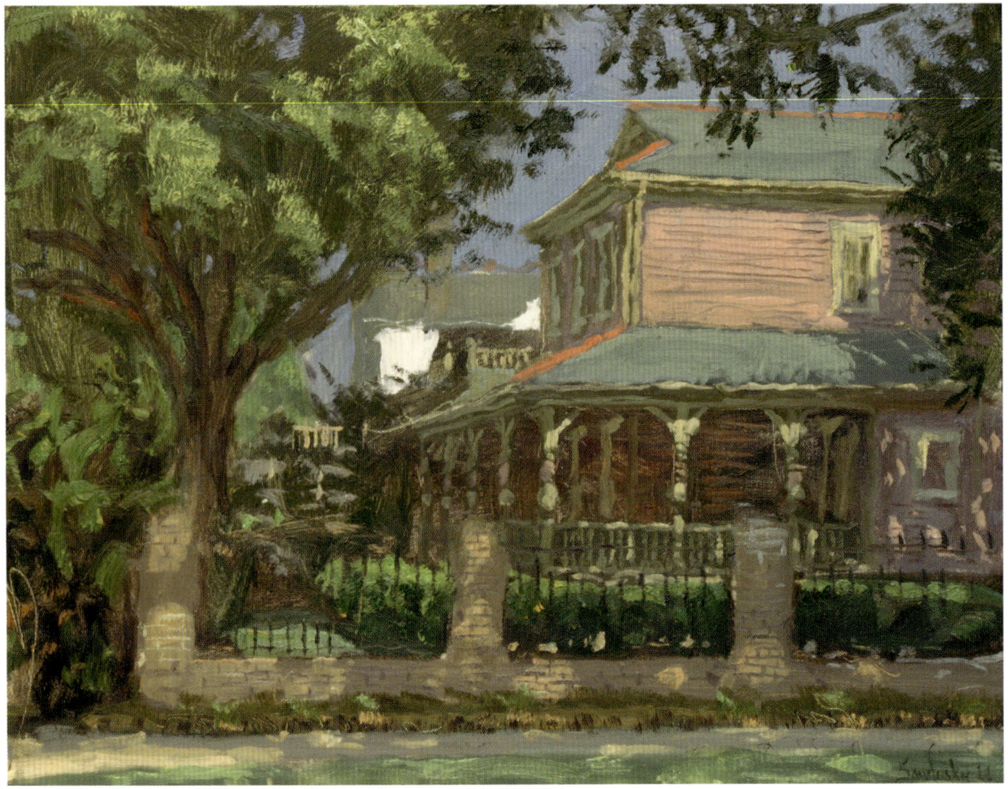

House on the corner of Camp and Robert streets 16" x 20" There is an earlier painting that I did of this house reproduced in my first book, New Orleans en Plein Air. The house has a different color scheme now and it's amazing how tall the tree on the left has grown.

qualifiers, many of which we can think of clustering together into molecules like "softness" (petals) and "sharpness" (thorns). But qualifiers fatigue immediately and unconditionally, only serving to help select memories that perhaps contain similar qualifiers that will refresh those that are fatiguing, but most importantly, will contain mandates for our volitional behavior such as "nurture" and "protect" evoked in response to "softness," and "reorient body for safety" in response to "sharpness." Without these mandates the rose's image could just as well be reflected into an empty mirror instead of your eyes. Think of a dense dust cloud moving in your direction. Being an opaque homogeneous field of grey with fuzzy edges swallowing more and more of the periphery as it approaches, it seems much less interesting schematically than a rose. But your rapidly increasing mandates to "breathe" and to "flee," as the object size of the gray pattern increases, makes this a powerful visual experience. Whereas the multitudes of qualifiers intermittently rise and then unconditionally fatigue, the elastic mandates by comparison are fewer in number and persistently build to engage you. They pull and torment you for a significant period until they either win for their cause by summoning some remembered behavior that will lower (or satisfy) them, or effectively give up when they *eventually* fatigue. In short, the quality of our vision lies in its emotional components (mandates).

To summarize, where the image is only schematic, our vision has not only a schematic component but also a behavioral mandate (emotional) component that is considerably more important. We have seen that there is no sharp demarcation between the schematic and emotional components of our vision, and that vision as well as all of our other senses are infused and inextricably interwoven into our cognition. If this is the case, what even is vision? Perhaps vision would be best defined as the aspect of our cognition more heavily qualified by information originating from the eyes. Further, we have demonstrated that our vision (whatever it is) is formed mostly from memory. An important conjecture that we can make from this is that, because we all have different memories, we must each *see* something *different* when we look at the same view.

The Time Dependency of Vision

Earlier we noted that vision must have at least some time dependency, given that the small high-acuity center of vision must move all around the view, as our eye moves, to gather information over time. Here we will explore the full extent of that time dependency. It's easy to appreciate how sound plays out in

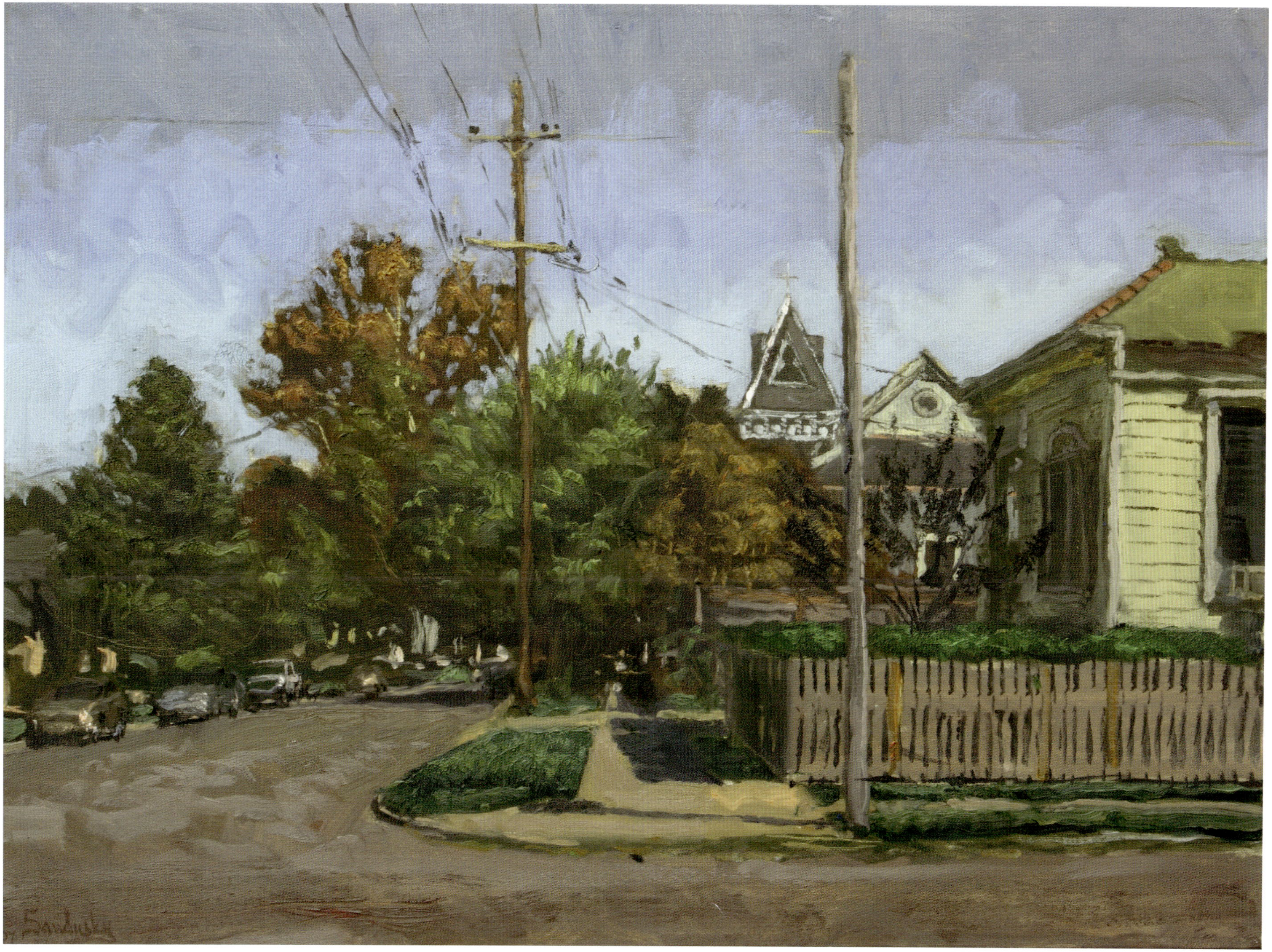

VIEW FROM THE INTERSECTION OF VALENCE AND CONSTANCE STREETS 18" X 24"

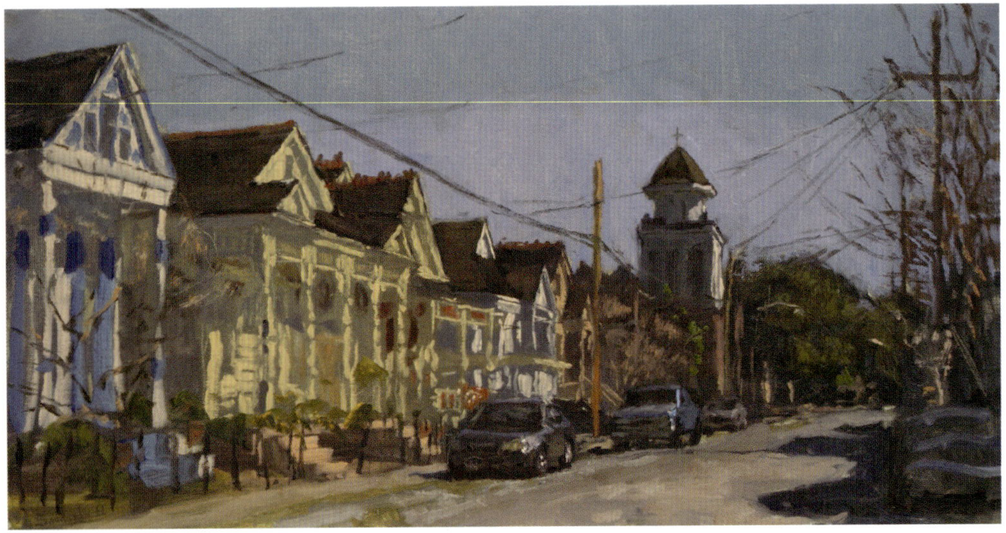

LOOKING DOWN COLISEUM STREET FROM A POSITION NEAR VALENCE STREET 15" X 30"

time because our auditory sensation and perception is simple compared to our vision. If you were to quickly open and close a door to a soundproof room in which you were standing, you would not be able to identify the sounds that you heard outside. But if you glanced outside the door for this brief period, your raw visual senses and memory would supply layers of organized visual information. It would not be the same information or likely as much information as could be provided in a photograph but there is more than enough to help foster the illusion that you have photograph-like images in your mind.

When you first glance at a certain view you are startled by the contrast between the breadth of it and your previous view. Perhaps your eyes were focused on objects in the cool shade and now they've been turned up to a view in the blazing sunlight. We have learned that we cannot see things absolutely. Vision, as well as all of our senses, registers only change. As the impact of this initial big sweeping change begins to evoke many qualifiers and perhaps even some mandates (perhaps a mandate to "protect eyes"), in the next instant you begin to register contrasts between the different parts of this new view: how the big areas within it resonate in form, scale, color, and texture. Your eyes scan all around the bigger view producing great numbers of qualifiers and some mandates that pertain to it as a whole. All corners of your vast library of memories are queried for similarities to be compared and contrasted to these fledgling perceptions so that at first basic recognition can be achieved followed by a grand perception of the whole subject charged and flavored by memory. This is the freshest and most vivid the subject will seem and it will seem different to each one of us because we all have different memories. We impressionists have found that a strong, succinct statement of the whole with few details brings viewers to this pinnacle of perception and holds them there.

However, our vision is not just this one crisp first impression. After taking in the big view, our attention begins to be drawn to aspects and smaller parts of it. To a great extent it is each individual's unique library of memories, or more specifically the mandates within (or referenced to) these memories, that determine to which of these aspects and parts of the bigger view our attention is drawn. For a car salesman the initial first impression of his neighborhood street might have had more qualifiers evoked from memory having to do with circles and shiny metallic effects, because these qualities are prominent in cars, which are more abundant in his memories. These particular qualifiers have in the past figured prominently into lowering, or satisfying, such mandates for his volitional behavior as "maintain or strengthen position in group" (as the most valuable salesperson in the dealership), many others, and ultimately "hunger." Accordingly, his attention and eye-scanning become focused more upon parts or aspects of the view (in this case, cars) that evoke more of these specific qualifiers. Imagine how different a landscape architect's vision of this neighborhood street would be. As we each scan the view differently depending upon our memories, each smaller part or aspect of the bigger view to which our attention is drawn becomes a new whole.

In general, we register the qualifiers and mandates evoked

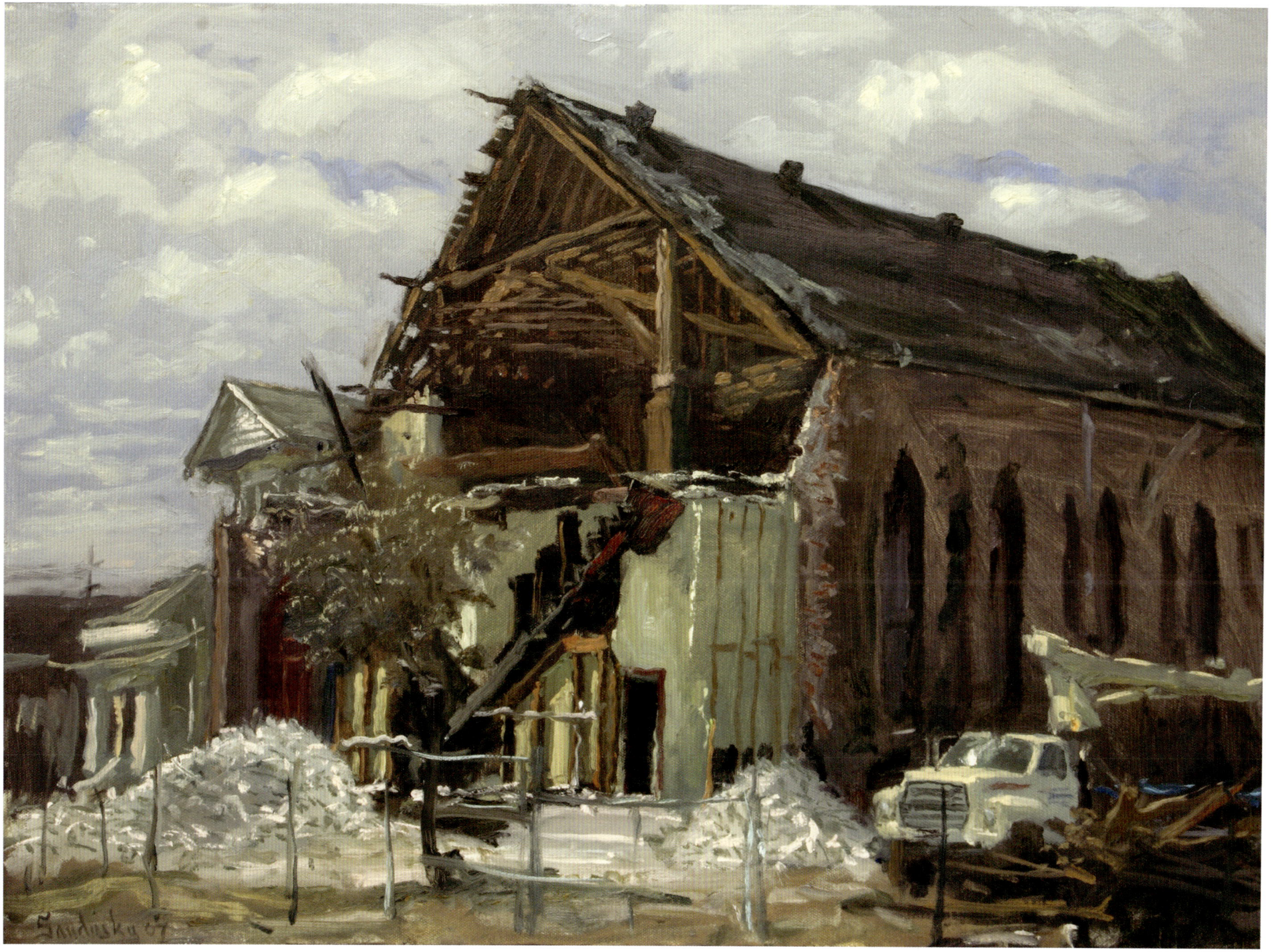

CHURCH DECONSTRUCTED (SEEN FROM THE CORNER OF VALENCE AND CHESTNUT STREETS) 18" x 24"

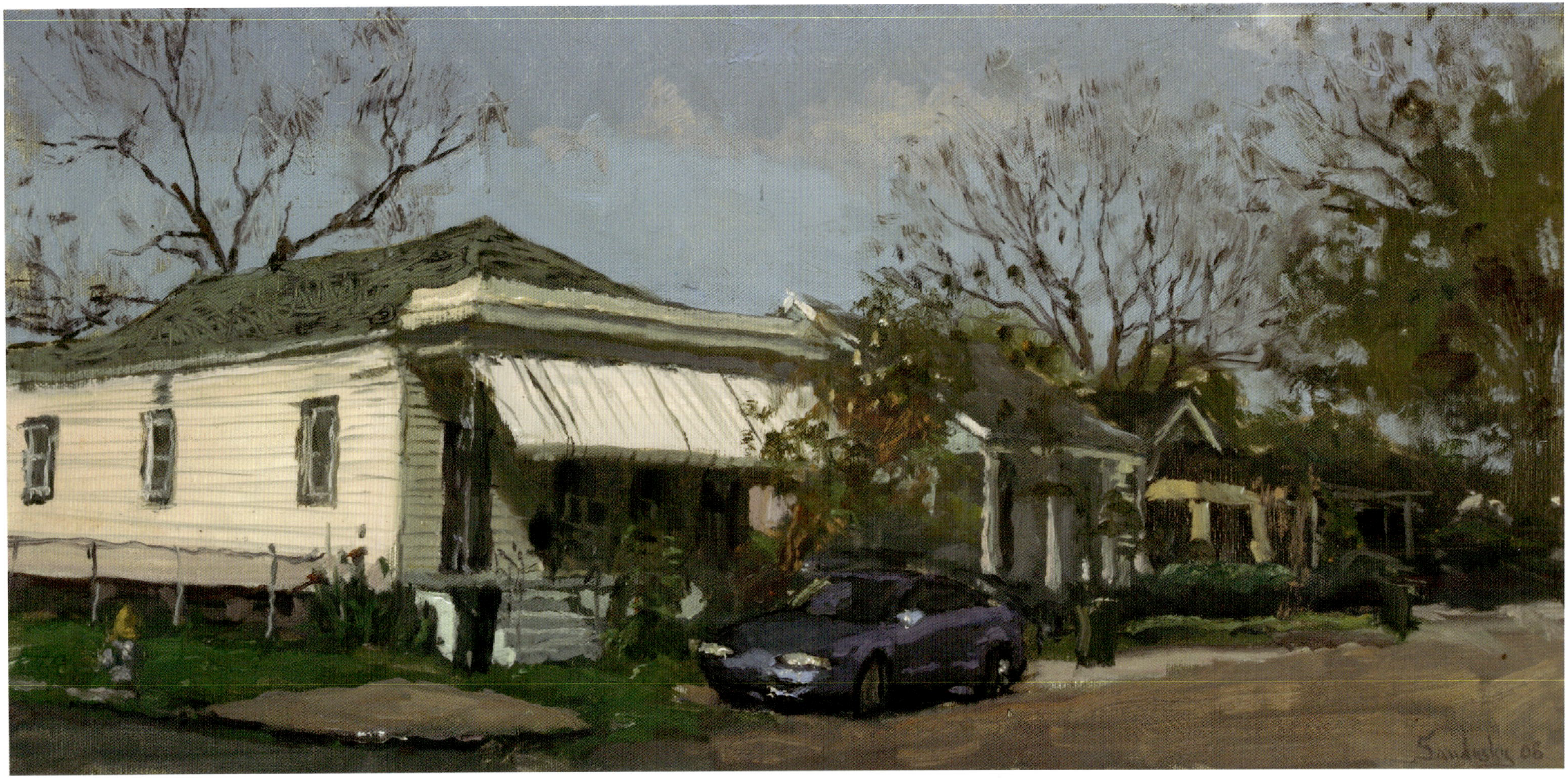

View from the corner of Laurel and Delachaise streets 12" x 24." These houses have recently been renovated and remodeled and the view is only recognizable now by the trees and the roofline of the closest house.

from our eye-scanning and memories over time, not all at once. The first wave of qualifiers and mandates are registered when we turn our head from one big view to another. More waves are registered in succession as we begin to scan our eyes around to juxtapose the big parts within the new big view. And then more waves are registered as our scanning is drawn into the smaller parts. Intermittently our attention is drawn back out to the bigger view and eventually to an entirely new view. We are aware of a great many waves of mandates and qualifiers at any one instant, but the more recently evoked ones are more prominent in our perceptions. There is no point where enough qualifiers and mandates have been accumulated that our cognition can take the measure of them to summon learned behaviors that will satisfy the preeminent mandates. This would imply that some total picture or accounting is drawn up in our mind to which we would respond. But learned behaviors are constantly being summoned, and most are overwritten before they can be acted out. Think of how often you've aborted an under-the-breath verbal utterance to either say something entirely different, or nothing. Our cognition is constantly and continually doing the best that it can with what it has.

Through a series of simple perceptual experiments conducted in the early twentieth century, Max Wertheimer, the founder of Gestalt psychology, demonstrated that smaller perceptions that *seem* to fall under the umbrella of a bigger perception cannot be added together to form the bigger perception. The motto of the Gestalt psychologists, and what would eventually be called "the first principle of gestalt," became, "The whole is different than the sum of its parts." The application of this timeless principle of perceptual psychology to vision comes to bear when our attention is drawn in to the smaller quarters of a larger view. As we begin to scan and assess each object in a view separately, these smaller perceptions cannot be added together to replicate the initial experience that we had when we first laid eyes upon the bigger view. The best proponents of impressionism have at least intuitively realized this and have made paintings with only

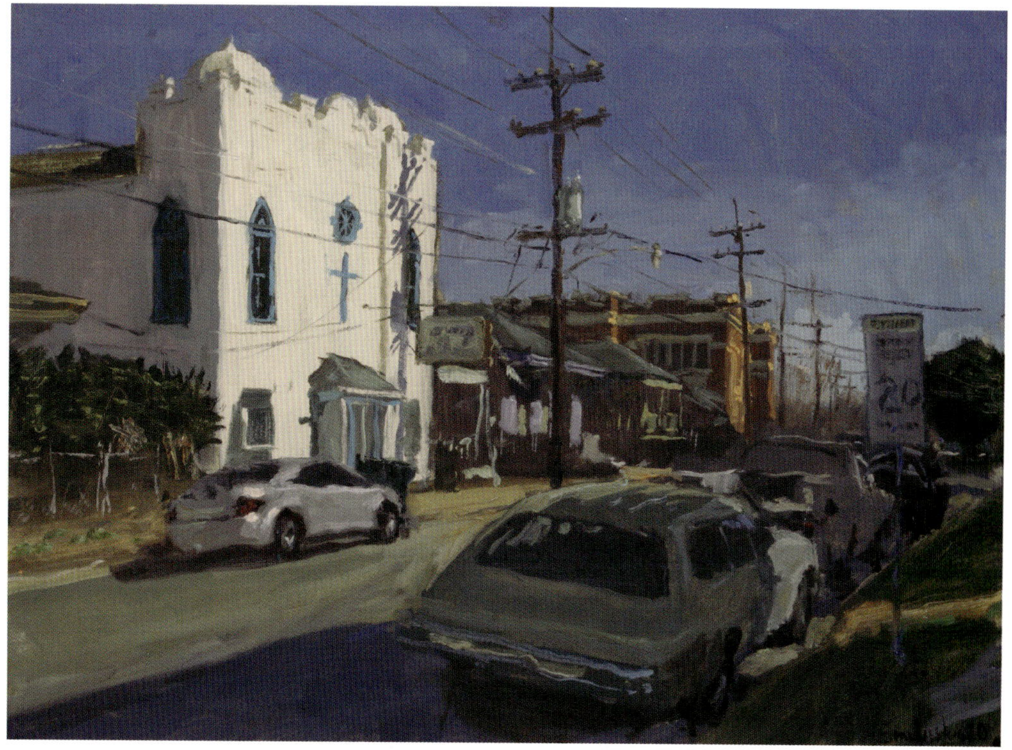

ZION TRAVELERS SECOND BAPTIST CHURCH ON LAUREL STREET NEAR PENISTON STREET 18" x 24"

the whole in mind. The parts of their paintings are often either brash, indistinct, or rather odd when viewed from up close but are painted as such so that when seen from a distance together, they form a powerful whole. But the impressionists have chosen to design an image on their canvas that evokes just this one distinct experience. A great dilemma of more traditional forms of representational painting is that one canvas has been used to evoke many different distinct experiences associated with the same view that happen in succession. In these paintings, individual parts of the bigger view are articulated to evoke a sense of what we would see when we focus our attention on each of them separately. These paintings read well when viewed from up close, so that the smaller parts can each be seen separately. But when we view these paintings from a distance, the whole is usually less

(Continued on page 47)

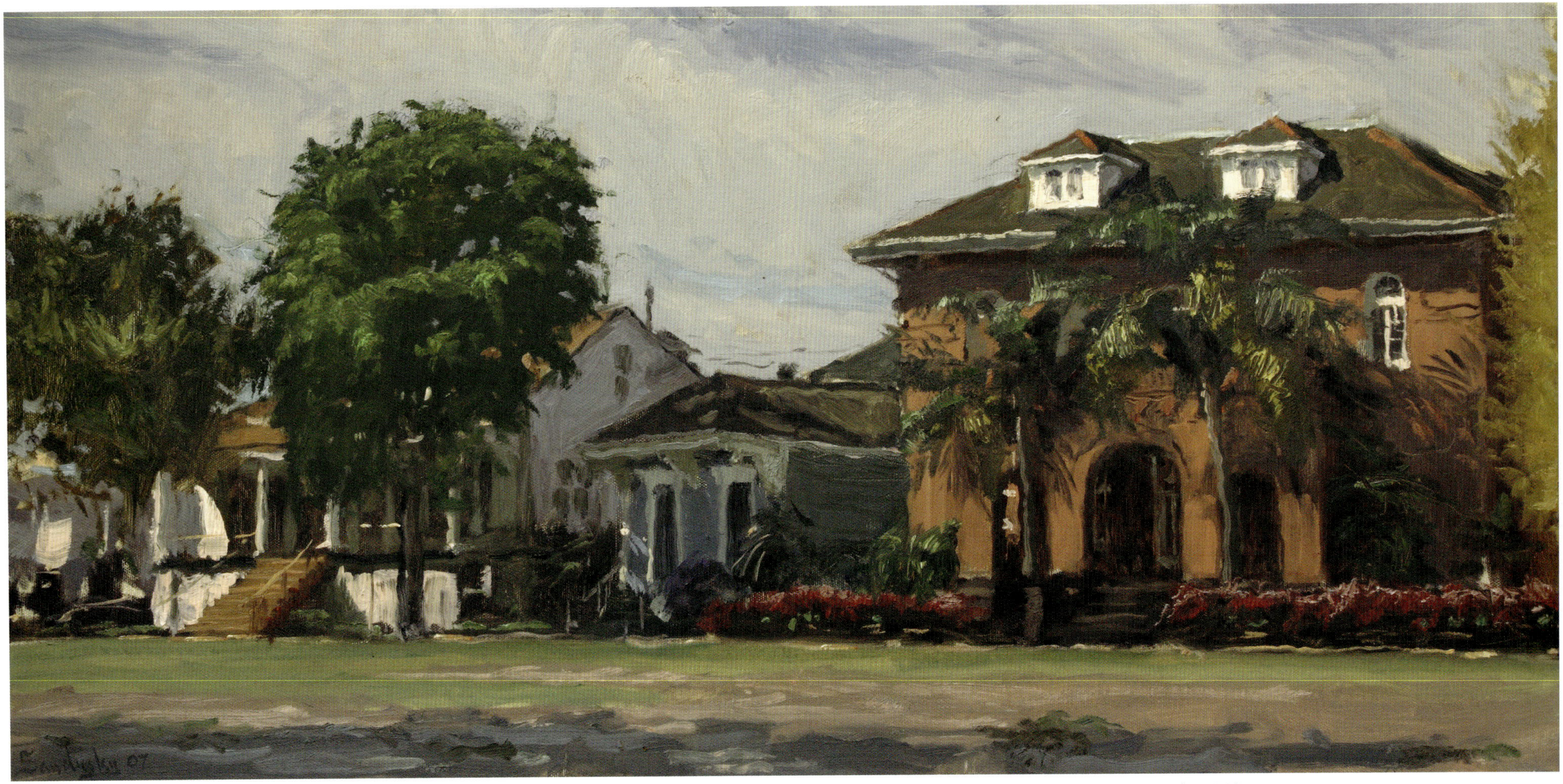

Houses seen from across Laurence Square on Napoleon Avenue between Camp and Magazine streets 15" x 30"

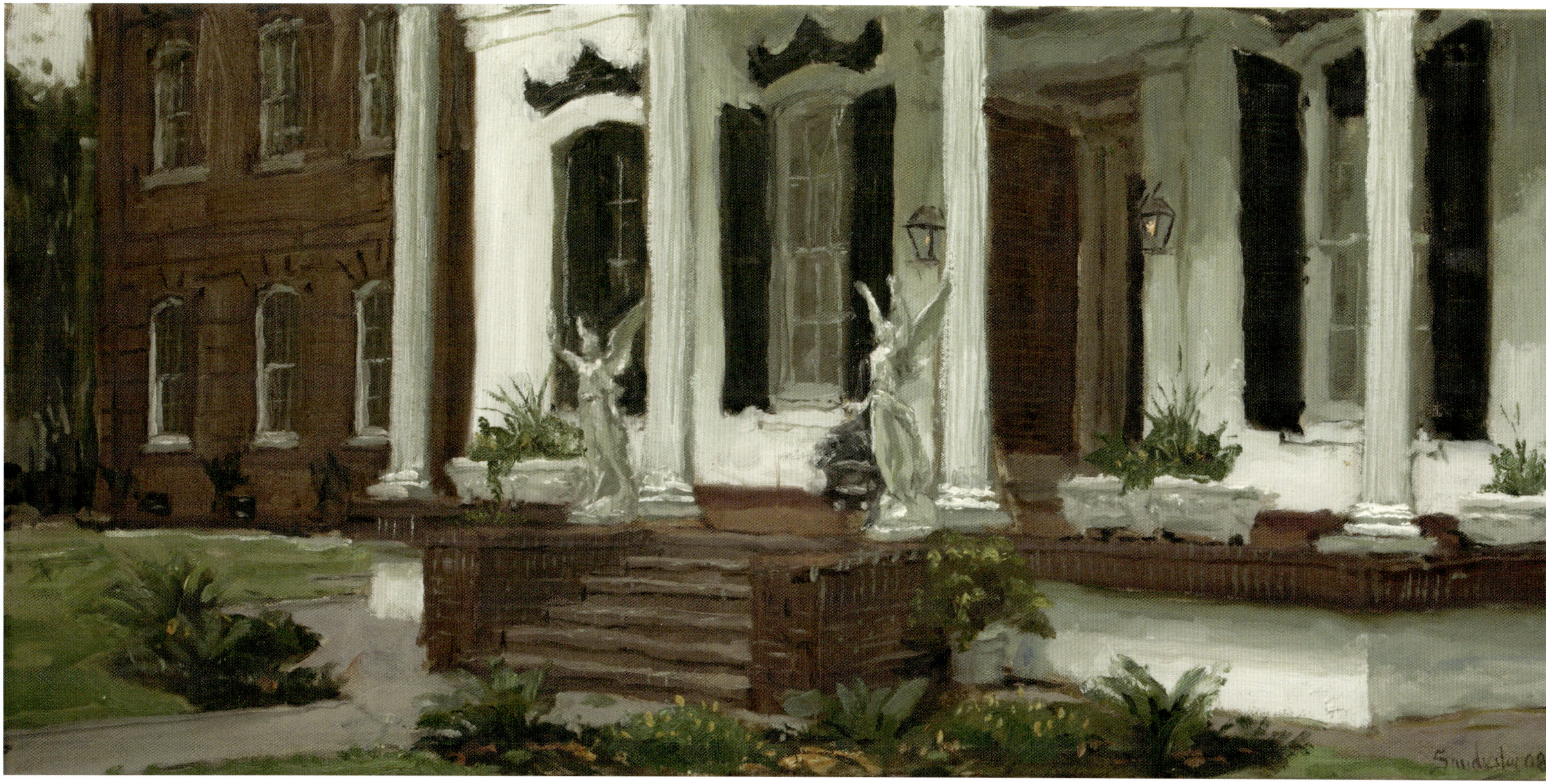

St. Elizabeth's seen from Napoleon Avenue close to Prytania Street 15" x 30"

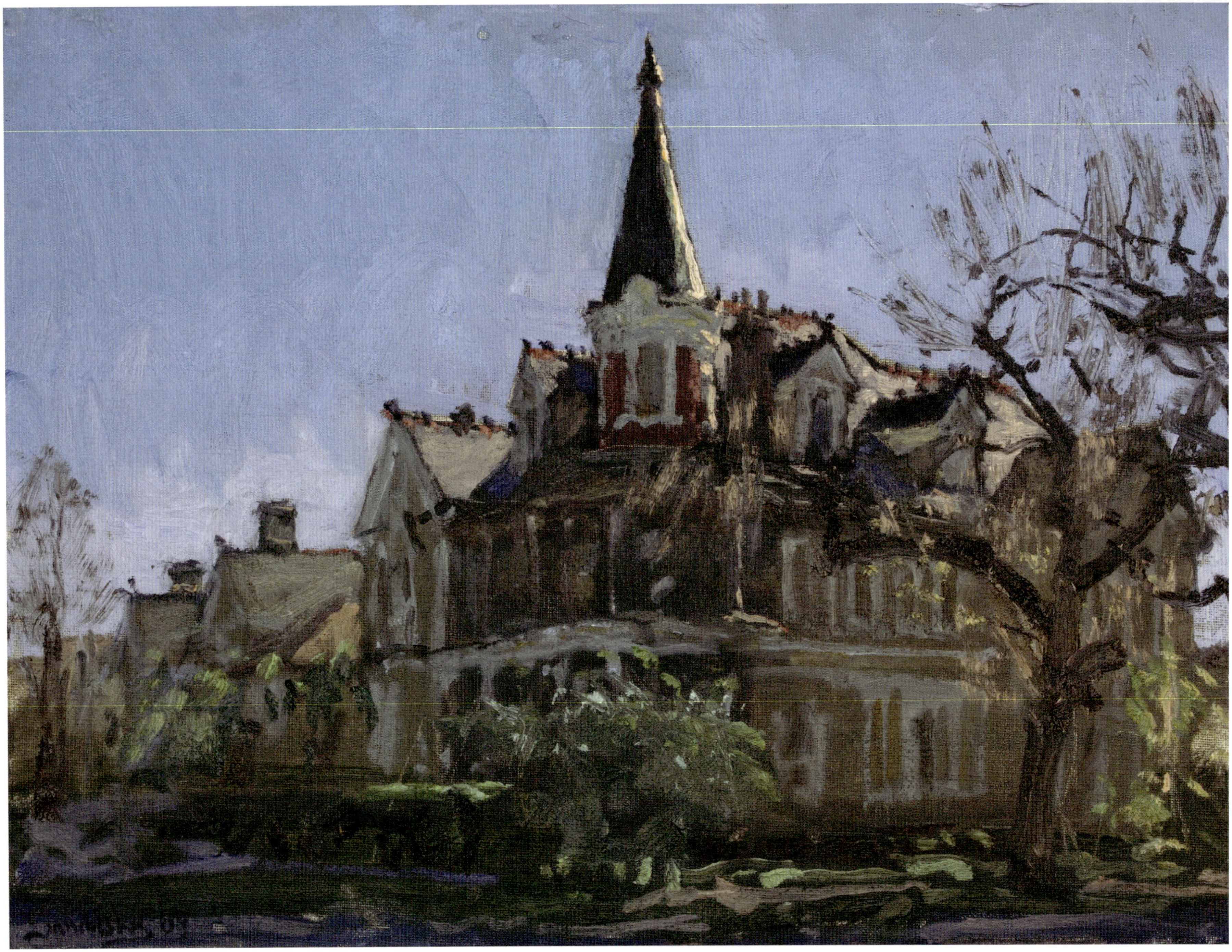

House on the corner of Marengo and Prytania streets 14" x 18"

evocative than each of the individual parts. We know that if every note in a musical composition were to be played all at once there would be nothing but meaningless noise. But when too many notes of our visual perception are stated coincidentally upon the same canvas, as is often the case in more traditional forms of academic realism, there is a dubious fallback position. The artist can avoid producing meaningless *visual* noise by aligning his painting with the *objective image* instead of vision. The objective photograph-like image is not bound by the first principle of gestalt or any mechanics of our visual psychophysics. It is not relative, but absolute. It has no time dependency, existing as it is in its entirety in one instant, every part being equally distinct. This is why traditional more meticulous academic paintings when seen from a distance often look a bit boring and photograph-like compared to small preparatory studies that were done of the same view or good impressionist paintings of similar subjects. Yet, these more traditional pieces that contain more information still remain the only *conventional* vehicle for communicating the breadth of vision as it plays out in time. But the best proponents of this type of painting don't allow the whole to be *completely* compromised by the parts. They skillfully negotiate between the whole and the parts, allowing the parts to have more voice, but not *too* much more. They allow the parts to be a little less interesting each in themselves so that the whole can still have good impact. The Cubists Pablo Picasso and Georges Braque made a stab at showing how our vision occurs in bits and pieces over time. But in my opinion their end result was unsuccessful, because they placed different perceptions on the same canvas, producing an overall effect that resembled seeing the world through a cracked mirror. As modern technology becomes better integrated into our future esthetics more options will open. Perhaps time-based painting presentations better aligned with real time-based human vision will provide a better vehicle than Cubism or the traditional *meticulous* painting for communicating the breadth of our vision as it plays out in time. Imagine a series of impressionist vignettes of different aspects and parts of the same view, each a near perfect

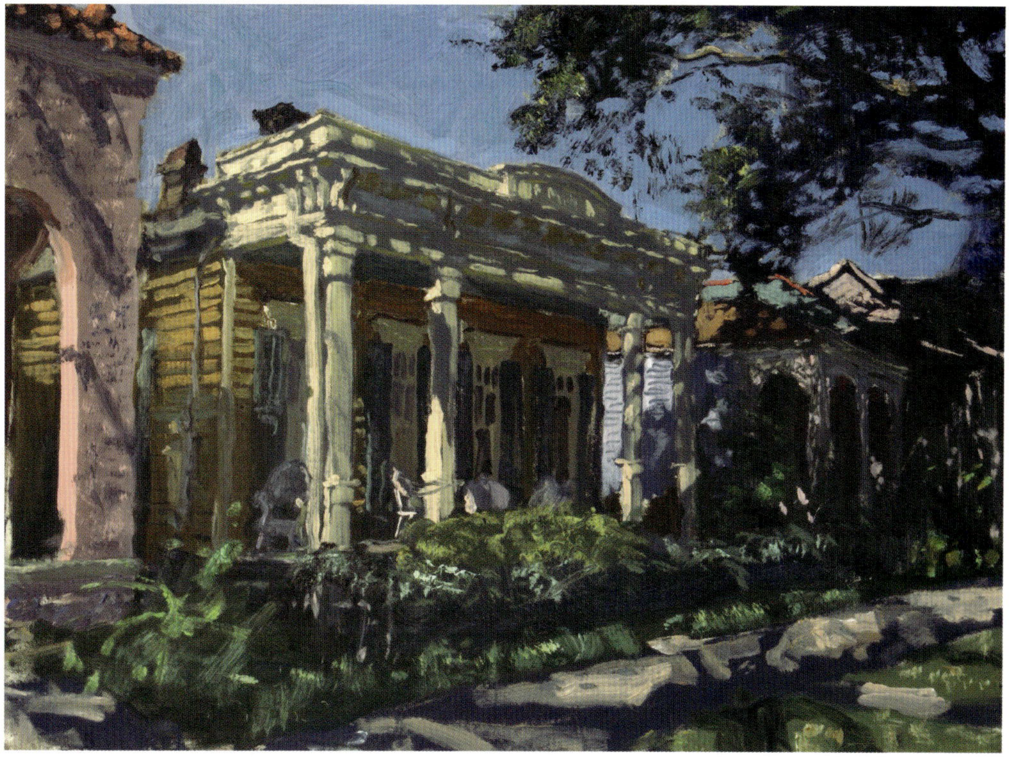

COTTAGE IN DAPPLED SUNLIGHT ON NAPOLEON AVENUE NEAR CHESTNUT STREET 18" X 24"

uncompromised whole, presented sequentially on something like an iPad or wall-mounted flat monitor. Each vignette would be like a chord in a piece of music, presented sequentially as in real human vision rather than all at once as in the objective image.

Events and Objects

The grand illusion that we have been trying to dispel that vision is like photographic images in your mind would be more accurately compared to video, given the dynamic nature of our experiences. Your vision might seem more like a video camera, registering many frames in succession showing objects in motion and constantly changing your view by panning as you move your head and eyes around.

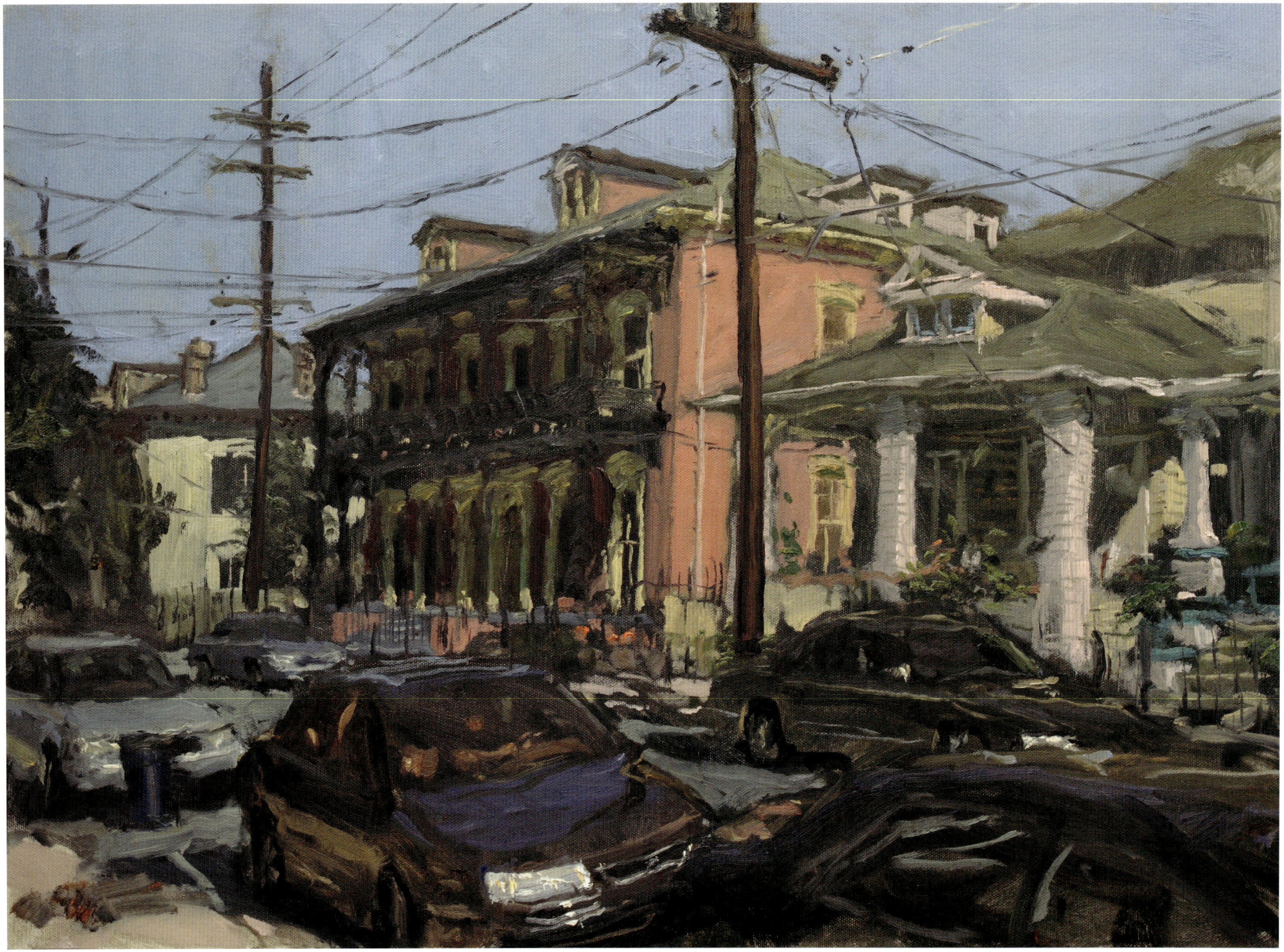

Old apartment building on St. Andrew Street viewed from a position between Camp and Chestnut streets 18" x 24"

Our perception of objects seems more intuitive than that of events because we *seem* to have images that represent objects stored in our memory, and events seem to be the more abstract substance that reports the behavior of those objects. It is easy to conceptualize as mandates and qualifiers the intangible qualities that inter-relate objects, describe their movement, and their usefulness to us or the threat that they pose. Objects are more difficult. Though we know that objects are solid, our perception of them can only be composed of a large number of corollaries of distinct little perceptual *events* that are cross-referenced to each other. This idea is a bit easier to digest when we consider that all we know of any aspect of the world, event or object, is provided by our senses which sample in bits and pieces over time. When you first glance at an object you notice only the big overriding qualities that juxtapose it to the surroundings, such as its relative scale and its overall shape and color. These overriding qualities we might think of as occupying the first row of a *matrix* of qualifiers. Succeeding rows of the matrix could be formed over time as you gather more information about the object from your senses and juxtapose it to memories. Physical events and the physical objects that are participants in those events are both only *perceptual* events cognitively. This conceptualization of objects as events is not new. Impressionist painters of the late nineteenth century, such as Eduard Manet and Claude Monet, transitioned from rendering solid forms in 2D using traditional modeling and chiaroscuro techniques to making paintings that evoked a sense of the subject as a perceptual event that they referred to as the "fleeting moment" or the "sensation." This was perhaps our first formal recasting of concrete objects as perceptual events, although there were individual painters such as Frans Hals who touched on this idea long before the impressionists. Consideration of a writer describing an object with a verbal narrative that plays out in time may help you to better intuit the way that matrices of qualifiers and mandates registered in quick succession, if not almost simultaneously, could create your perception of a solid object.

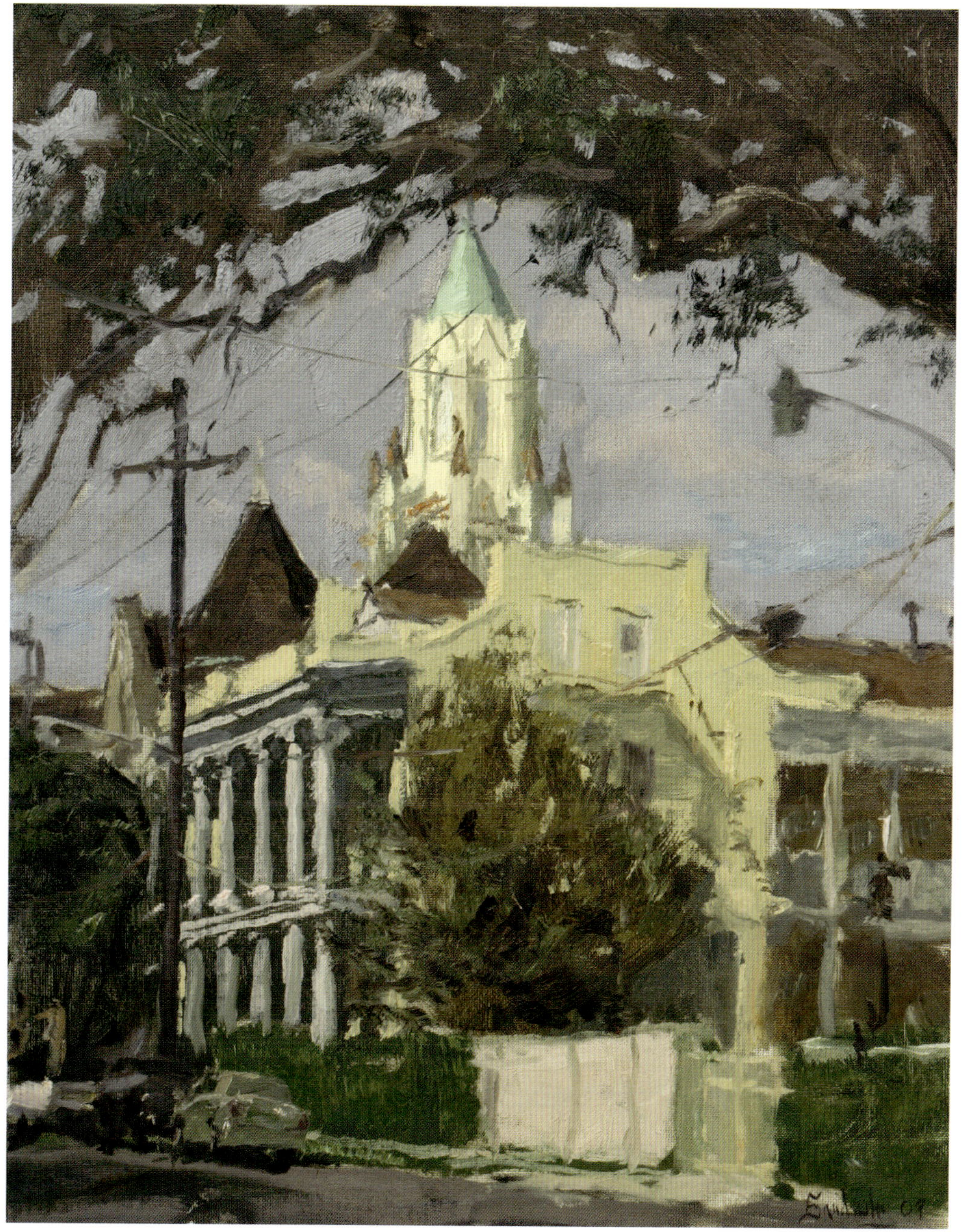

View from Prytania Street close to St. Andrew Street 18" x 14"
The church, whose spire is seen in the middle of the canvas rising above the Greek Revival mansion, was destroyed by fire about a year after I did this painting.

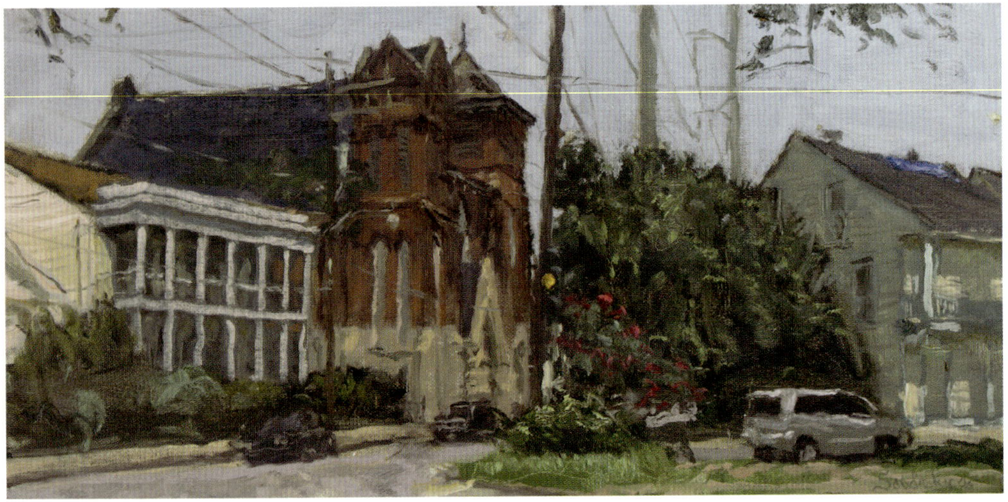

View from Felicity and Camp streets 10" x 20"

The Image Fallacy

Now we have laid enough groundwork that we can confront the grand illusion that I think of as the image fallacy. We have posited that as modern humans inundated with flat photographic images and artists' renderings to which we respond similarly to light reflecting off of three dimensional physical objects, we likely have the misconception that such images are in our mind. Amazingly, children's drawings may hold the key to a more accurate conceptualization of vision. When you step outside and look up into the sky, it seems that there must be a big blue pattern somewhere in your mind. A child who has had no art instruction typically draws the sky as a blue bar at the top of the paper and the ground as a green bar at the bottom, with a great void of blank paper between the two. He doesn't seem to *see* that the sky goes all the way to the horizon, where it meets the ground. Certainly when the child scans a view with his eyes there are sensory evoked qualifiers issued corresponding to where the sky meets the ground such as "blue adjacent to green," (or perhaps more accurately, "difference between blue and green," because our senses only register change). But the qualifiers, "blue / up / all over" and "green / down / all over," are much more prominent in his memories because they relate to what is always close by: frogs and bugs jumping around in the grass beneath his feet and birds and tree limbs above his head. Even when the horizon is visible and not blocked by nearby objects, it is of little consequence to him. He can't touch it or even throw a rock at it, and he knows that as far away as he walks there is always sky above him and ground below him. The qualifier "blue adjacent to green" is one of a few sensory evoked qualifiers and mandates that initiate an avalanche of arrays of qualifiers and mandates from the child's memory, rich with occurrences of "blue / up / all over" and "green / down / all over" but not even a faint echo of "blue adjacent to green." After completing its expeditionary mission, that qualifier had become an aberrant data point to be disregarded by the child's cognition / vision. Even when the child followed with his eyes a flock of birds flying off into the distance, he would have likely never seen them *adjacent* to the horizon but rather only *far away*.

Yet, the child is not satisfied with his childish drawing. It is an output of his neural processes that is inadequate to be used as input to re-evoke those processes, because it is missing at least one important catalyst that is invisible to him: "blue adjacent to green." When he is shown how to draw the sky and ground more convincingly with the sky color filled in all the way to the ground, "blue adjacent to green" becomes more prominent in his memory perhaps because it becomes a key qualifier in satisfying the mandate, "maintain or strengthen position in group" (as more proficient draftsman). With more such experiences under his belt, his vision of the sky will expand beyond a simple triad of qualifiers. But just because his experiences become more heavily qualified, and he has learned to color the sky in his drawing all the way to the ground, it doesn't mean that he *or you* will ever have anything like contiguous patterns of color in your minds.

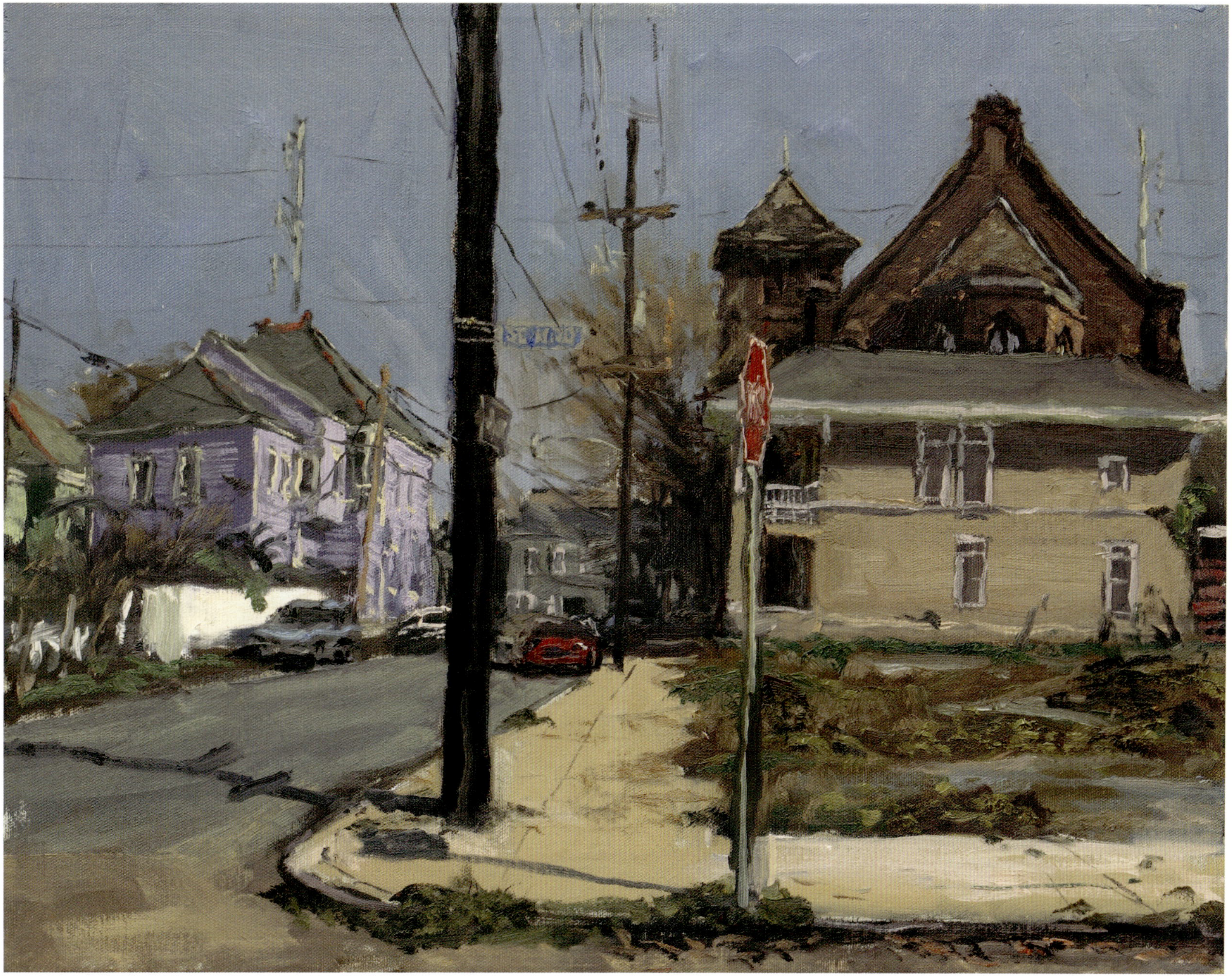

View from the corner of St. Mary and Chestnut streets 16" x 20" This majestic view of the back of Felicity United Methodist Church rising above the middle ground house was revealed only for about a year or two when a house on the corner burned and was razed. A new house has since been built, re-interring this amazing view.

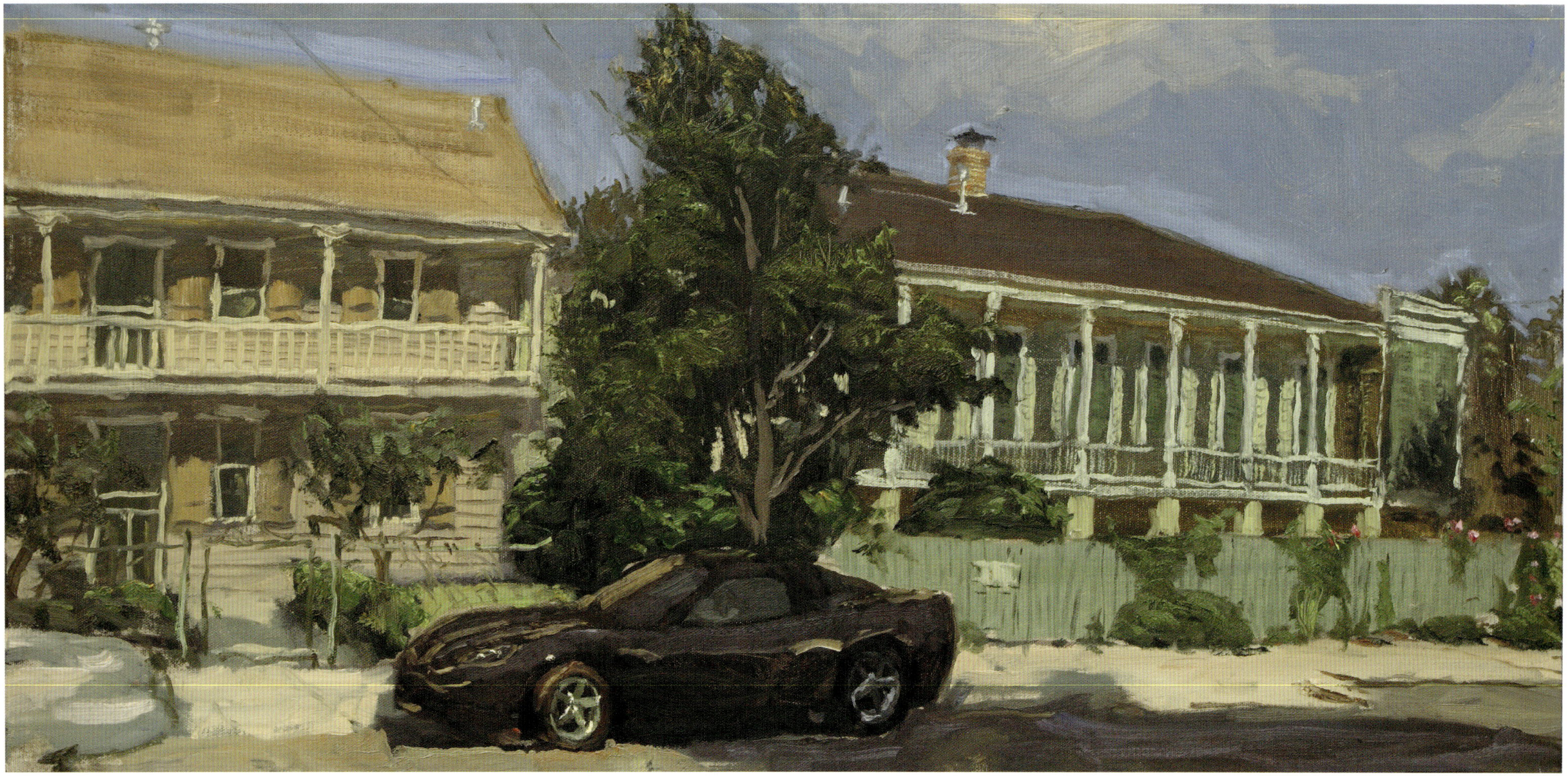

Black corvette on Chestnut Street close to Jackson Avenue 15" x 30"

We could keep deluding ourselves that the untrained child is not drawing what he sees, or we could observe the round, primitively stated face in his stickman drawing and think of the neural circuit that tests for object patterns that resonate like a human face. We could think of legions of qualifiers and mandates pulled up from memory and herded by the cracking whips of squadrons of qualifiers and mandates evoked by eye-scanning, simultaneously and sequentially feeding the child *and you* information over time—little aspects, big overriding aspects—all of which can be pretty powerfully re-evoked by turning around into view a flat photographic print made by a camera pointed in the general direction in which you were looking. But you must struggle to discern *cause* from *effect.* Instead of photographic images like this in our memories, we have cross-referenced mandates and mutually exclusive dense matrices of qualifiers providing enough descriptors so that our responses can be finely tuned. The point is that our vision and our visual memory, if there is any distinction between the two, are not images, but images *can* evoke them. A great majority of the same qualifiers and mandates are evoked from your exposure to a photograph or painting as would be evoked from your exposure to the first-hand experience. And because such images are more portable than the great big world out in front of our eyes and much more tangible than matrices of qualifiers and mandates, they become imposters that represent our vision.

Our *experience* of flat photographic images and artists' renderings must figure prominently into our memories, because they are most people's primary visual connection to the world outside of their own close environs. The memories formed from our experiences of their various properties, such as what would pertain to their 2-dimensionality; their every part being highly detailed and distinct all at the same time; *their filled-in contiguous color patterns;* and their obliqueness in ¾ view, become cross-referenced through so much of our visual memory that they effectively encapsulate

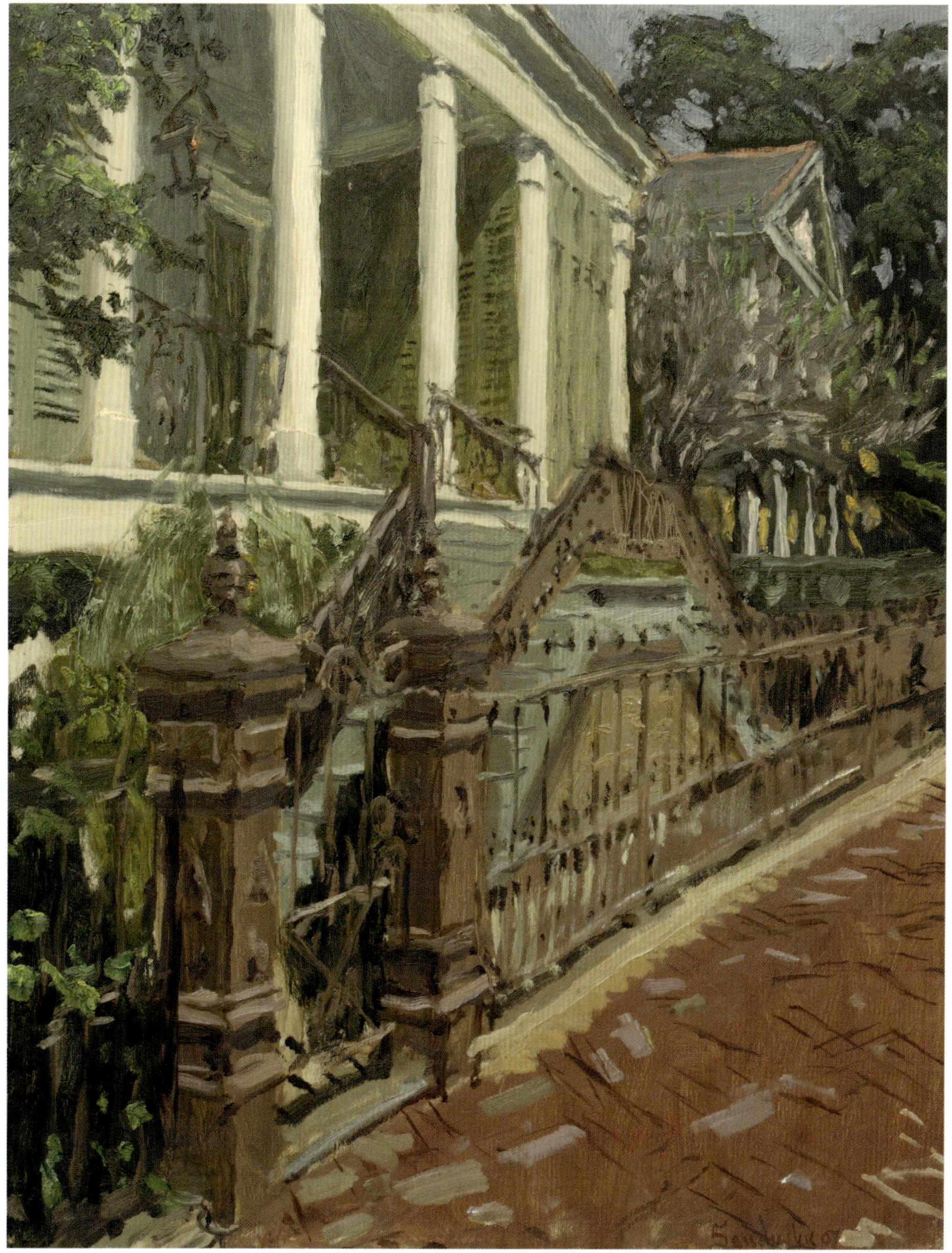

House on the corner of Jackson Avenue and Chestnut Street 24" x 18" This is a close-up view of the house to the right of the black Corvette on the facing page.

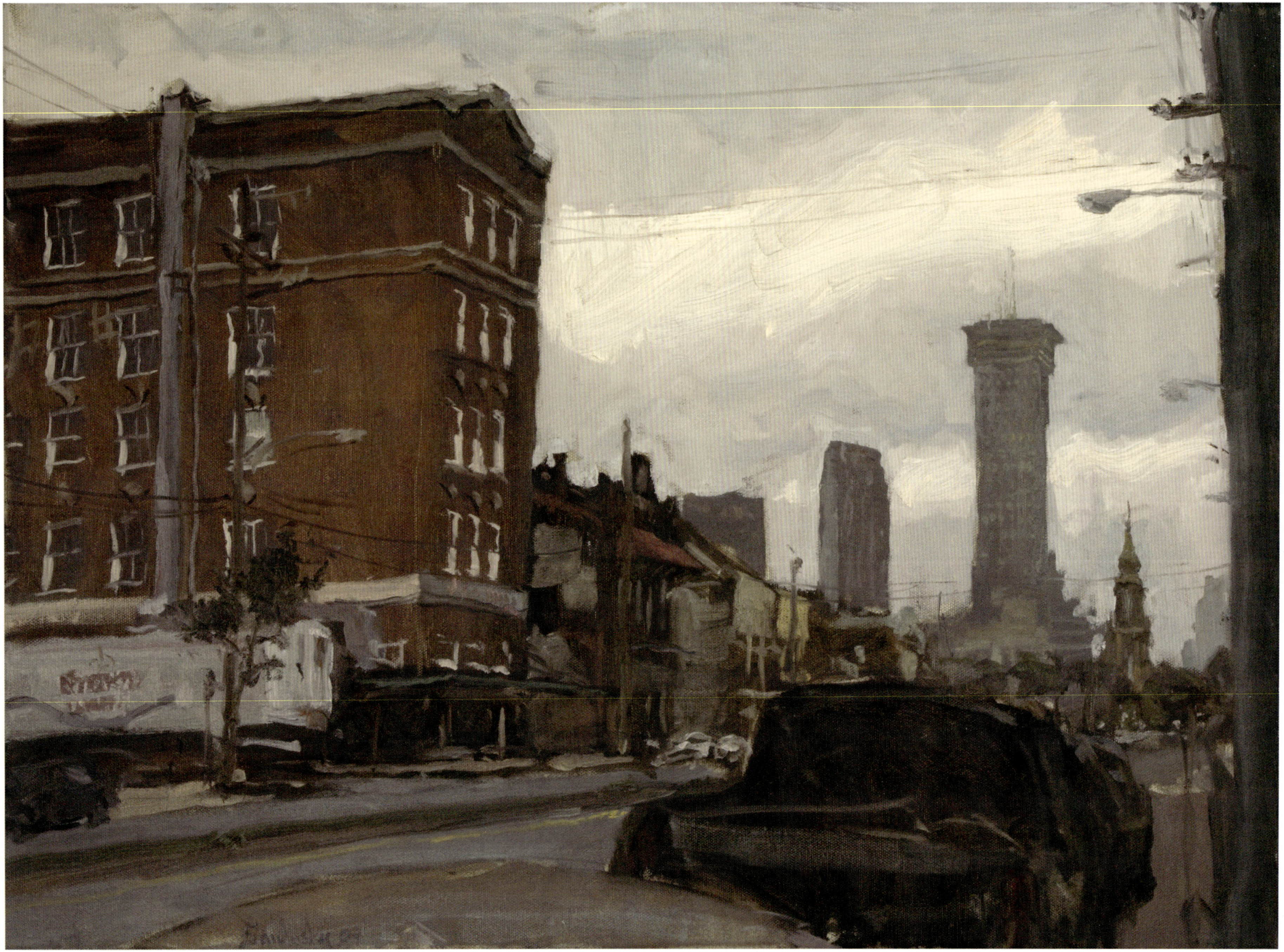

Oretha Castle Haley Boulevard at Felicity on a gloomy day 18" x 24"

our visual memory and make it difficult for us to perceive our vision as what it actually is, elastic mandates for our volitional behavior and successively occurring dense matrices of qualifiers, not stacks of little photographic images. How would the dense arrays of visual qualifiers manifest without your memories of images such as photographs, video, signage, and paintings? Perhaps something a bit closer to blue high, green low, pie faces, sticks, diagonals, circles, and very much more, constantly changing but well ordered. Although, as we saw earlier, these things are not actual qualifiers, but rather they are efficient economically created stimuli that can evoke the most prevalent qualifiers that exist mostly in our memory. We have seen that the qualifiers in themselves are much less interesting than the stimuli that evoke them. But given that qualifiers are boring, why do our experiences seem so rich?

Qualia

"Qualia" is a term used by philosophers to name the phenomenological or subjective aspects of our experiences such as the blueness of the sky, the warmth of the sun, or the sound of a musical note. Daniel Dennett, a prominent neuroscientist and philosopher of the mind, says that "qualia" is a most *unusual* term to name the things that are the most *usual*. How can mere qualifiers and mandates, which correlate to nothing more than simple pulse telemetry, account for the multitude of qualia that we experience, such as when we are in a restaurant: the color of the menu, the feel of the surface of the table, the look of the table's wood grain, the color of the waiter's hair, the clanking sounds of dishes coming from the kitchen? To answer this, let's cut one of these qualia out of the herd. One of the color patterns on our menu is blue.

Earlier we traced a color from its external physical inception through its basic processing in the neural circuitry to our final perception of it seen through the lens of our memory. You might at first think that the blue pattern on the menu is the ideal type

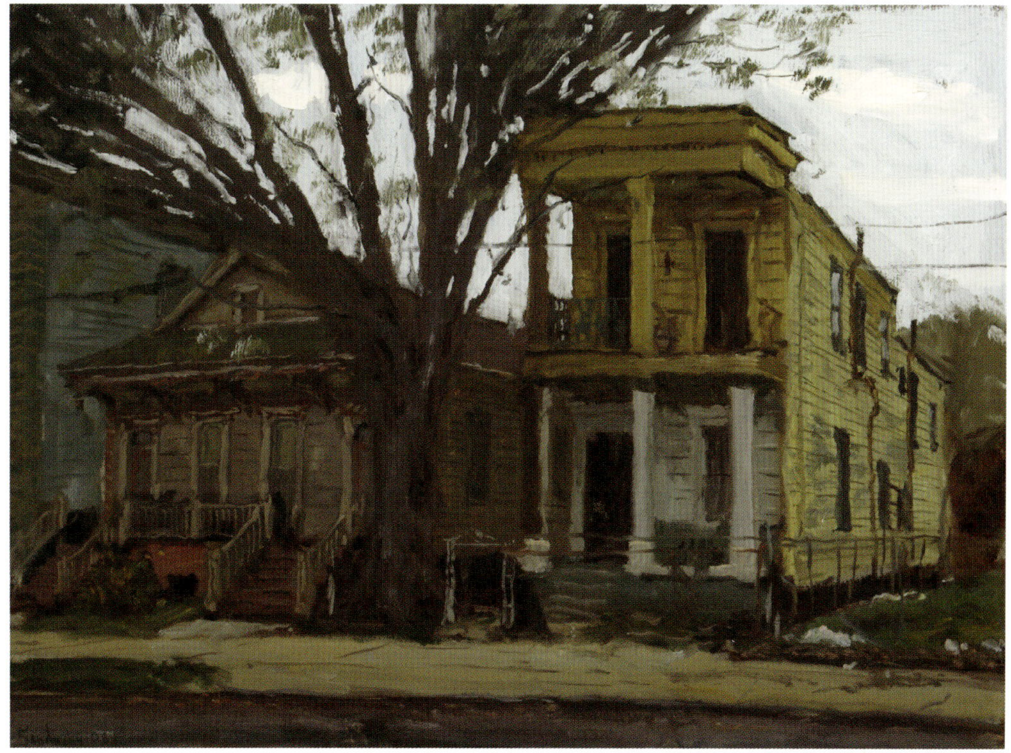

Blighted House on Carondelet Street near Felicity Street 18" x 24"

of color pattern not to be altered too much from its objective reality by memory. First, it has distinct boundaries, making it easy to juxtapose to adjacent color areas. Secondly, there are no memory associations that suggest that a color pattern on a menu has to be any particular color. Yet we have already seen that our experience of such an *arbitrary* qualifier as this "blue" can be at least somewhat dependent upon memory.

We begin with the naked qualifier "blue." (Actually there may be at least a few different blue qualifiers considering that we can detect about 150 different hues in the visible spectrum.) Throughout your life you have accumulated many memories formed from experiences of things that are blue. One of the most universal human experiences is seeing a large body of water such as a lake or ocean that is given its

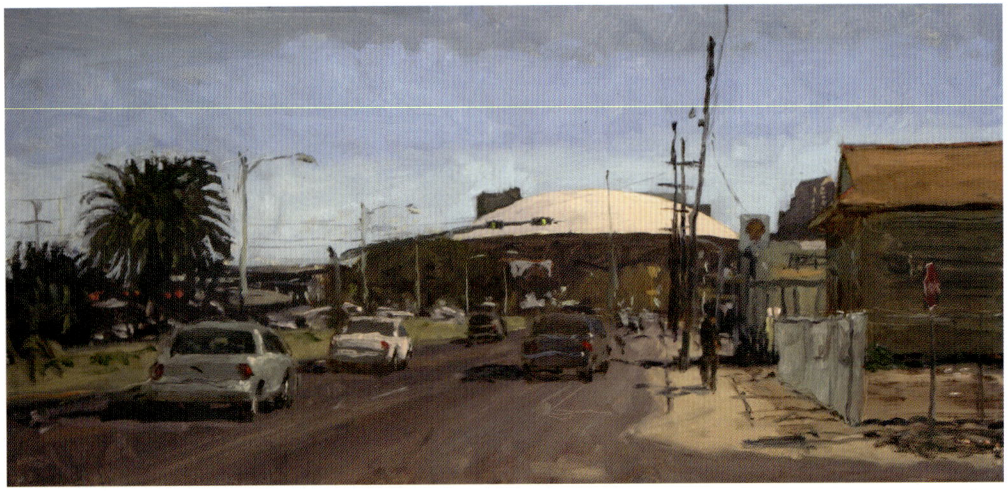

SUPERDOME ON A CLOUDLESS DAY SEEN FROM SOUTH CLAIBORNE AVENUE 15" X 30"

bluish color by the way it reflects the sky. There must be many qualifiers and mandates associated with the "blue" ocean. Most people have memories formed from experiences like swimming or learning to swim. Mandates such as "swim, don't drown" and "breath" (when underwater) might be significant players. Cross-referenced to these memories are memories formed in response to indirect experiences of people drowning, which might evoke the additional mandates, "protect" and "gain control." Memories of the *coldness* of ocean water contain the mandate to "seek warmth" and memories formed by experiences of a blue lake on a hot summer day contain the mandate to "cool down." But such opposite mandates don't cancel each other because of the way that they are qualified in the memories. Memories caused by experiences of fish (that swim in blue water) with qualifiers such as "triangle" and "ellipse" (corresponding to the form of the fish) may be cross-referenced. The lack of qualifiers that indicate similarity to the human form, such as might be caused by the fish's lack of feet and arms, may produce the mandate "ostracize" that in turn might be crucial in evoking memories formed in response to experiences of fishing that contains such mandates as "chase" and "masticate." These fish memories may be cross-referenced to memories formed by experiences of dead fish out of water that may contain a mandate "escape from bad odor." Thus far we have only barely started down one path of the "blue" forest. You have experienced other prominent things in your life that are blue, such as the sky, that might evoke memories caused by your experiences of falling or skydiving, containing such mandates as "gain control." These memories could be cross-referenced to memories formed in response to your experiences of birds containing qualifiers that relate to the shape and movement of the bird, and perhaps the mandate "gain freedom of movement."

Of course, when glancing at the blue pattern on your menu, you don't think of the ocean, swimming, drowning, fish, the sky, height, falling, etc. In a fleeting instant you only perceive the unique quality of blueness. Over the course of your life, especially early in your life, a matrix forms consisting of the most common qualifiers and mandates associated with your experiences of things that are blue. It is this unique "blue" matrix that is referenced when you passively glance at your menu. It may be difficult for you to fathom that a simple blue qualifier is accompanied by other qualifiers and different mandates like "breath" and "seek warmth" to form the unique quality "blueness." But, just think how much deeper and richer are a dense matrix of qualifiers and mandates than a lone signal from a neural circuit reporting only the certainty with which it has found a color difference within its receptive field. The "blue" experience is at least a little different for each person, because we have all had different life experiences forming different memories, making different associations to things that are blue.

However, the human experience generally and our experience of color specifically is, to some degree, universal. We all seem to consider reds, oranges, and yellows as being warm colors, probably because the most common associations to these colors are that of fire and the sun. Similarly, purples,

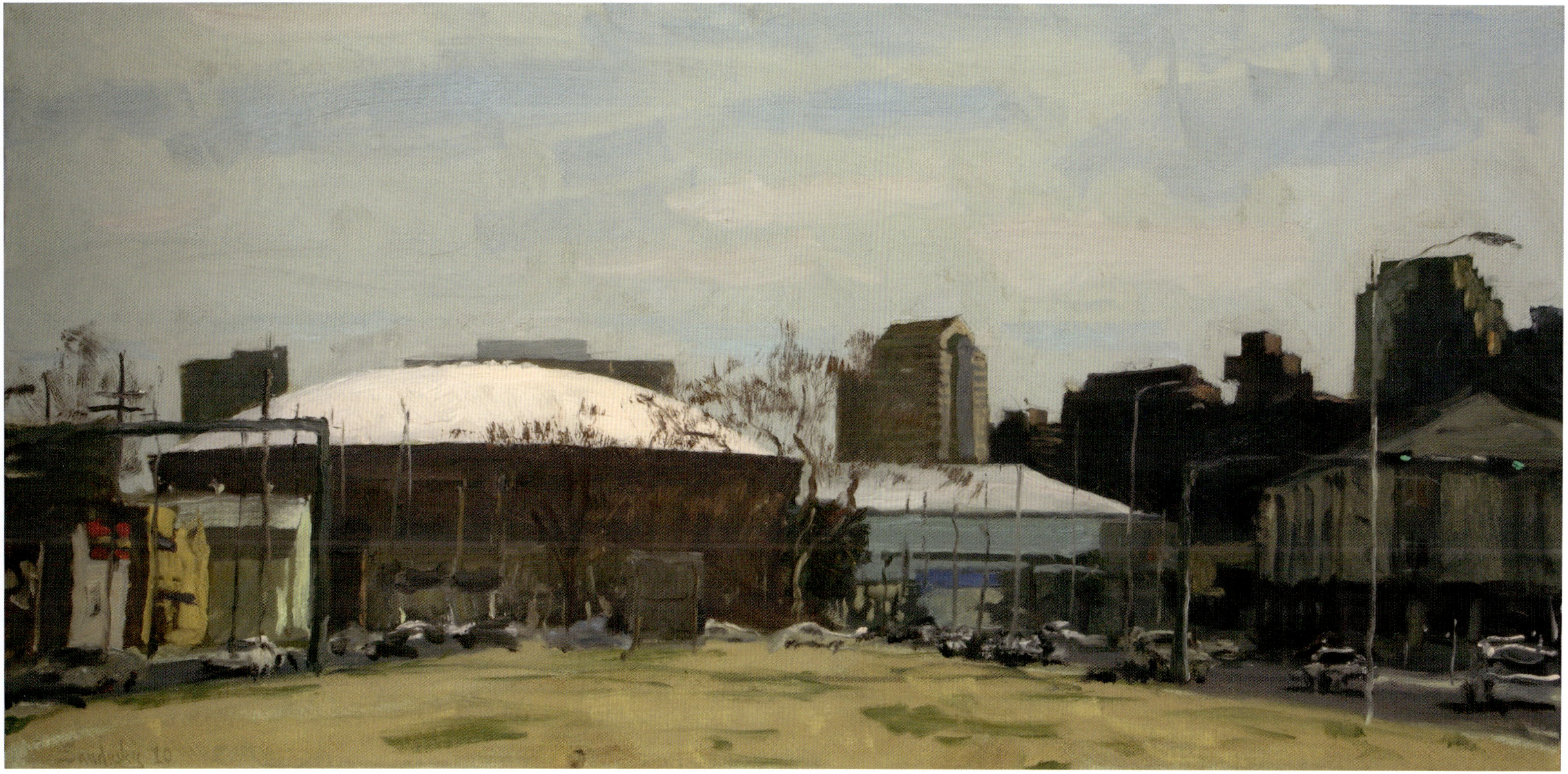

Buildings of the Central Business District viewed from the South Claiborne Avenue neutral ground 15" x 30"

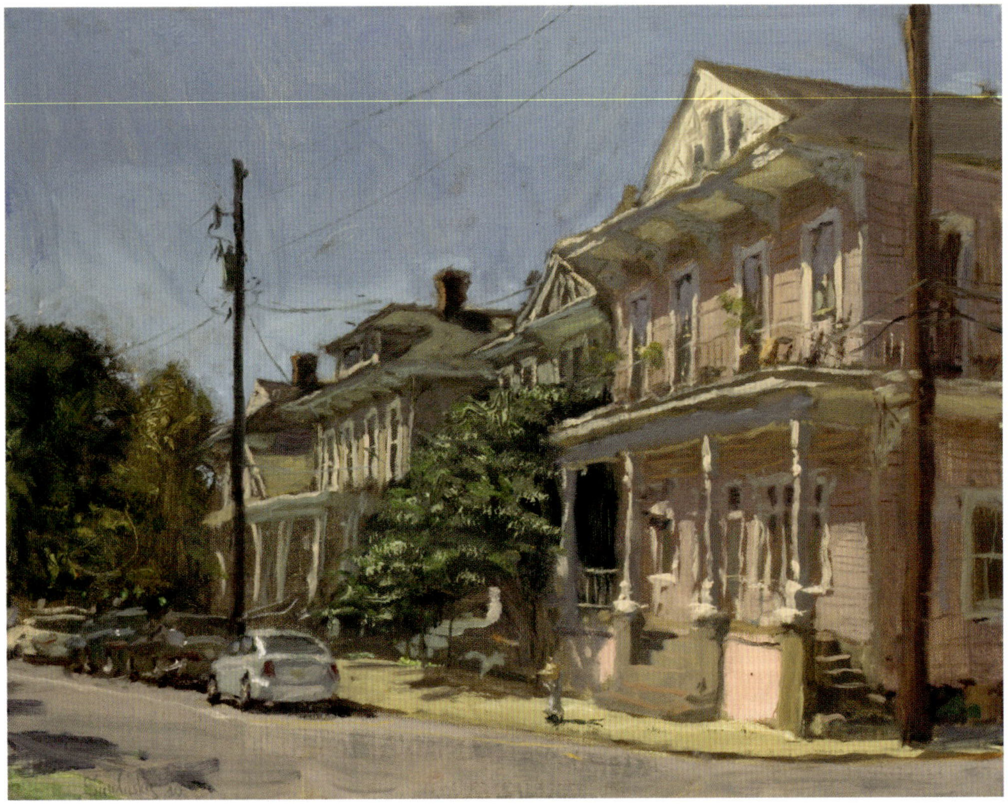

Lower Garden District houses seen from Erato and Coliseum streets 16" x 20"

blues, and blue-greens are likely thought of by most people as cool colors because they're unlike the sun and fire and more often associated with cool water and shade. This implies that an infant just developing color vision might begin with only the elemental qualifier "blue," having never seen the sky, water, or fire. This basic experience of blue would then be further augmented by life experiences.

The objective physical properties of our surroundings mask the differences that we each must have in our experience of any quale (singular form of qualia) such as "blue." The clear sky today is almost the same as the clear sky yesterday and is similar to its reflection in the water, to cars painted a certain pigment, an acetylene flame, to varicose veins, etc. Each of us experiences "blue" differently, but we all call these things "blue." Generally, we can each point to the same stimulus and call it the same name, but from that point blossoms out in each of our minds a different delicious phenomenological cocktail that can only be deciphered by artists. There is a chapter in Herman Melville's novel *Moby Dick* called "The Whiteness of the Whale" that shows the breadth of such a matrix of qualifiers and mandates for a certain quale (in this case "white") formed by an individual's life experiences. When you understand how different and complex is each person's perception of something as elemental as an isolated swatch of blue, you gain a greater appreciation of just how differently we must each see a larger, more meaningful view.

The Naked Qualifier and Mandate

We have argued thus far for the reduction of the qualia of our experiences to qualifiers and mandates as we have defined them, but to fully understand our vision we must reduce it even further. It is natural to think about qualifiers and mandates macroscopically in their usual context, such that the mandate to "relieve epidermal irritation" is considered greatly different than an auditory qualifier such as "middle c," which is considered greatly different from a visual qualifier such as "blue." Actually, the fact that they manifest as simple electric signals in our neural circuitry suggest that naked qualifiers and mandates are only slightly different from each other.

We have seen that the depth of the quale of blue is formed throughout our life by matrices of such qualifiers and mandates often associated with the physical color of blue such as "seek warmth," but what of the irreducible qualifier "blue" that is only an imperative to juxtapose a certain abstraction of the raw senses to its counterparts in memory? An infant just developing color-vision has not formed a matrix of qualifiers and mandates associated with blue that constitutes

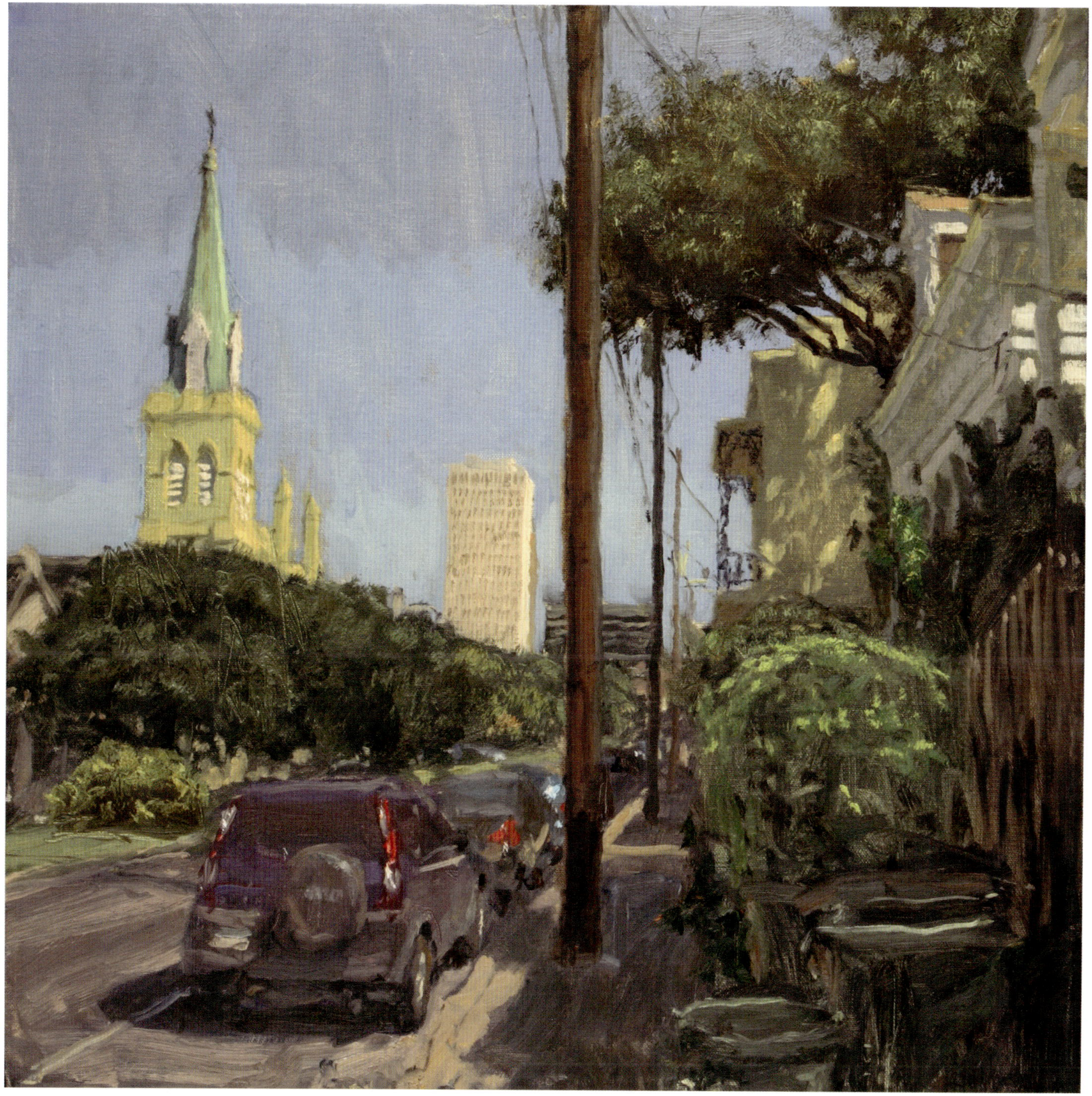

View of One Shell Square and Theresa of Avila Church from Camp Street near Thalia Street 20" x 20" The equal luminance (equiluminance) of the sky and background buildings in this painting by the sun creates an eerie effect. This is because our vision has difficulty establishing the position of patterns using only color contrast with no contrast in lightness or darkness (value).

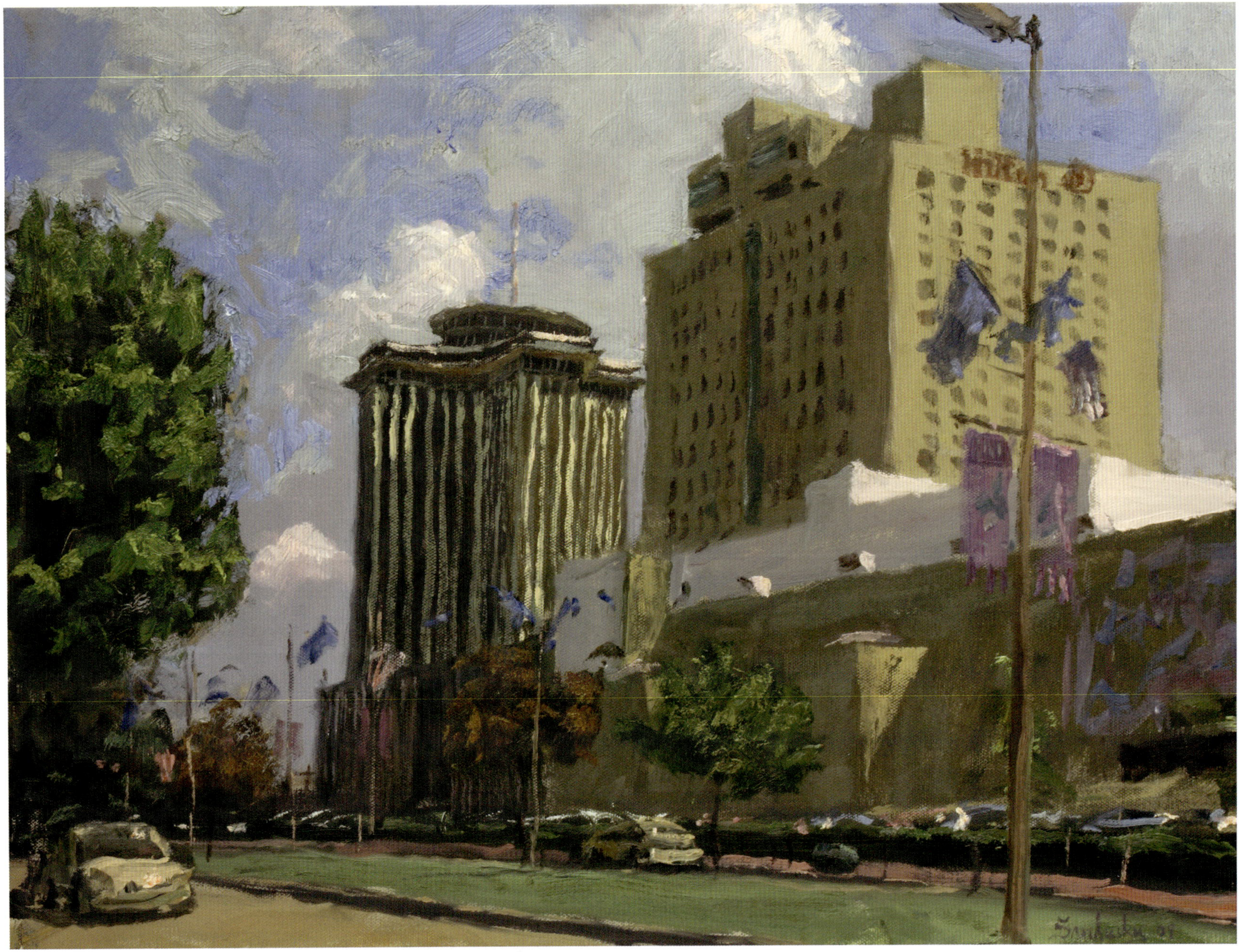

The ITM and Hilton Buildings seen from Convention Center Boulevard 16" x 20" For me the ITM building is the most beautiful high-rise in New Orleans.

our richer, mature experience of blue, but there still must be some distinct blue quality to his experience of blue that is different than his experience of other colors, other visual qualifiers, or other families of qualifiers such as smells, tastes, and sounds. To understand this it might be helpful to look to our elastic mandates such as "hunger" and "breath." Although they are connected to matrices within our memory, as are qualifiers, they seem not to be as densely interlocked into those matrices. They seem to have less baggage. While hunger evokes associations to things like thick juicy steaks, or more specifically the matrices of qualifiers and mandates associated with things like thick juicy steaks, we also seem to be, perhaps even more predominantly, aware of the naked elemental hunger mandate. Imagine now an infant's distinction between blue, blue-green, and a given pitch of sound as being something like the distinction that you make between "hunger," to "breathe," and to "gain freedom of movement." There would be little metaphoric color, just simply a distinction. The qualifiers of our mature cognition are so densely interlocked into matrices that paint a picture of the world around us through sight, sound, smell, and taste that it is difficult to comprehend how blue and any given pitch of sound would distinguish themselves from each other in how we *feel* them, out of the context of these matrices, in the way that an infant might. We are so used to the visual qualifiers being repeatedly type cast in their signature roles, all performing in a theater that seems to reside in the location of our eyes—this apparent location also being no more than matrices of qualifiers and mandates—that it is difficult to grasp that at their most elemental level any given color qualifier and any given sound qualifier are nothing more than two distinctly different feeling prods. "Prod" is a good word to use because a prod is uninteresting. Different prods are only distinguished from each other in the bluntness of their points and the pressure applied. There is no color to the naked "blue" qualifier other than that it is simply *different* from any other qualifier. All of its personality, its metaphoric color, its *quale* is formed through its juxtaposition in matrices of other qualifiers and mandates formed by our life experiences.

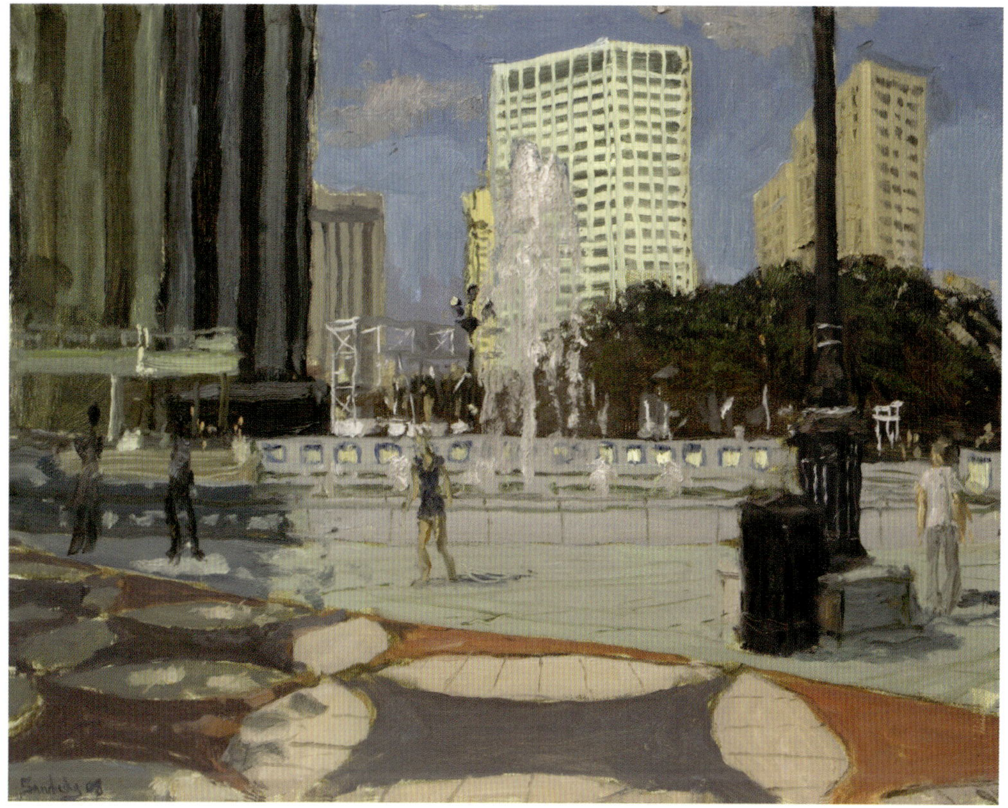

THE SPANISH PLAZA 16" X 20"

The most interesting aspect of my job as an artist is reducing a significant visual experience to several seemingly insignificant patterns of color that will re-evoke the experience when placed next to and on top of each other in the picture plane. Most artists, even in this age, have been taught that the whole is *greater* than the sum of its parts, the popular bastardization of the First Principle of Gestalt that replaces the word "different" with "greater." What I wouldn't give to go just a little further starting at these insignificant individual colors and extract from them that seemingly irreducible bit of meaning that clings to them like dampness to a wrung out sponge.

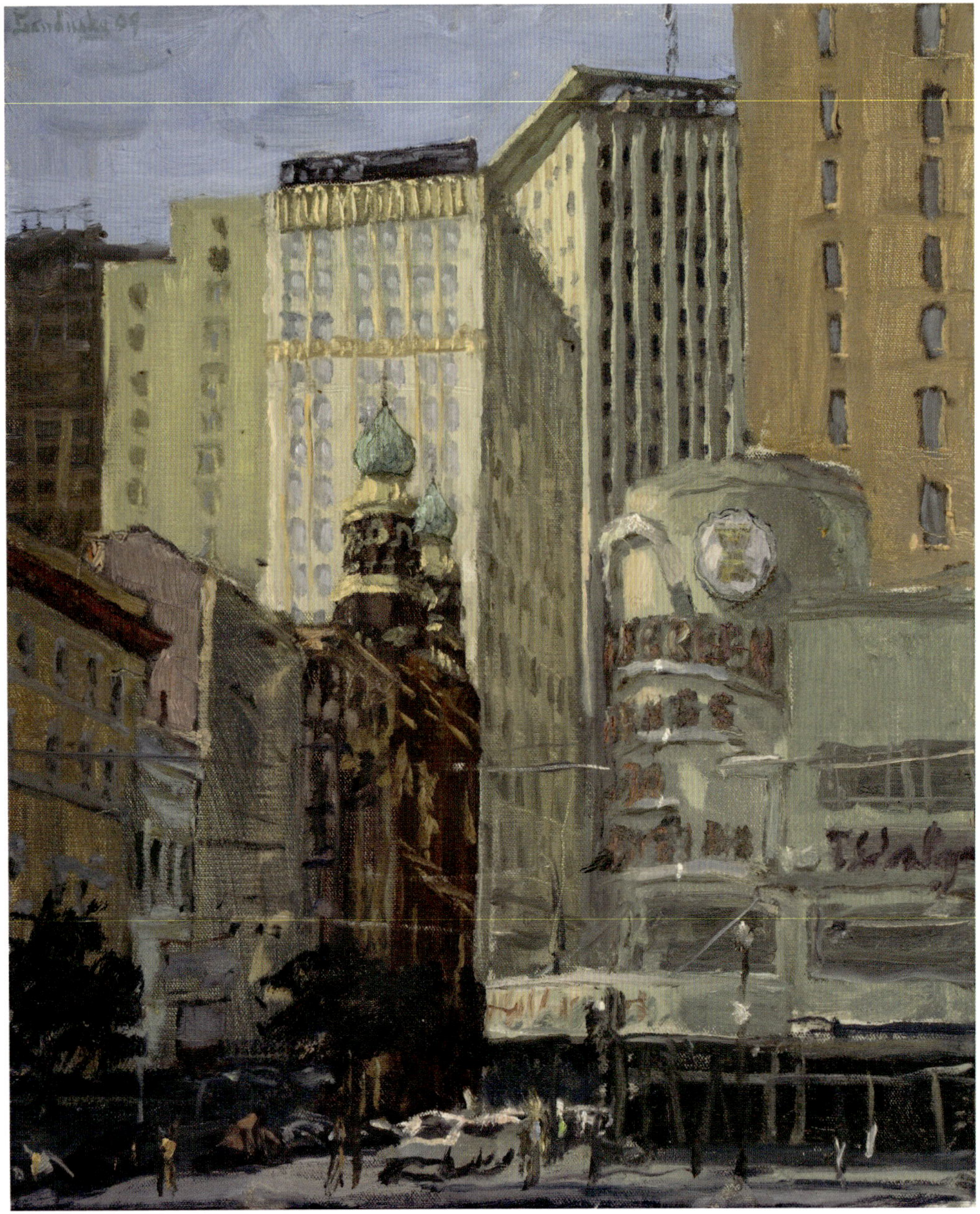

The Old Walgreen's seen from Canal Street at Dauphine Street
20" x 16"

As you take in the painting on the facing page (ships anchored on the Mississippi), you may be reminded of such things as crisp clear days, massive ships anchored in the water slowly swaying back and forth by their bow lines, expansive views, wind blowing through grass, and big rivers meandering through industrial flatlands. I hope that you are drawn into it so completely that for a brief moment you are aware of little else in your environment. In the moment that you make such a connection with this painting, the three significantly different colors that resonate to create the effect of the sky become more meaningful/important. If they weren't painted as such, at the very least the painting would not be as effective in evoking the memories that were formed by your experiences of similar clear sunny days. In the worst case scenario, stating these three different colors unconvincingly could destroy the effect of the whole painting, making it no more than a packet of dissonant colors on the page, evoking only memories caused by your experiences of peripherally noticing diagrams and illustrations in books. However, in the painting as it is, these three significantly different colors in the sky are very distinct and important. Let's deliberately demote these colors in importance now by taking them out of the context of the painting. In figure 3 (see page 64), you see samples of these three colors isolated by the white of the page. The small diagram at the top of the page shows you where the colors were sampled from the painting. These color swatches now become more expendable. Only slightly different matrices would be evoked if you removed one or the other of the swatches or even replaced them with different colors. This is because this illustration of the isolated swatches forms only a small contribution to your overall experience of this page, which includes your hands clasped around the book, the room you are in, your contemplation of the ideas put forth in this text, etc. The three isolated swatches, unlike the painting, are incapable of drawing you in and, even for just a moment, being a principle evoker of memories.

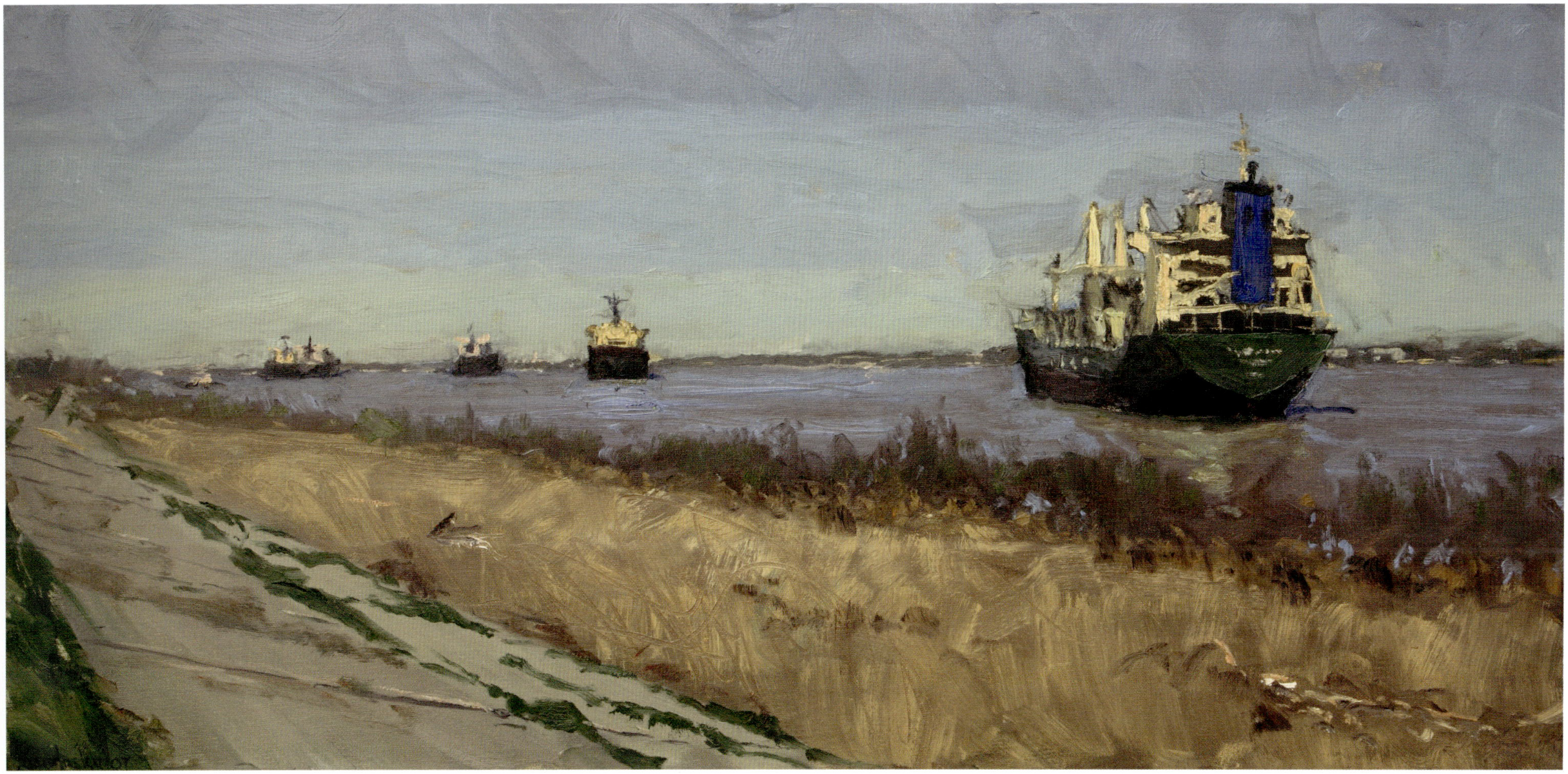

Anchored Ships on the Mississippi River 15" x 30"

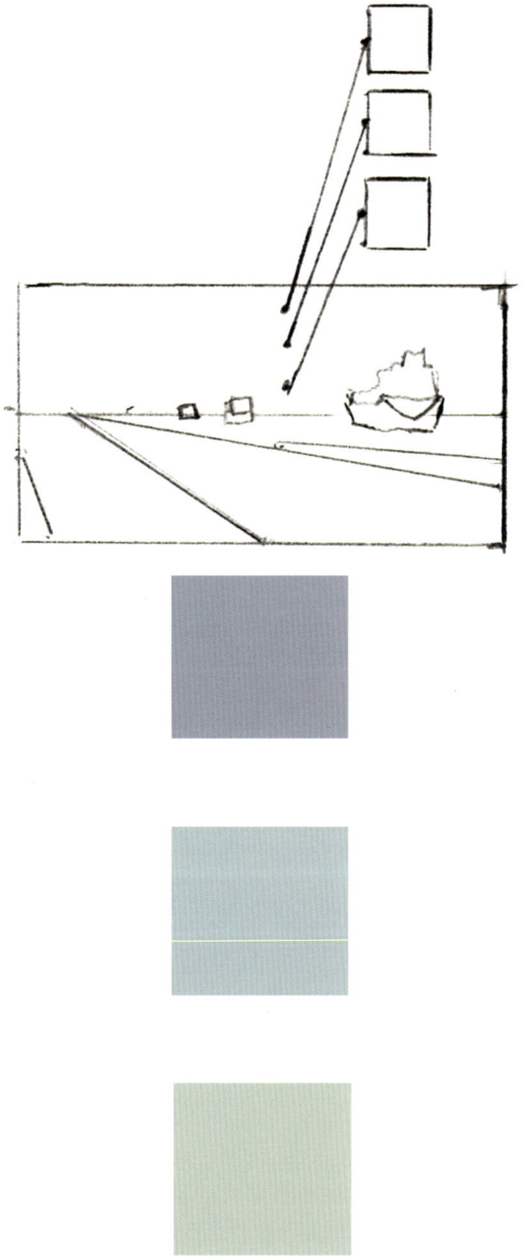

Figure 3 Color swatches and small schematic of ship painting with locations of swatches

Similarly, as with these color swatches, we can extract a lone note (monotonal sound) out of a piece of recorded music and make it less important and less evocative than it is within the context of the music, by sounding it once by itself with complete silence before and after. Certainly at the level of the painting and the piece of music, any given color and any given sound seem much more interesting and therefore as qualia more distinguished from each other. But by removing the color from the beauty of a clear, crisp blue sky and removing the lone sound from the beauty of the music and all the associations we make to these things, we make them less interesting and therefore less different. They become less instrumental in evoking memories. Unfortunately we seem to be able to extract no more interest or dissimilarity out of two such qualia. It seems impossible for us to reduce a given color and sound any further until they are but two distinctly different feeling prods as they certainly must be as naked qualifiers. Taking the most grayed out, and presumably least pervasive, of the three colors from the sky in the painting, the one closest to the horizon, and our lone monotonal sound, we close our eyes and hear the sound. Then the sound stops as we open our eyes and see nothing but a field of the grayed out color. And then again we hear only the sound in darkness followed again by seeing only the color in complete silence, again the sound, again the color, the sound, the color, the sound, the color. . . . Alas, the sound still seems like a sound and the color still seems like a color.

From your infancy every time you have covered your ears sound has been lowered, and every time you have covered or closed your eyes every perception revealed by light is removed. These most basic experiences have resulted in distinctly different memory matrices that provide the highest level of distinction between these two families of qualifiers that tie them to different locations on the body. These matrices can contain not only qualifiers but also elastic mandates such as "protect eyes," "acquire sound information," "acquire

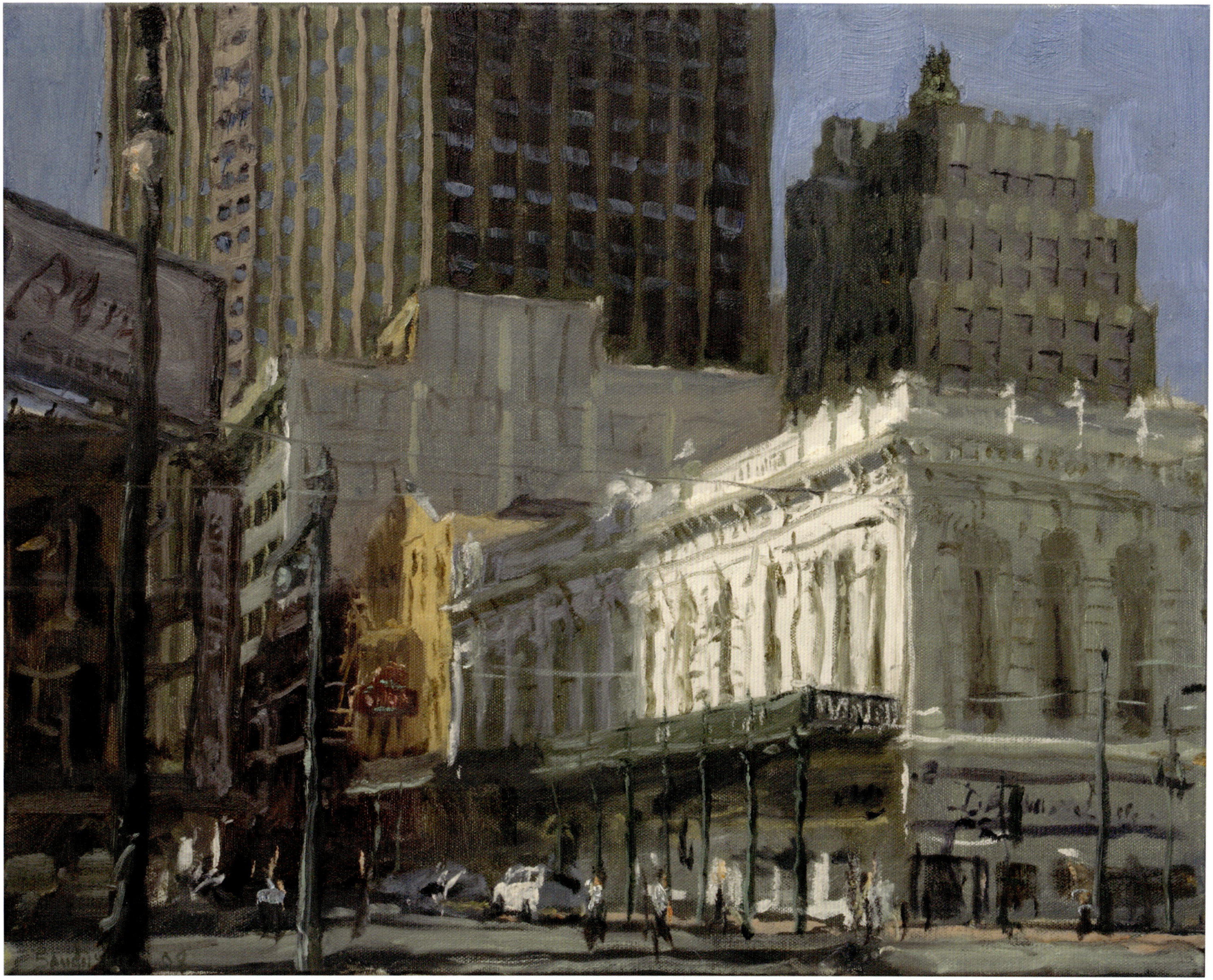

VIEW FROM CANAL STREET CLOSE TO ROYAL STREET 16" x 20"

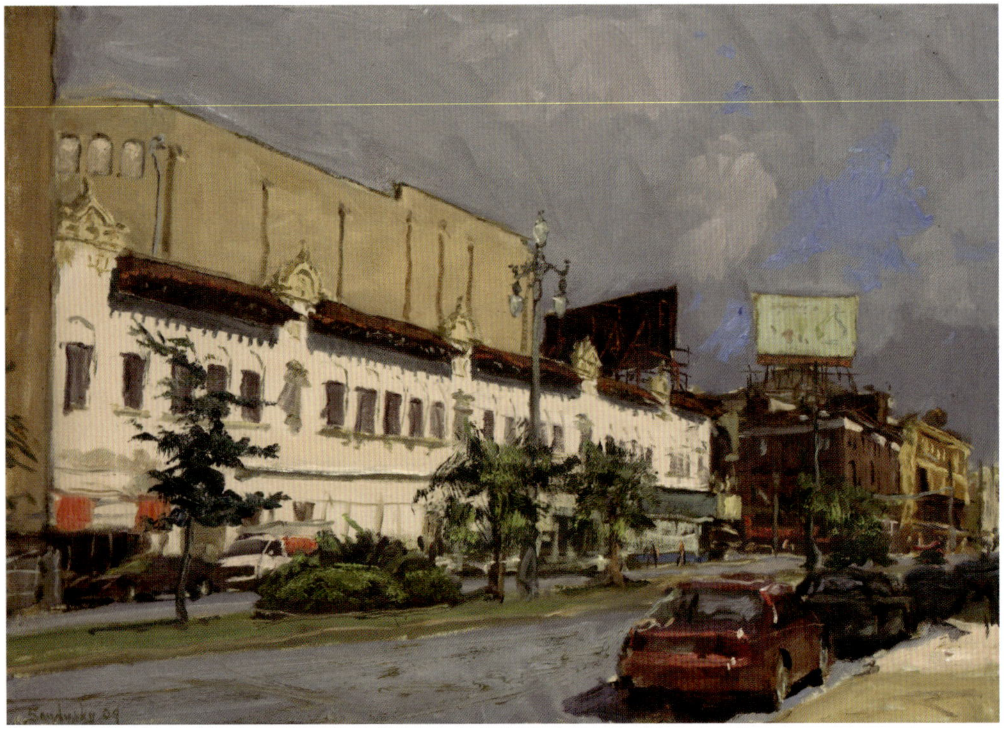

THE THEATER DISTRICT SEEN FROM SOUTH RAMPART STREET LOOKING TOWARD CANAL STREET 18" X 24"

visual information," and "protect hearing." Beyond this first level of distinction, basic universal experiences of light that are different than that of sound create different matrices that further distinguish qualifiers of vision from those of sound. For example there are things such as the sun that reveal themselves by light but make no sound and there are things that reveal themselves by sound but have no luminance, such as the wind blowing in your ear. No qualifier exists in memory by itself. It can exist in memory only as parts of matrices of qualifiers and mandates. As we single out any lone quale, such as a swatch of blue, and focus all of our attention upon it, it will bring along its usual posse of referenced qualifiers and mandates that give it its *metaphoric* color, depth, and richness. Perhaps we can alter this posse a little to slightly modify the way a qualifier feels. For example, a sound that usually seems high in pitch can be made to seem low in pitch if it is preceded for some time by nothing but sounds that are even higher in pitch. However it would take some serious psychotropic drugs to bypass or alter a posse of referenced qualifiers and mandates enough to make a color feel like a sound.

It's too bad that we can't talk to an infant (or perhaps even a fetus) just coming into his senses, although, even if he *could* talk, he wouldn't have very much to report. All we non-infant humans can do to acquire *some* visceral connection to the naked qualifiers is to build special memories that help us de-contextualize them. The diagram in figure 4 linearly extrapolates the sound and the color from their most meaningful distinction through their less meaningful distinction to help you visualize how they could exist in their most elemental form, as being only slightly different from each other.

As great as the difference might still *seem* between any given sound and any given color, there is no sound in your head, or color, or shape. The pure elemental irreducible qualifier and mandate likely needs only an identification and value. The value for the qualifier may be no more than the certainty that it has been located within a receptive field. The mandate's value would be its increase or decrease in magnitude. It is their juxtapositions in matrices that make their distinction seem complex. That distinction manifests *apparent* lines, circles, blues, reds, middle Cs, hunger, and assist. What other way would they be perceived? It wouldn't matter if they manifested in some other way, as long as they're consistently different from each other in the same way. They would still *seem* every bit as interesting if not amazing in how they cluster together to form our perception of the universe.

Perhaps we are leaving one final loose end in our explanation of vision if we do not offer an explanation of why complex, continuously changing arrays of qualifiers and mandates seem *interesting if not amazing* to us. What is the evolutionary reason for our feelings of interest, excitement, amazement, and their counterpoints, boredom and ennui? A desktop computer doesn't feel interested in the complex inter-functionality of its parts and software—why should we? There is one possible explanation that I can offer. One of the many ways our brain is different from a desktop computer is that it does not degrade with use but rather with lack of use. Just as nature trails infrequently walked upon become overgrown and disappear, our dense biological neural circuitry needs to be used or it will atrophy. In the quiet times between our bouts for survival when our mandates have been lowered or satisfied (including a supposed mandate to rest), it makes sense that there would be an imperative for mandates to be raised so that our neural pathways can be reinforced *and possibly even improved.* When this imperative is raised we feel bored. To satisfy or lower this imperative, providing us with a feeling of interest, excitement, or amazement, we voluntarily act in ways that might raise mandates by deliberately making ourselves a little vulnerable or grappling with esoteric problems when no practical ones are presented. This prospective imperative to raise mandates would certainly be lowered, creating a feeling of interest when contemplating the complexities of the mind and vision, and would explain a wide gamut of other human behaviors such as solving crossword puzzles, sky diving, reading, looking at art, wondering about far away places, and it would allow—within a cold pragmatic biological latticework of imperatives, mandates, and qualifiers—for the warm spirit of our humanity to emerge: a mother's love, a hero's journey, a sonnet, a requiem mass, an impression sunrise.

(Continued on page 74)

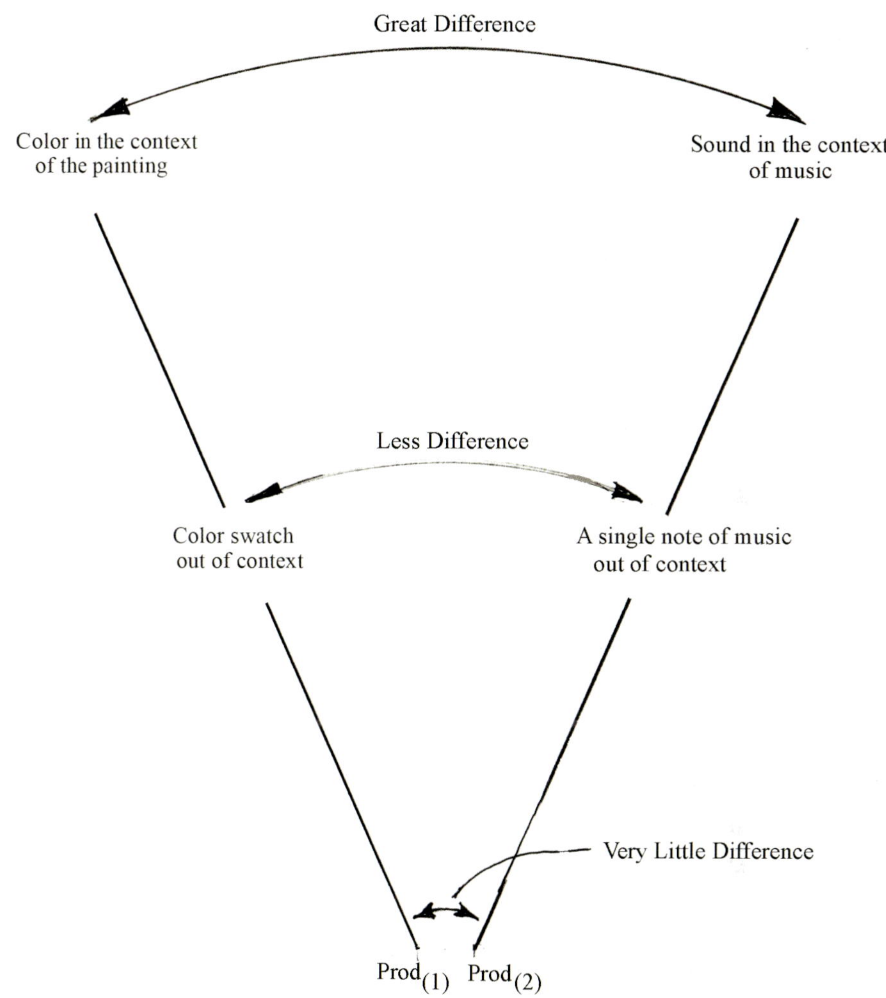

FIGURE 4

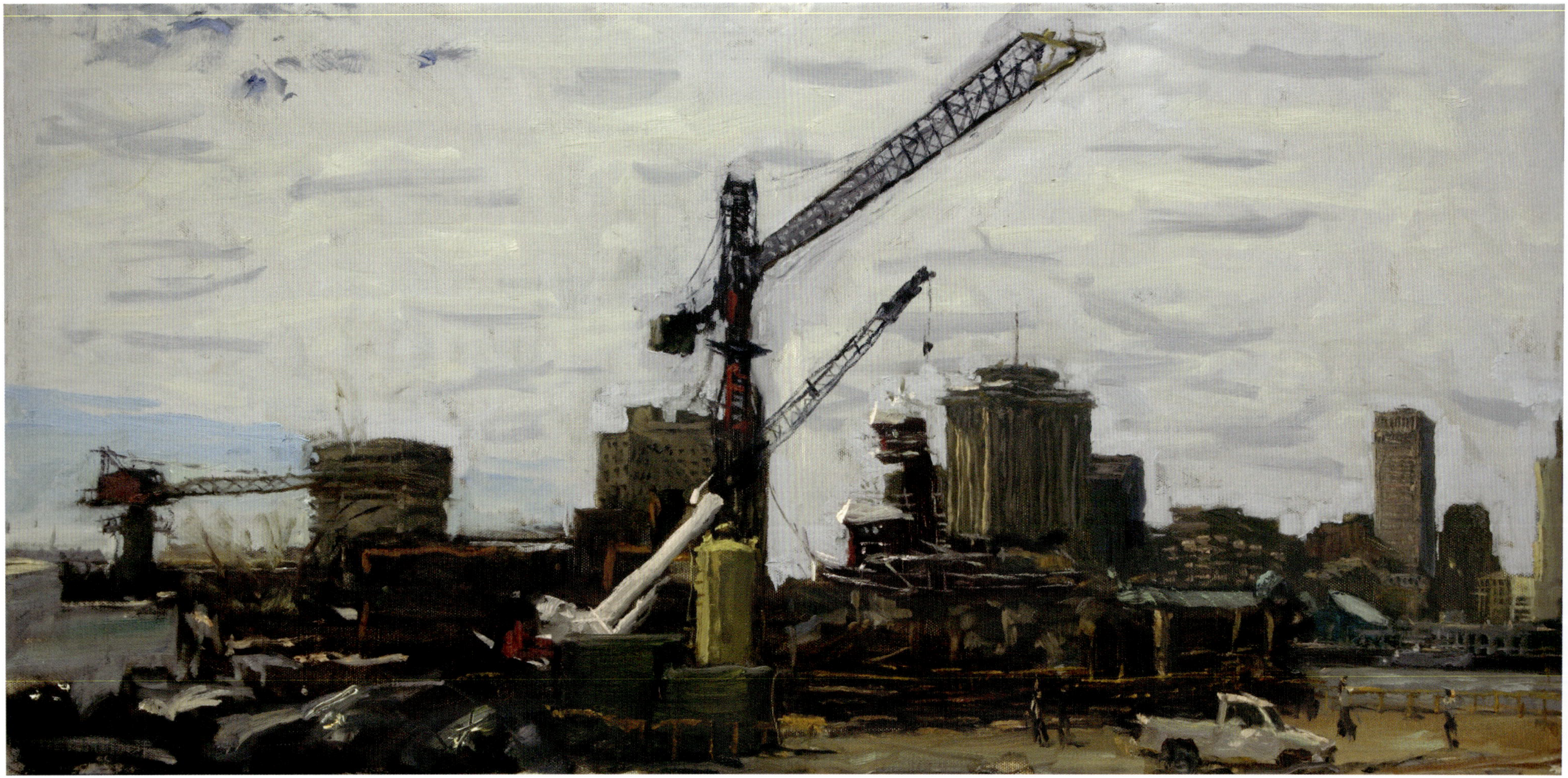

BOLLINGER SHIP YARD IN ALGIERS POINT 15" X 30"

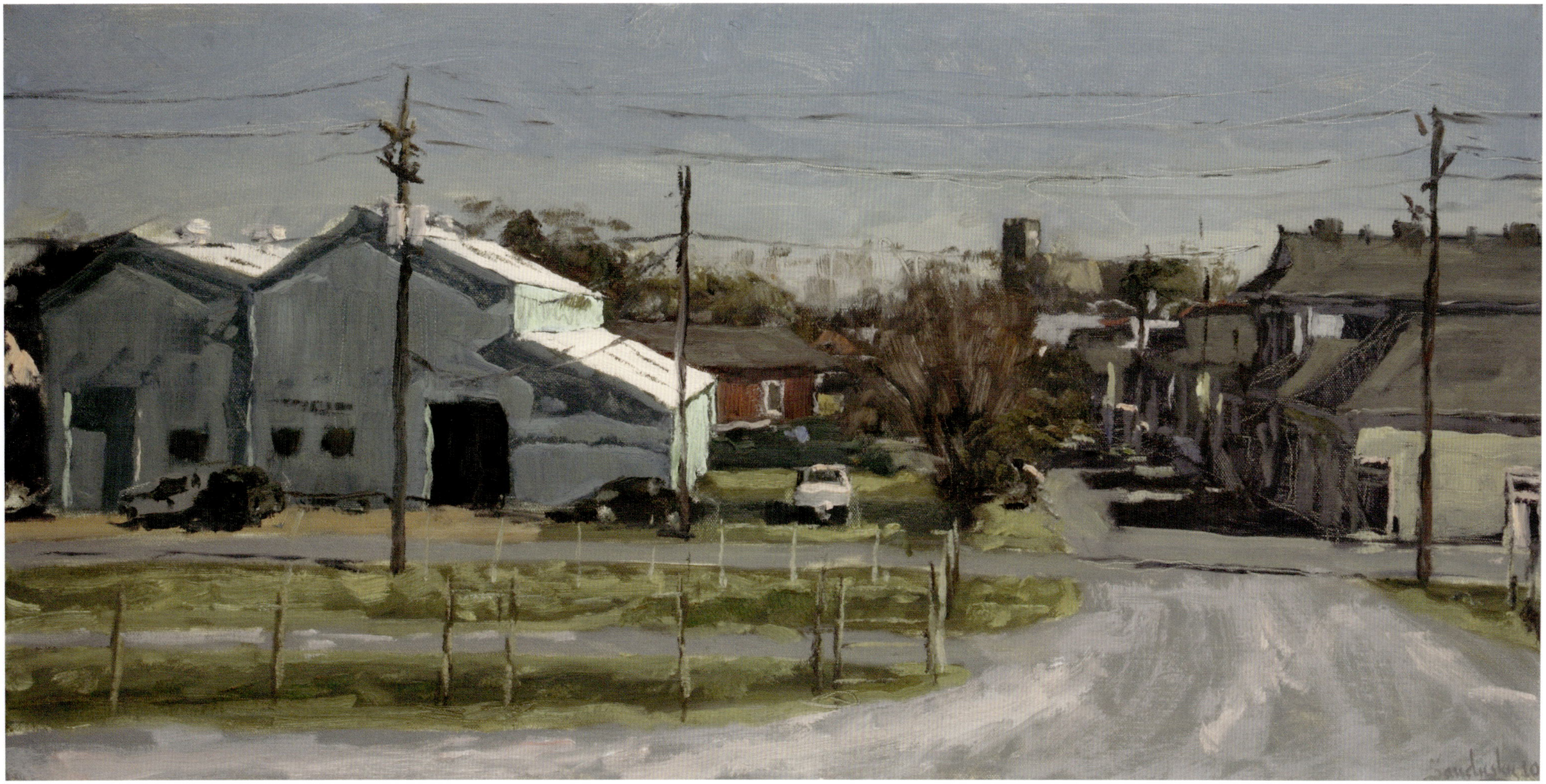

Algiers Point. View down Alix Street from the levy 15" x 30"

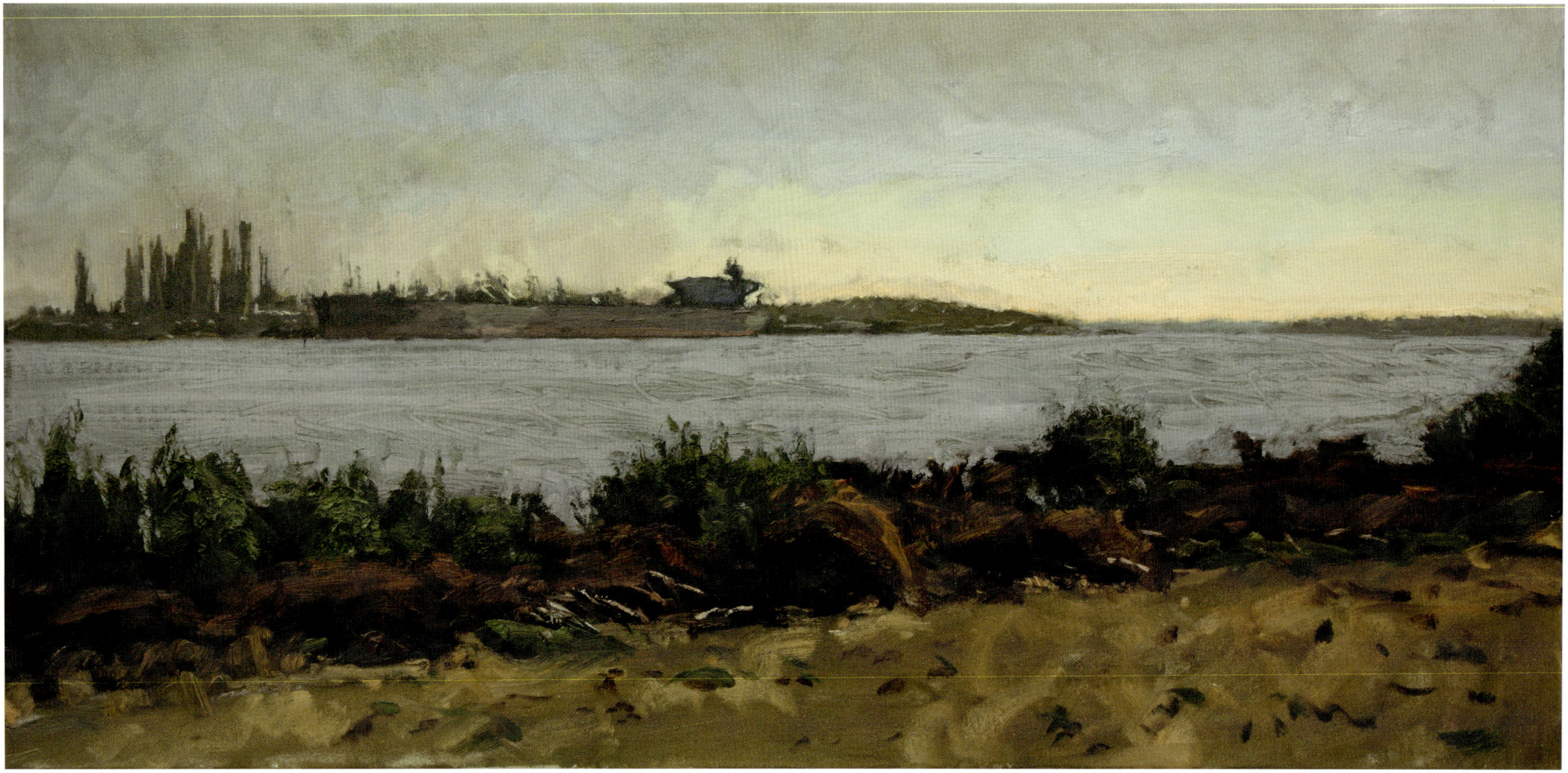

Oil tanker at the Chalmette Refinery 15" x 30"

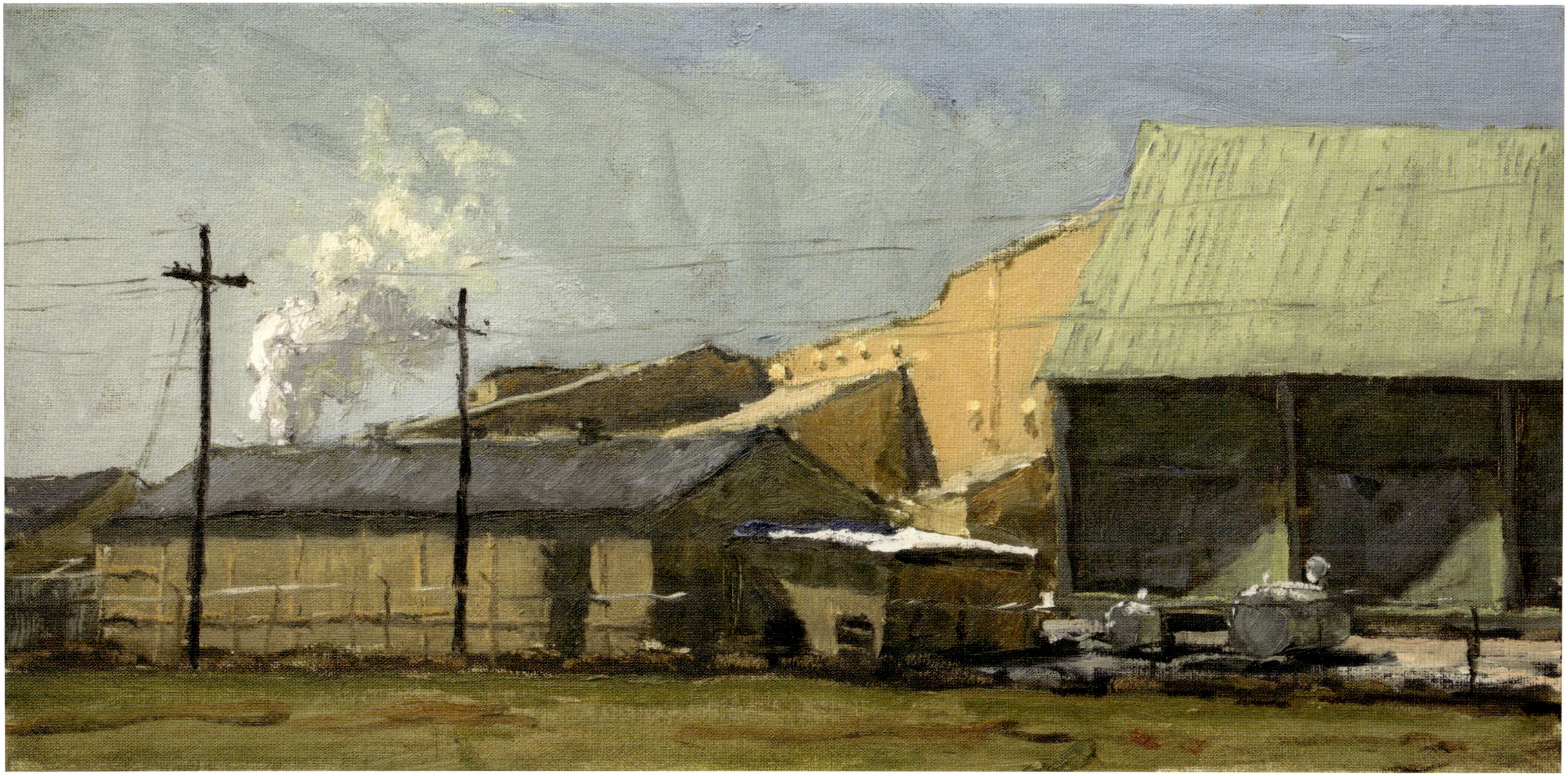

Gypsum plant in Westwego 10" x 20"

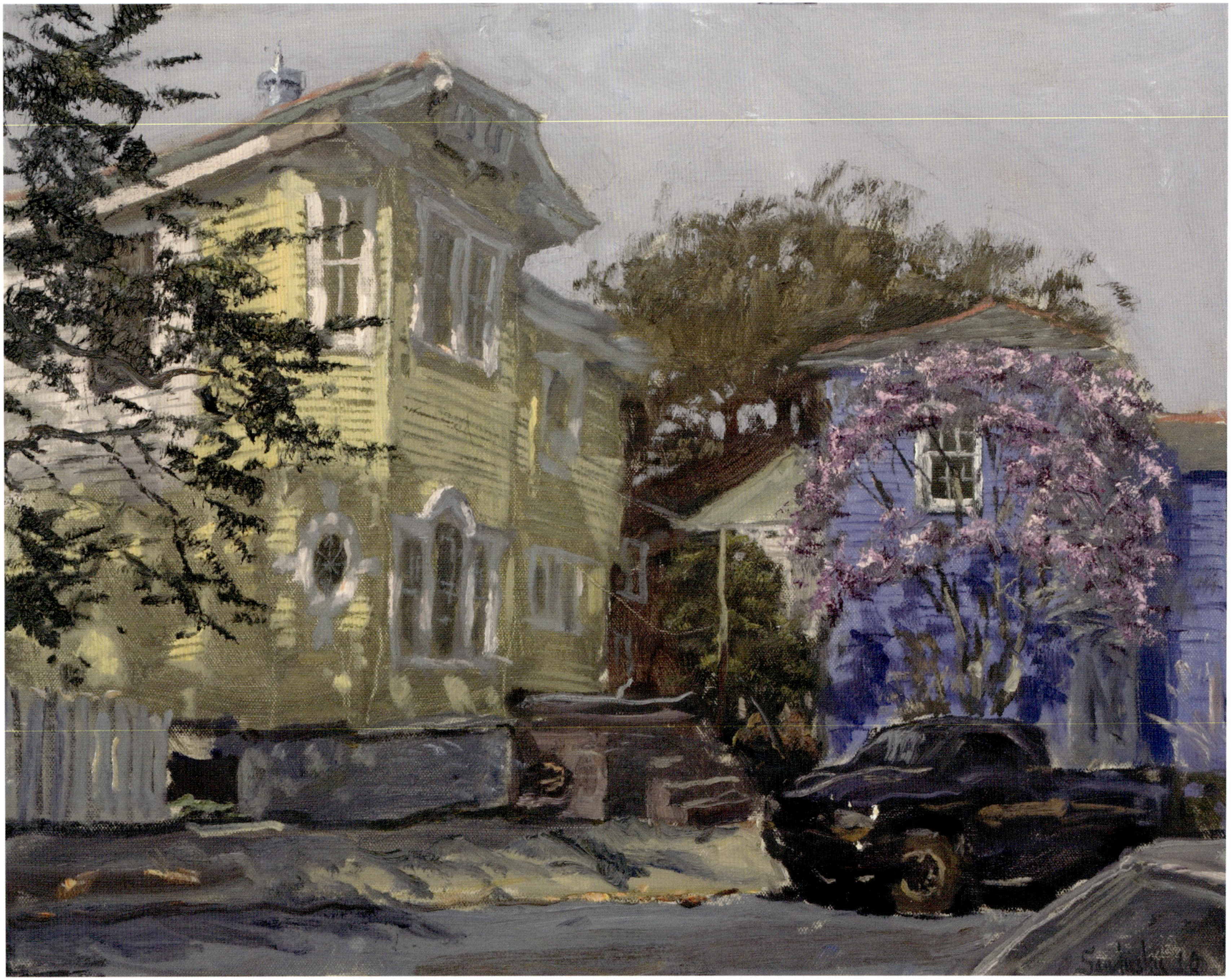

Houses in Algiers Point on Verret Street 16" x 20"

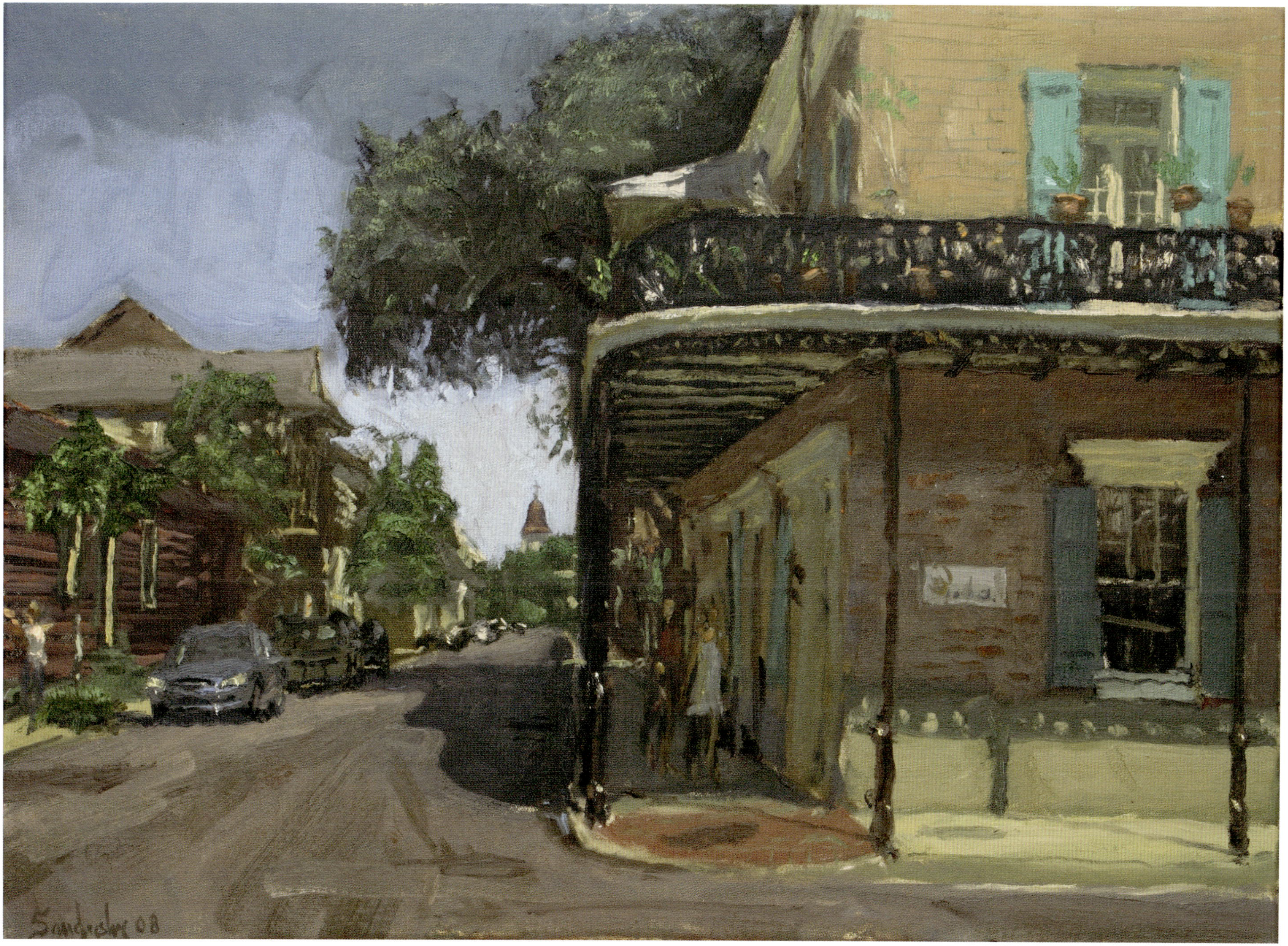

View from the corner of Governor Nicholls and Dauphine streets 18" x 24"

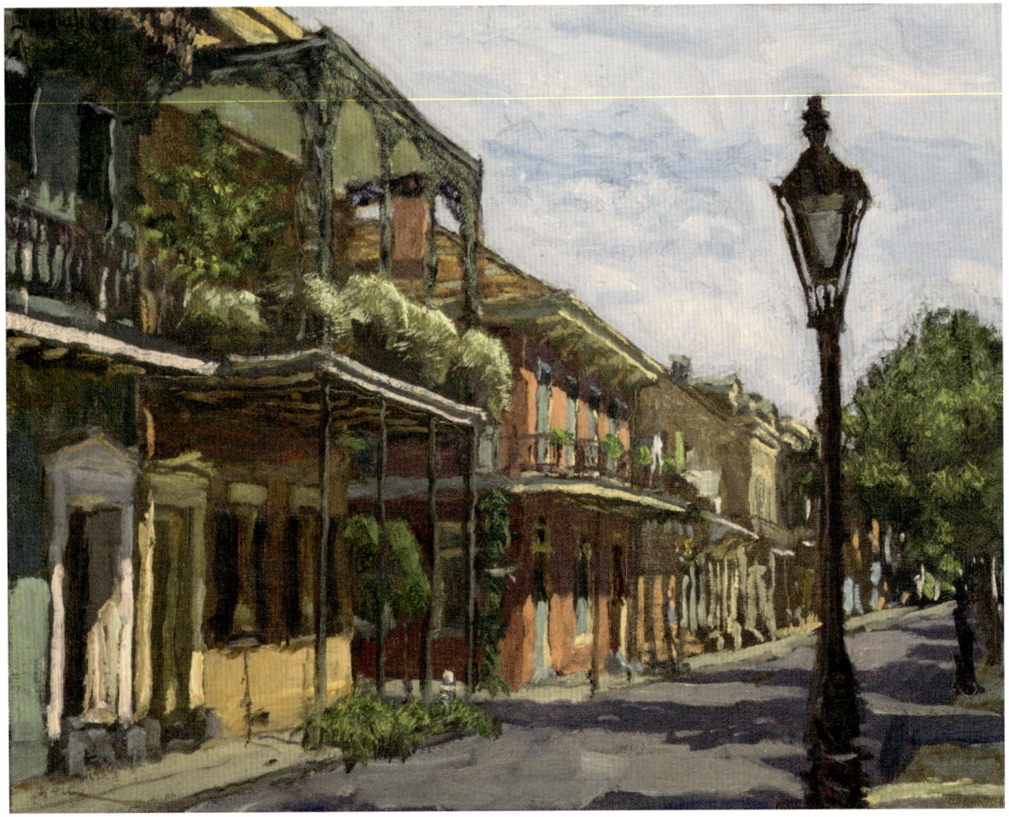

Houses along Bourbon Street at Governor Nicholls Street
14" x 18"

Summary of How the Objective Image Is Different than Our Vision

The relationship between the image and our vision:

The image is no part of our vision but provides the raw material for our eye-scanning. The relatively small number of qualifiers and mandates produced by eye-scanning summon a vast confluence of qualifiers and mandates from memory in a way that keeps our vision connected to our environment with respect to our body's survival needs. Suppose we try the analogy that for our vision the qualifiers and mandates produced by eye-scanning are to those supplemented by memory as a conductor is to the orchestra. But this analogy would only work for a democratic orchestra, because our memories also have great influence in *directing* our eye-scanning. Memory provides the meaningful vision unique to each person, but it also becomes a filter that enables each of us only to see a very small portion of our environment.

There are specific ways that the image is different than what we see:

1. There are no image patterns in what we see, only qualifiers and mandates (emotions). There is no mandate (emotional) component to the image; it is only schematic.
2. Where the image is absolute, what we see is relative. Qualifiers and mandates are evoked from eye-scanning only in response to *juxtapositions* of various properties of the image. Also, qualifiers and mandates are evoked by the differences between images, but there is no information in any given image about the difference between it and other images.
3. The image exists in its entirety all in the present instant in space. What we see, *even for an unchanging view,* exists in time. Waves of qualifiers and mandates from the raw senses and memory are constantly being evoked. The new waves are more prominent in our perceptions as the older ones fatigue.
4. The image is the same for everyone from the same vantage point. What we see, the set of qualifiers and mandates, is formed almost entirely from memory and, considering that everyone's memories are different, what each person sees is *different* for the same view.

Despite a small but important causal influence of the image on what we see, the two are so different that they almost seem opposite.

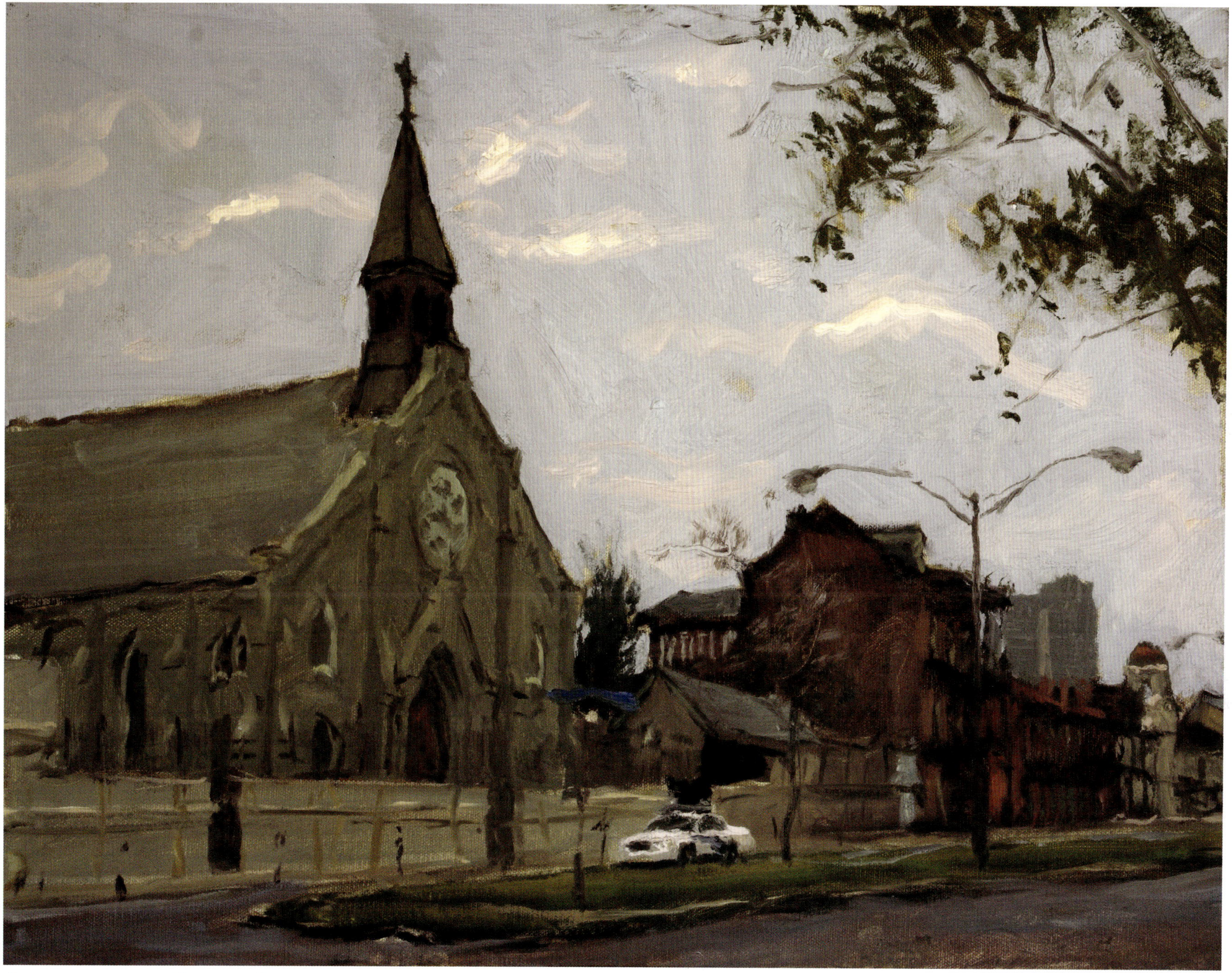

Perimeter of the French Quarter along North Rampart Street close to Esplanade Avenue 16" x 20"

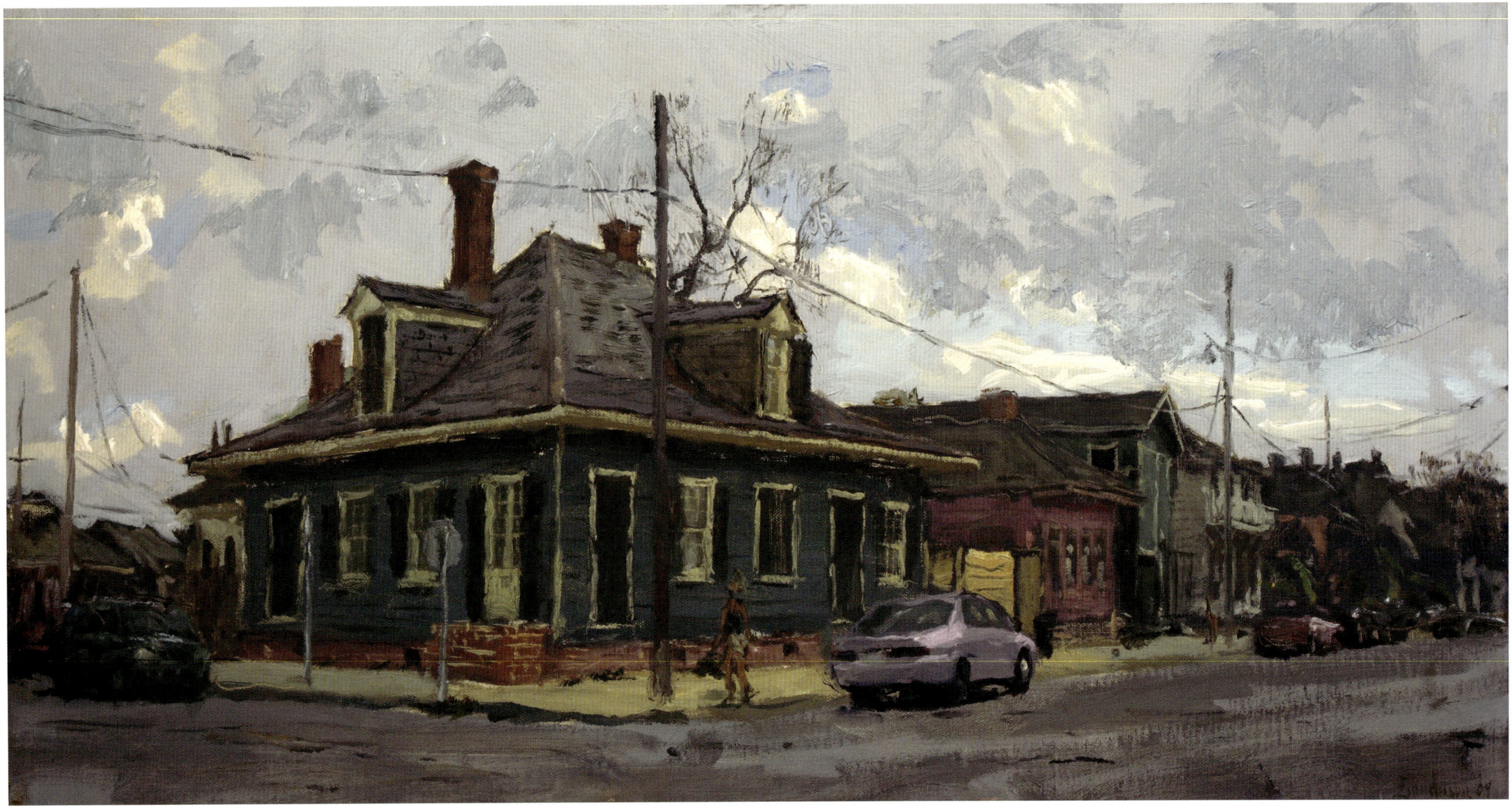

View from the corner of Burgundy and Kerlerec streets 15" x 30"

The Artist's Uneasy Alliance with the Image

In light of the fact that our vision is nothing like images, it's ironic that the only conduit from the visual artist's mind to the minds of other people is an *image* designed by the artist. Each way that the image is different from vision presents a different face of this vexing conundrum that few artists have directly confronted. There can be no emotion in the molecules of pigment that the artist applies to the canvas. So, he must design a set of overlapping and adjacent patterns of color that will evoke the qualifiers and mandates that reconstitute his own vision in the minds of the viewers of his work. But reproducing the objective image cannot accomplish this.

We will see that the limitations of certain academic approaches to drawing and painting have, perhaps accidentally if not serendipitously, forced artists to align their statement more with *vision* despite having to use an *image* as the vehicle for communication. Regardless of their approach, successful artists must communicate their point of view. To accomplish this, the artist must infuse his statement with his unique personal memory, which is perhaps the most important property of his vision that the objective image doesn't have.

We have seen that elements of children's and novices' drawings, such as parallel horizontal lines, blue bars high on the page with green bars low, and stick men, become effective visual stimuli that evoke the most prominent qualifiers and mandates in our memories. Yet they do not evoke a complete set of qualifiers and mandates that could provide the *nuance* of any other experience than looking at naive drawings. Revisiting yet again our previous example of the beginning art student's drawing of the house, the most prominent qualifiers evoked by his parallel horizontal lines tells us that there is a ceiling above the floor, the house is level, and every part of the roofline is the same distance above the ground. But these parallel horizontal lines also evoke qualifiers that tell us that either he is standing directly in front of the house, rather than viewing the house from the corner, as he is, or that he is viewing the house from far away, rather than viewing it from up close, as he is. While his parallel horizontal lines successfully evoke the most prominent qualifiers from his memory/vision, they also evoke qualifiers ambiguously from other experiences having nothing to do with the present experience that he is trying to communicate visually. However, a set of diagonals much like the objective rendering of the house would unambiguously evoke all of the more important qualifiers from memory: being close, viewing from the corner, *and* most prominently that the house is level. This in a nutshell is why representational artists' renderings are *similar* to the objective image and why representational artists spend much of their career making the qualifiers evoked

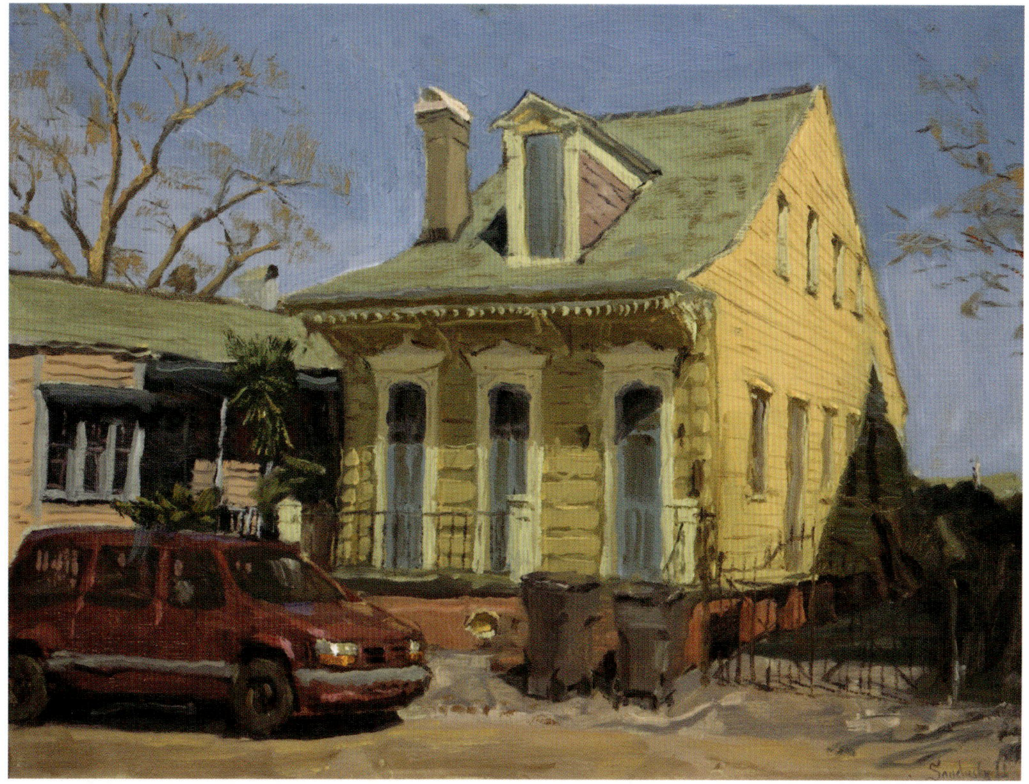

House on Kerlerec Street near Dauphine Street 18" x 24"

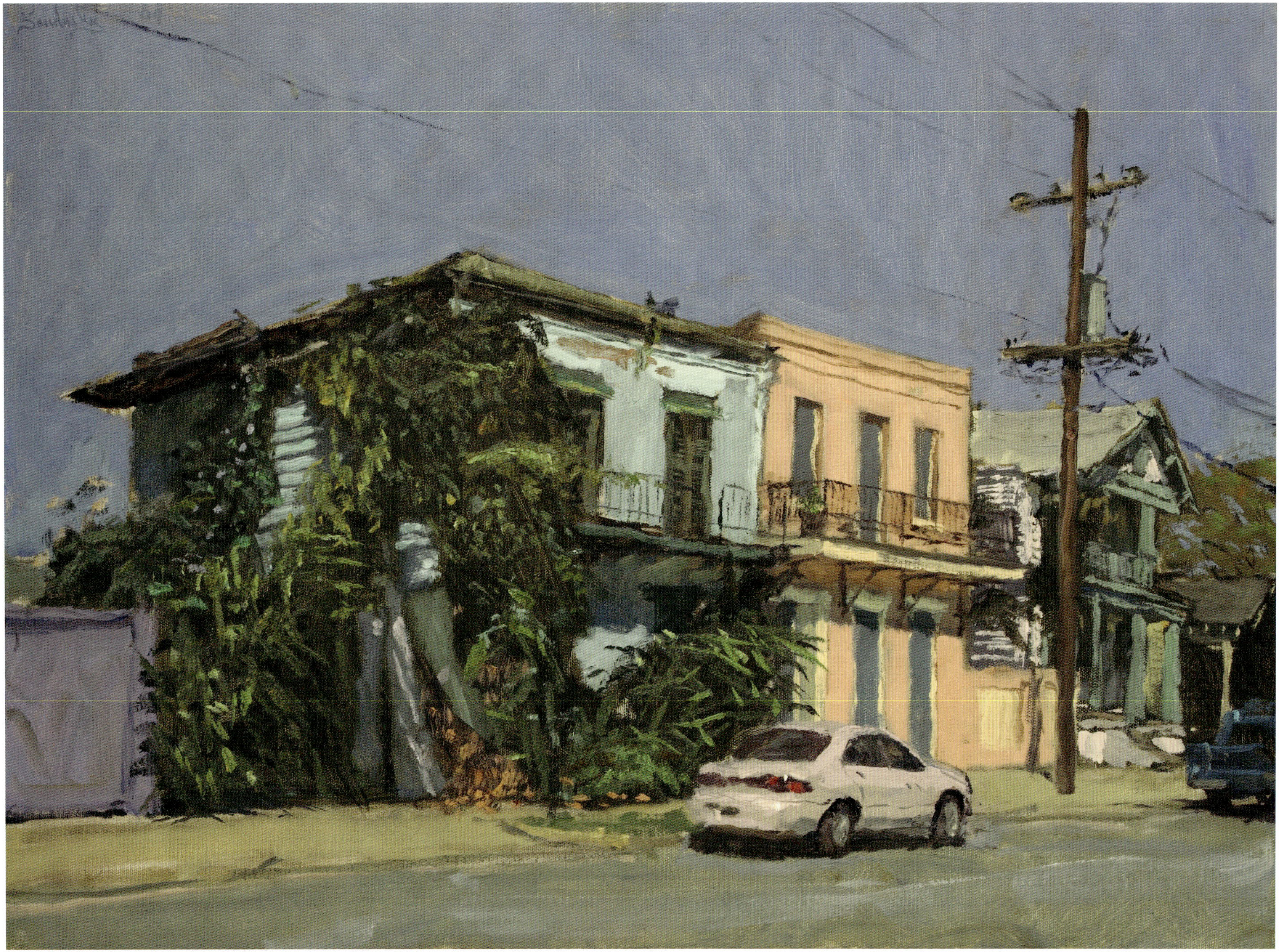

HOUSES ALONG PAUGER STREET NEAR DAUPHINE STREET 18" X 24"

directly from eye-scanning more prominent in their perceptions (memories). This is why they use sight sticks and view finders, learn linear perspective, and in this age of photography, draw a human face from a photograph that has been turned upside-down so that they can better see how flat image patterns can be used to evoke a sense of this most familiar of all objects.

However it is important that the sensory evoked qualifiers are brought forward in the artist's mind without allowing them to squelch the legions of qualifiers and mandates from memory that form the heart and substance of his unique personal vision. If he goes too far in his measuring, gridding, calculating, and matching, he bypasses his vision and provides no more than an accurate rendering of the objective image. Each viewer of his work will respond in their own way, rather than seeing the world as he does. The one great purpose of visual art that has survived the loss of its earlier more utilitarian function of documentation (usurped by photography) is to put the viewer of a work of art into *another* person's head, seeing the world as he does. We relish our delusions of flying off into space and finding exotic new places while often neglecting very *real* gateways that we have to parallel universes right at our fingertips. There is such an unfathomable amount of data and potential meaning in this world, let alone universe, that we each can see only a different tiny piece of it. To see someone else's slice of the world, to perceive this world differently by embracing another person's point of view, is even better than visiting another world. It is the greatest exploration. There are as many such frontiers to explore as there are human beings on the planet. An artist's point of view is no better than yours; he just knows how to communicate it. A reproduction of the objective image shows you what you already know. A work of art that engages an artist's vast and unique memory is like a window to another world. Memory is the soul of art and its conveyance should be art's sole purpose.

Representational artists can follow many paths for their training and work. We will examine two quintessential paths at opposite ends of the spectrum. The first and most difficult

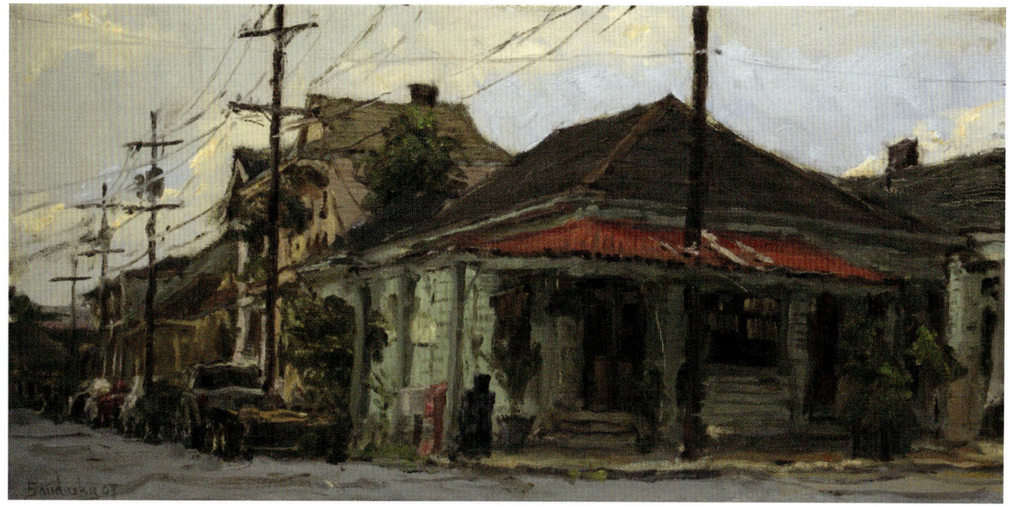

LA PENICHE RESTAURANT, CORNER OF TOURO AND DAUPHINE STREETS
10" x 20"

path allows the sensory evoked qualifiers to come forward in the artist's perception *without* squelching those evoked from memory. We will call this the "memory inclusive" path. The second and easiest path, which we will name "strictly objective," brings the sensory evoked qualifiers forward by *excluding* those from memory. If we consider that our vision is completely different from the objective image, we can think of these two paths as leading in very different directions. However, considering that an artist who takes the more difficult path must communicate what he sees with an image *similar* to the objective image, we might then juxtapose the two paths by the appearance of their respective artifacts. From this perspective the paths can be thought of as diverging in only slightly, albeit *importantly,* different directions. Before the advent of photography, the strictly objective path would have served a utilitarian purpose (documentation) but would have only been a bit easier at first, becoming difficult to maintain for very long in an artist's career. We will see that imaging tools and the changing of esthetics to accommodate fine art photography have both facilitated the strictly objective path and devalued the difference between it and the memory inclusive path. As a result, fewer artists are following the more difficult memory inclusive path and more artists are being drawn to the easier, strictly objective path, which has become the path of least resistance.

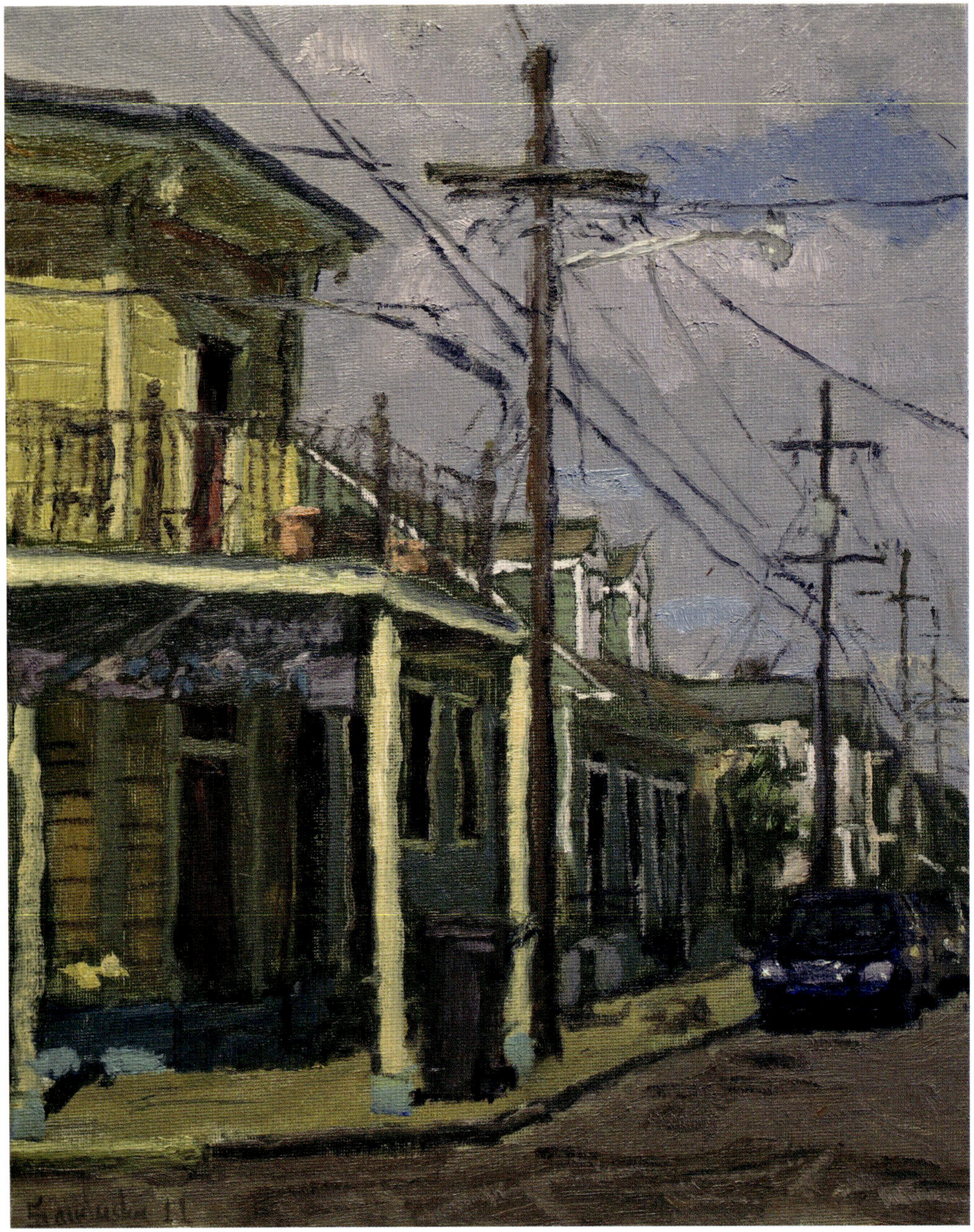

INTERSECTION OF TOURO AND ROYAL STREETS 14" X 11"

The Memory Inclusive Path

Before the advent and availability of photography, artists could only work from the live subject and memory. They had to gather information and learn from the live subject so that renderings made after the fact in their studio were accurate and convincing. They knew little about vision and paid little mind that different artists had different points of view. Their main concern was accurate documentation. In working from life, they were encumbered by having to deal with living things that were in constant motion, like human beings, or still life and landscape objects that were also constantly changing at least in how they were lit. For living things sight sticks and view finders were useful but limited, because proportions changed as the subjects moved. Even portrait models charged with being as still as possible would move their heads slightly during a sitting and slouch more as they tired. When artists attempted to render their changing subject by articulating each part separately, measuring with their sight stick to check proportions, there was at best a stiff, lifeless quality in their finished work. Similarly, when individual parts of a subject in changeable outdoor light were rendered separately over time, together they produced a disintegrated, nonsensical whole. Artists sidestepped such problems to some extent by obtaining and employing knowledge about anatomy, perspective, and light to depict the generalities of a changing subject convincingly from different vantage points. Working largely from learned formulas specific to each type of subject, they only needed the firsthand experience of a *specific* subject to articulate its unique nuances in the later stages

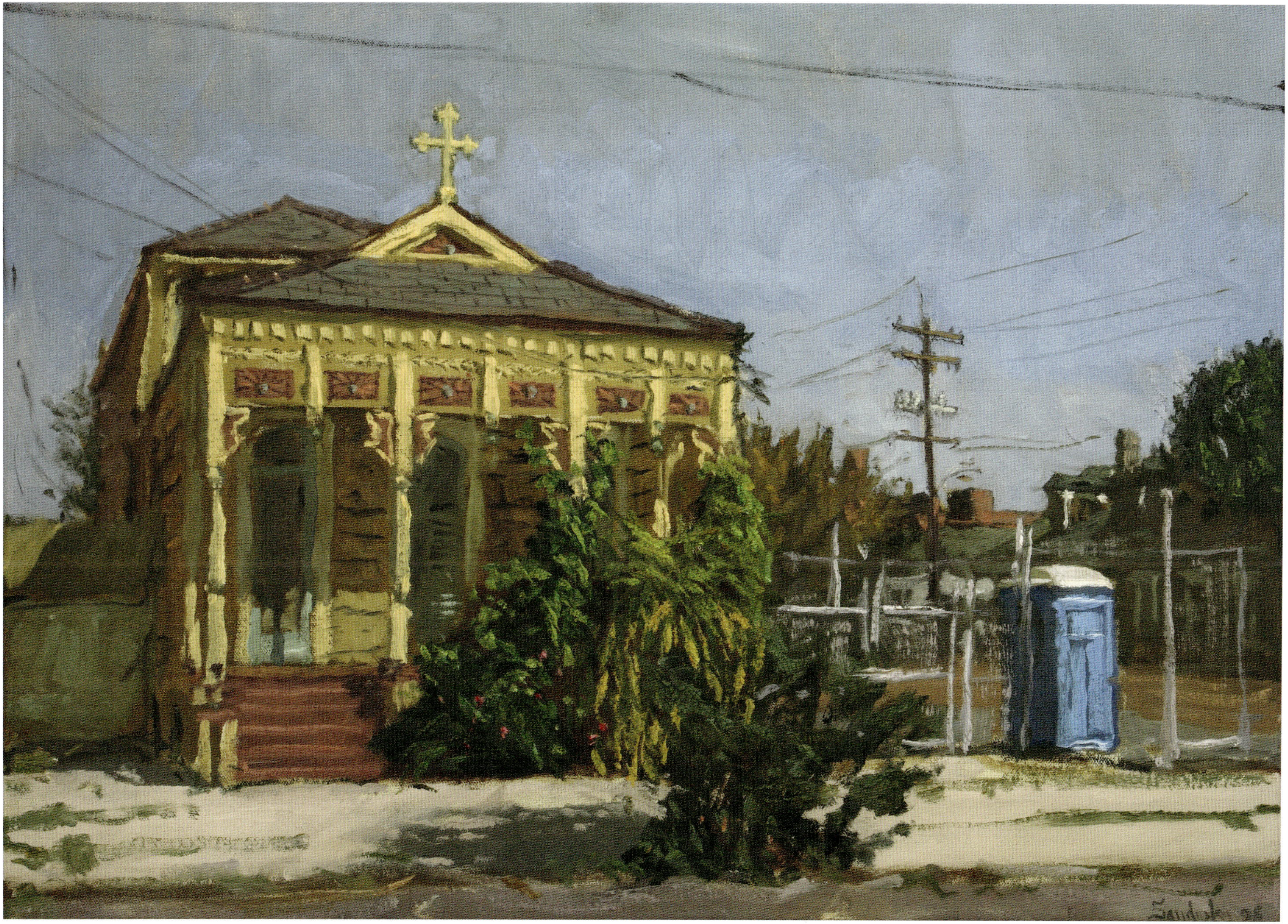

Rectory of Saints Peter and Paul Catholic Church, Burgundy Street close to Mandeville Street 18" x 24"

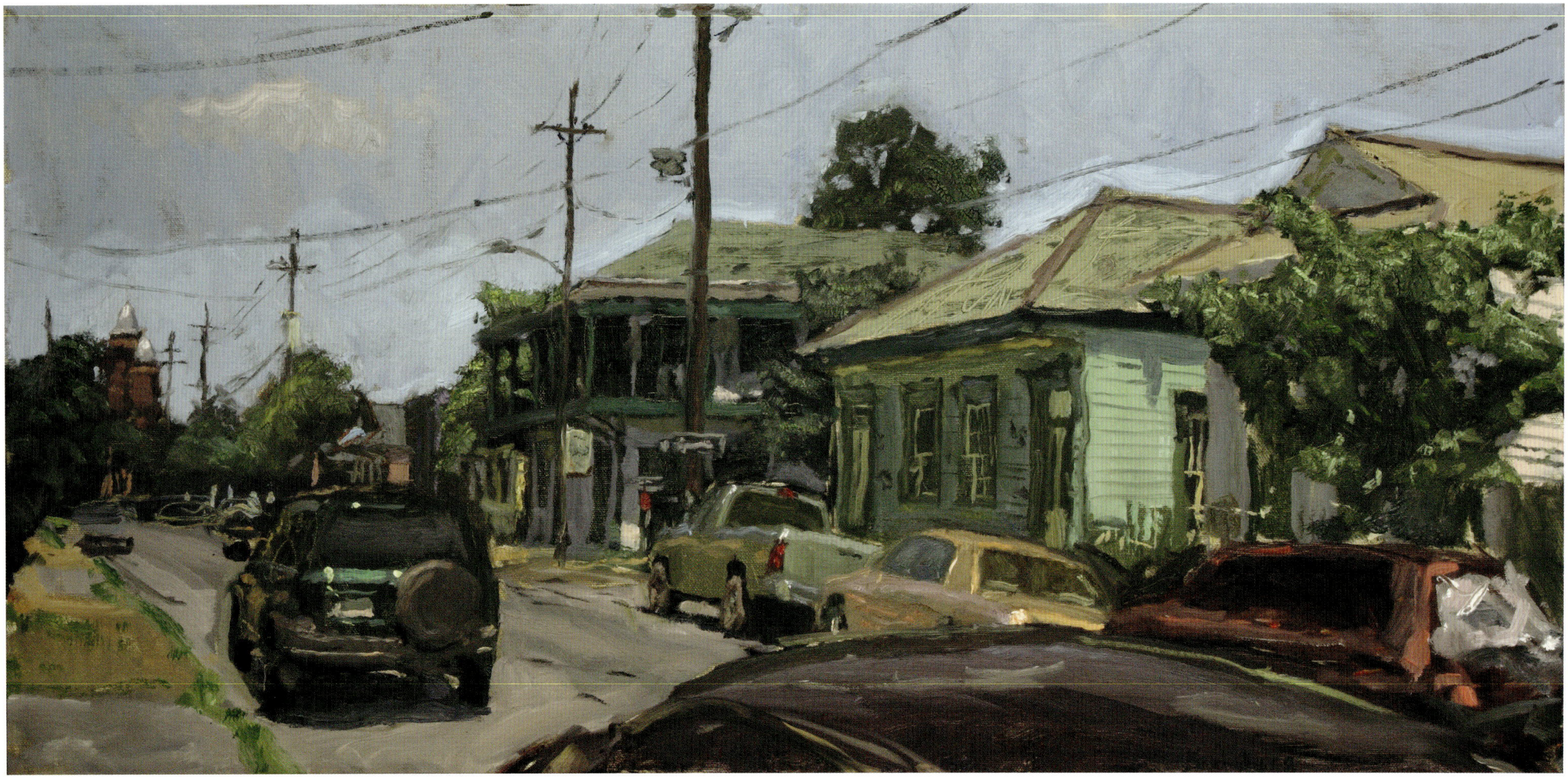

Burgundy Street close to St. Roch Avenue looking toward Saints Peter and Paul Church 15" x 30"

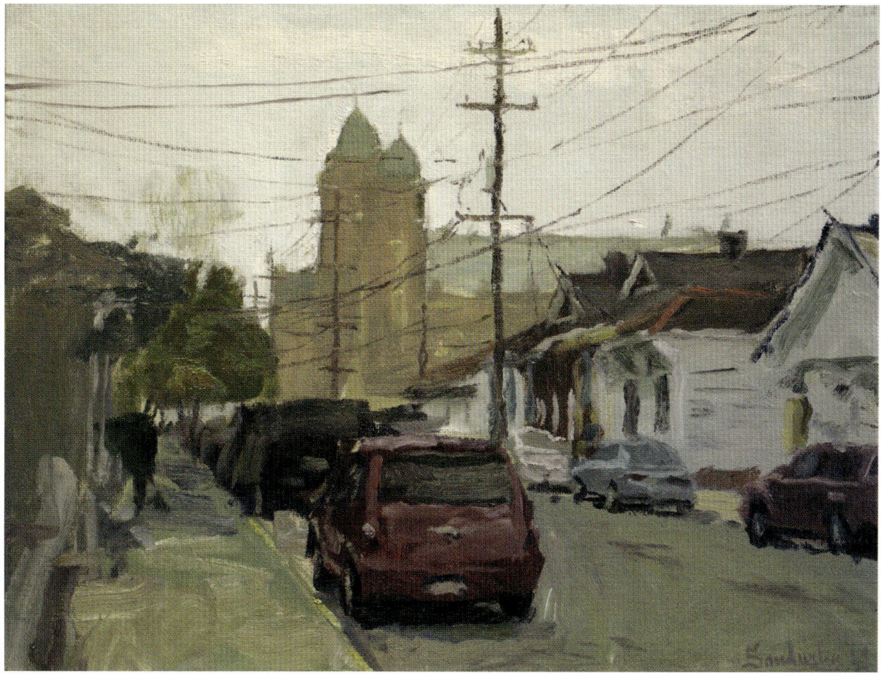

SAINTS PETER AND PAUL CHURCH ON A FOGGY MORNING 11" X 14"

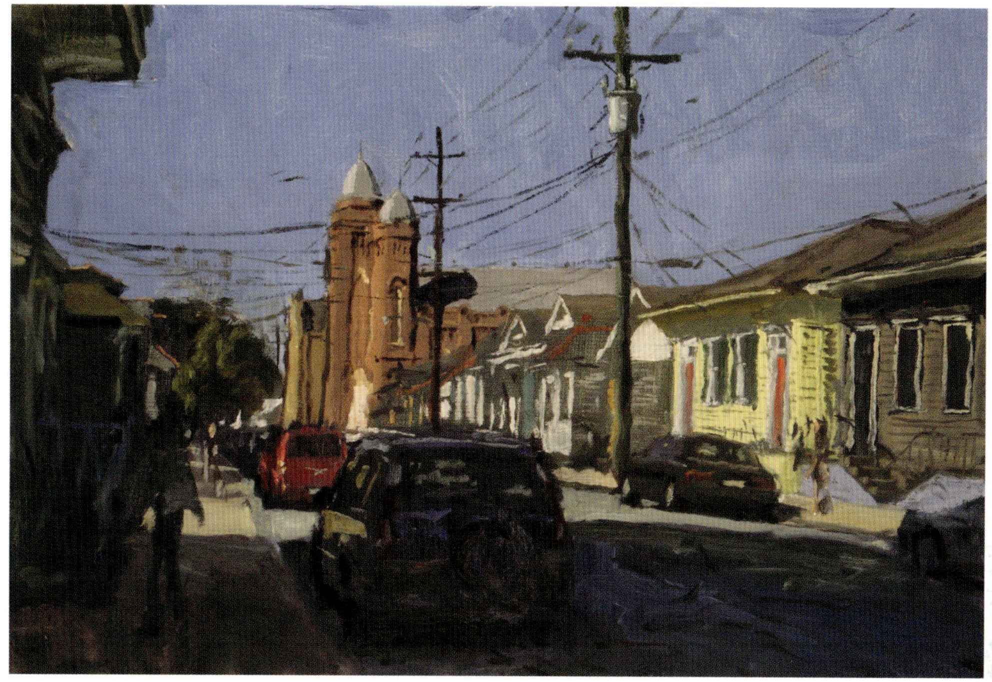

SAINTS PETER AND PAUL CHURCH ON A CLEAR MORNING 18" X 24"

of a work. This formulaic approach was dominant through the medieval and renaissance periods of art history. Although formulas are limiting, they reside in the artist's memory and therefore memory is engaged in the artist's process. Subtle inflections of the artist's own unique point of view can be ushered in with the formulas as long as the formulas are not too intrusive and dominant in the artist's memories.

For our keenest perceptions, canned formulas are inadequate to convey the subtle nuances that apply to the *biggest* aspects of a subject as well as the smallest. Therefore, the most effective way for artists to deal with a changing subject was to grasp it in its entirety at one moment and remember it as such throughout a painting or drawing session. But to grasp and remember all parts of the subject at once was impossible without first simplifying. This was done through various techniques of temporarily impeding the eyes' ability to gather information. Perhaps the most common is eye squinting. If you completely close your eyes and then slightly crack your eye lids until you can just barely see, you will notice that objects are indistinct. A complex view has been reduced to just a few big, simple patterns of light and dark. Another technique is to train your eyes away from the subject and notice it peripherally. Remember that our visual acuity is ten times less in the periphery than it is in the center of vision. Yet another technique more aligned with real human vision is to quickly glance at the subject and try to remember what you saw. It seems a bit counterintuitive that artists primarily interested in accurately rendering the subject would impede their vision, but these and other simplification techniques made it easier for artists to conceptualize and remember a fugitive subject as a whole. These techniques would also serve an alternate purpose of

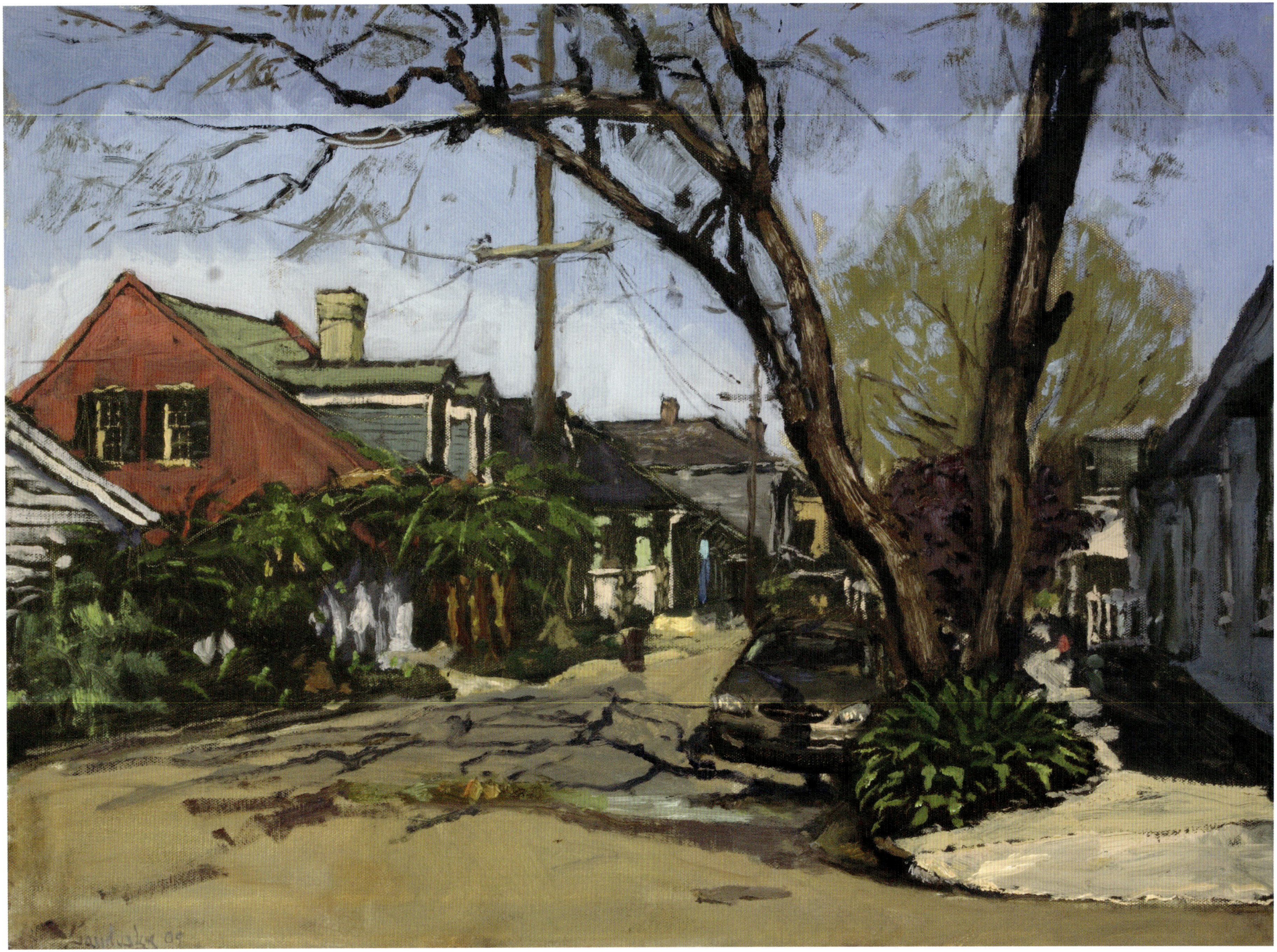

Intersection of Spain and Royal streets 18" x 24"

temporarily destroying the familiarity of the subject, bringing *certain* sensory evoked qualifiers forward in the artist's mind—a necessity for rendering a subject unambiguously and convincingly. But memory continued to be engaged.

If the eye's ability to gather information is impeded, the qualifiers and mandates evoked from memory are relied upon even more heavily. Long ago, when running at dusk on the dirt trail in Audubon Park, I was convinced that I could see better than just before sunset and more than well enough to continue safely navigating the treacherous ruts and tree roots. I wouldn't move over to the paved track until about 5 or 10 minutes before complete darkness. I changed this protocol when it occurred to me that most of my ankle injuries and falls had happened in the half hour or so before dark. During this period, my memory had done such an admirable job of forming a convincing and nuanced perception of my trail running that I didn't realize how useless information from my eyes was becoming. The sketchy and inadequate sensory evoked qualifiers were becoming incapable of whipping up the qualifiers from memory into accurately mapping the topography of the trail. Fortunately in art, nuance is much more important than accuracy. When an artist can only detect a vague shape of the human form through squinted eyes, memories from his experiences of not only human bodies but many other related things come forward to supplement the greatly reduced sensory evoked qualifiers. His artificial simplification of his subject closely emulates the normal state of our everyday vision as we see the world mostly in quick glances, never focusing on any one part of a view for too long. Conversely, it might seem that memory's vast contribution to vision should fade into the background when we intensely focus our attention on one part or aspect of our view such as irregularities in a dirt running trail. But in this case the memory evoked qualifiers and mandates just become more concentrated into smaller facets of the view being directed more scrupulously by the sensory evoked qualifiers.

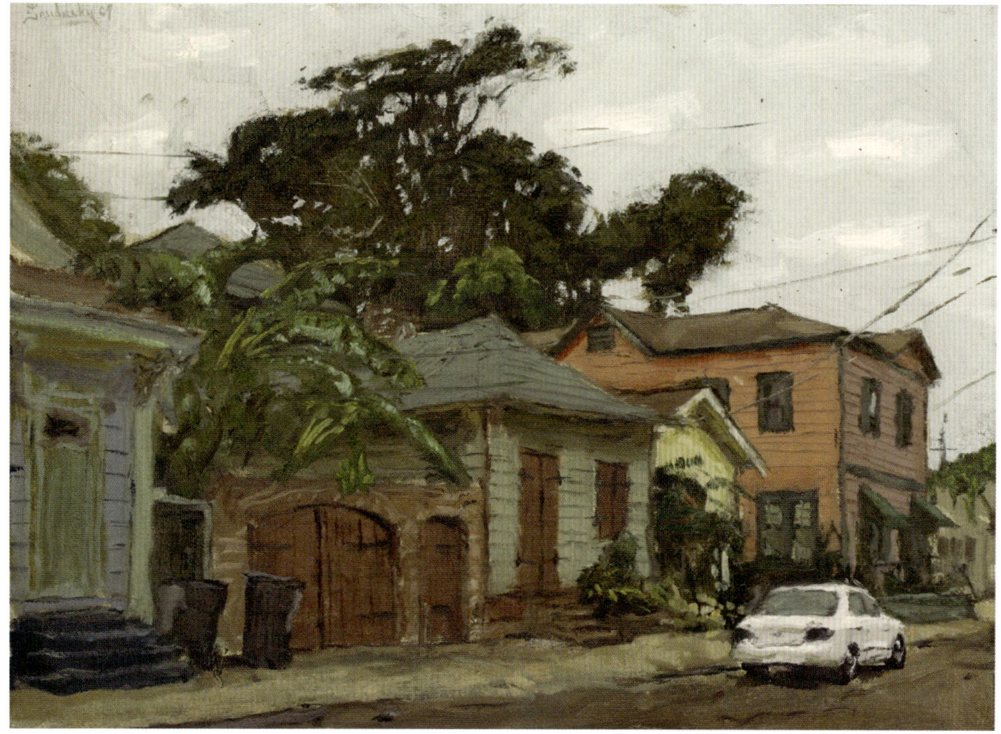

BURGUNDY STREET CLOSE TO ST. ANTHONY STREET 14" x 18"

Eventually, with much practice in simplification, artists could simplify a bit less, conceptualizing more parts of the subject at once as a whole, but they would gain a fond appreciation of simplification. Having obscured the details, they became attuned to the prominence in our perceptions of the big sweeping gestures and movements within the subject. As far back as the Baroque era, the best artists often painted fewer details in the subject, losing edges in shadow areas, for example. By using simplification techniques to accurately *and objectively* render a fugitive subject, they had accidentally become connected with the temporal aspect of vision. They might not have fully grasped that we don't see everything at once, but they began to understand that a statement often has more impact when it is a bit simpler than an exact meticulous copy of the image. This esthetic bent evolved and

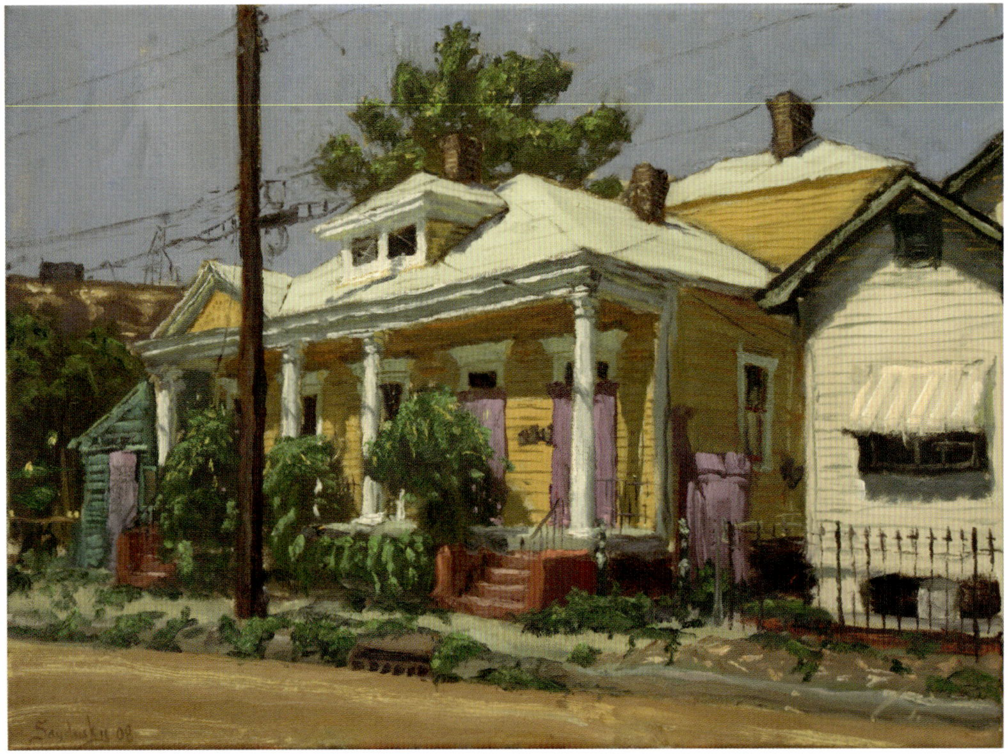

Brightly colored boarded up house on Montegut Street close to North Rampart Street 18" x 24"

expanded to become the central tenet for the Impressionists in the late nineteenth century called the "fleeting moment." It was supported by the work of the Gestalt psychologists in the early twentieth century and has been further supported by scientific research to present. In the latter part of the twentieth century the Minimalists attempted to reduce the temporal aspect of our perceptions as far as possible with the battle cry, "less is more!" However, we might surmise that there is an optimum point of simplification beyond which less becomes *ambiguous*.

Another limitation of the memory inclusive path, which inadvertently aligned artists' work more with vision, is that painted patterns on a canvas cannot come close to replicating the color contrast found in most live subjects, including those that are indoors. In the live subject the lightest values could be glints of sunlight and the darkest may be nearly void of light. Also there are colors in nature such as what would be found in certain flowers and filtered sunlight shining through the backs of leaves that are richer than any color of paint. This was especially true before the advent of new pigments such as alizarin (a very rich purple-red) in the late nineteenth century. Because artists working from life could not even come close to matching the colors in nature, their only option was to mix colors that *resonated* like the colors in nature. Remember that one of the ways our vision is distinguished from the image is that, while the image is absolute, our vision is relative. The qualifiers for color are evoked only in response to color differences, not to which colors are present. Memory was easily engaged because, in concentrating upon color differences instead of individual colors, the artist's process was aligned with vision, which is mostly memory. Also, memory *had* to be engaged from the standpoint that the colors in a successful painting could not have matched the colors of the live subject except by coincidence, meaning that the colors in the painting could have only been derived from memory.

Most artists who worked from life had to be attuned to the spatial differences in color that are registered more as you glance from one place to another within the same overall view. But many artists also became attuned to time changes in color. This was evident more during the impressionist era when occasionally paintings would have an *overall* warm or cool cast of the colors to evoke a transient effect that happens more prominently when one's entire view changes. Remember that certain qualifiers and mandates are evoked by the differences between images, though there is no information in any given image about the difference between it and other images.

In the memory inclusive path, we have seen that the limitations of working from a live fugitive subject have

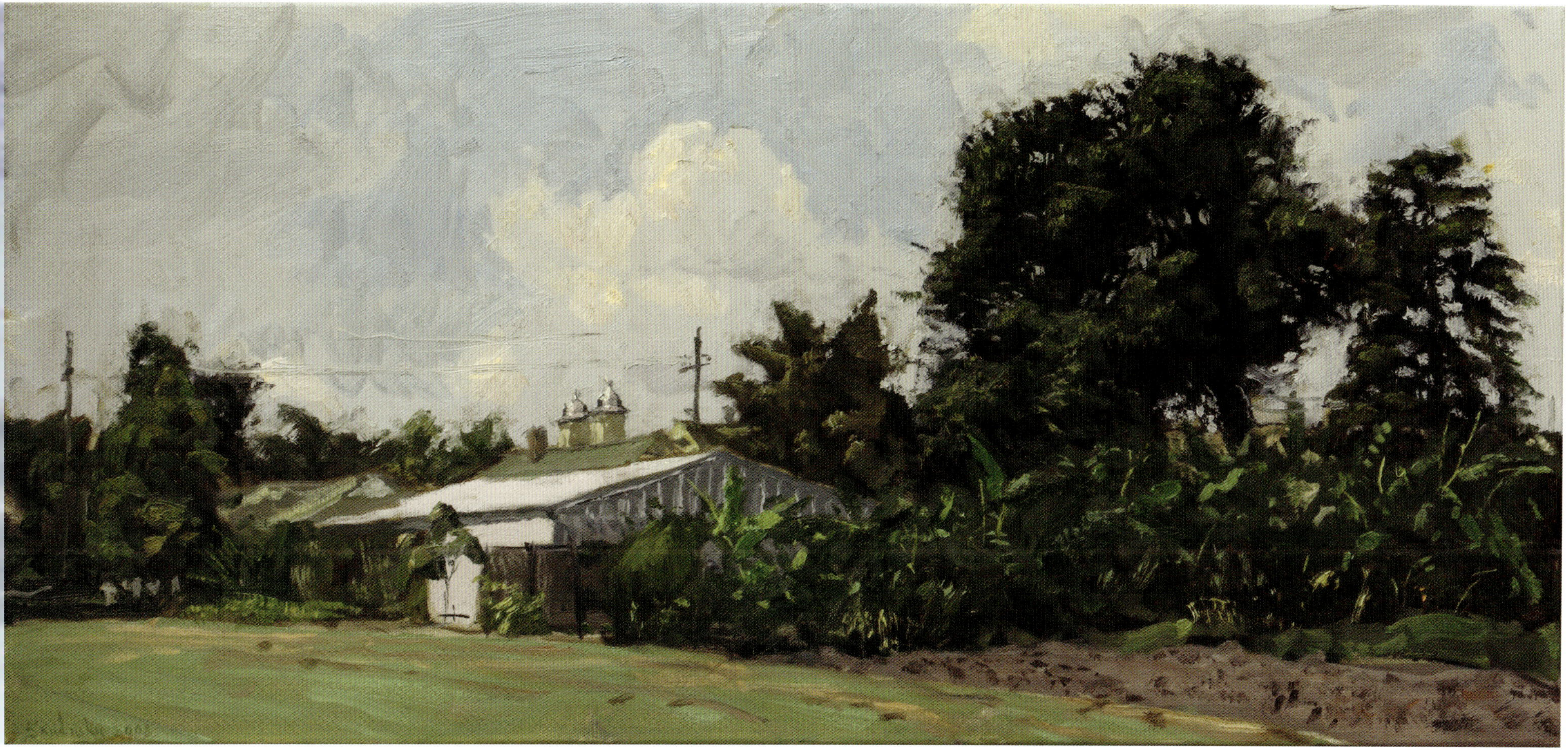

ACROSS AN OPEN FIELD AT PRESS AND NORTH RAMPART STREETS 15" X 30"

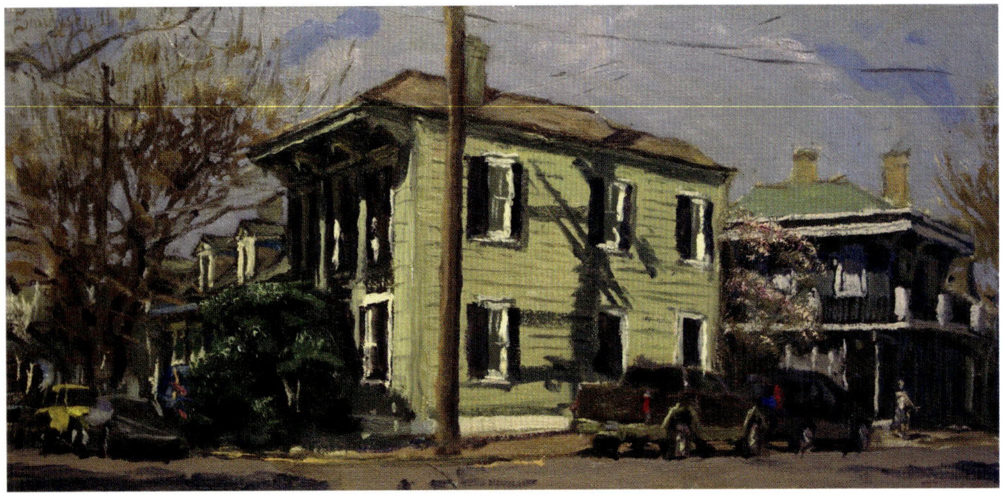

Intersection of Frenchmen and Dauphine Streets 10" x 20"

enabled the artist's statement to reflect the qualities of human vision that both transcend the objective image and have nothing to do with it. Even though the artist ironically has used an image to render his subject, and this rendering has been unambiguous and captured the nuance of a specific experience, it has been inadvertently inflected to enrich the viewer with a unique set of life memories (a point of view), and to evoke both the relational and temporal aspects of vision, producing a statement with a powerful visual gestalt. To see the benefits of the memory inclusive path firsthand, look at the work of great painters such as Rembrandt, Velazquez, Turner, Chase, and Sargent and compare the rendering of the subjects in these paintings to good quality photographs of similar subjects. Perhaps, what was the painting's *je ne sais quoi* has become a bit more tangible in light of our discussion of vision and the artist's process.

The Strictly Objective Path

Whereas the memory inclusive path engages the artist's memory and aligns his process and resulting painting more with vision, we will see that the strictly objective path uses a very small, easily learned skill set to copy the objective image, bypassing all of the rest of the artist's brain, including memory. Before photography, artists would have been able to approximate this path with sight sticks, view finders, and the camera obscura. But using such tools to render subjects that were live and changing and that eclipsed the value and color contrast capable of being achieved with paint, without infusing understanding and visual memory into the process, would have produced poor results. So the forbearer of the strictly objective path was the component of *some* artists' process devoted to measuring and matching with the tools of accuracy. This aspect of the artist's process trickled through art history as a small creek until the advent of photography, where it would begin to expand, and into the twentieth century where it would be fed by more tributaries swelling into a thundering river, eventually becoming the strictly objective path.

The emergence of the strictly objective path didn't happen overnight. When photography was invented, artists quickly saw it as a useful tool. It could aid in capturing the subjects that were the most changeable such as animals in motion and infants and child portrait subjects who were incapable of being still. There is a surviving photographic reference that Sargent used to paint a man rowing a gondola under a bridge. Photographic references also became a surrogate for very-important-person portrait models whose time was too valuable to pose. But the best of these artists who began to use photography were trained in some derivation of the memory inclusive path. They did not copy the photos by rote but observed them along with, and in the same way as, their experience of the live subject. The first painters who used photos referred to them as "memory aids." Later they would more commonly be called "photographic references." The earliest photographs could be of no more use than this to artists because they were monochromatic (only in black and

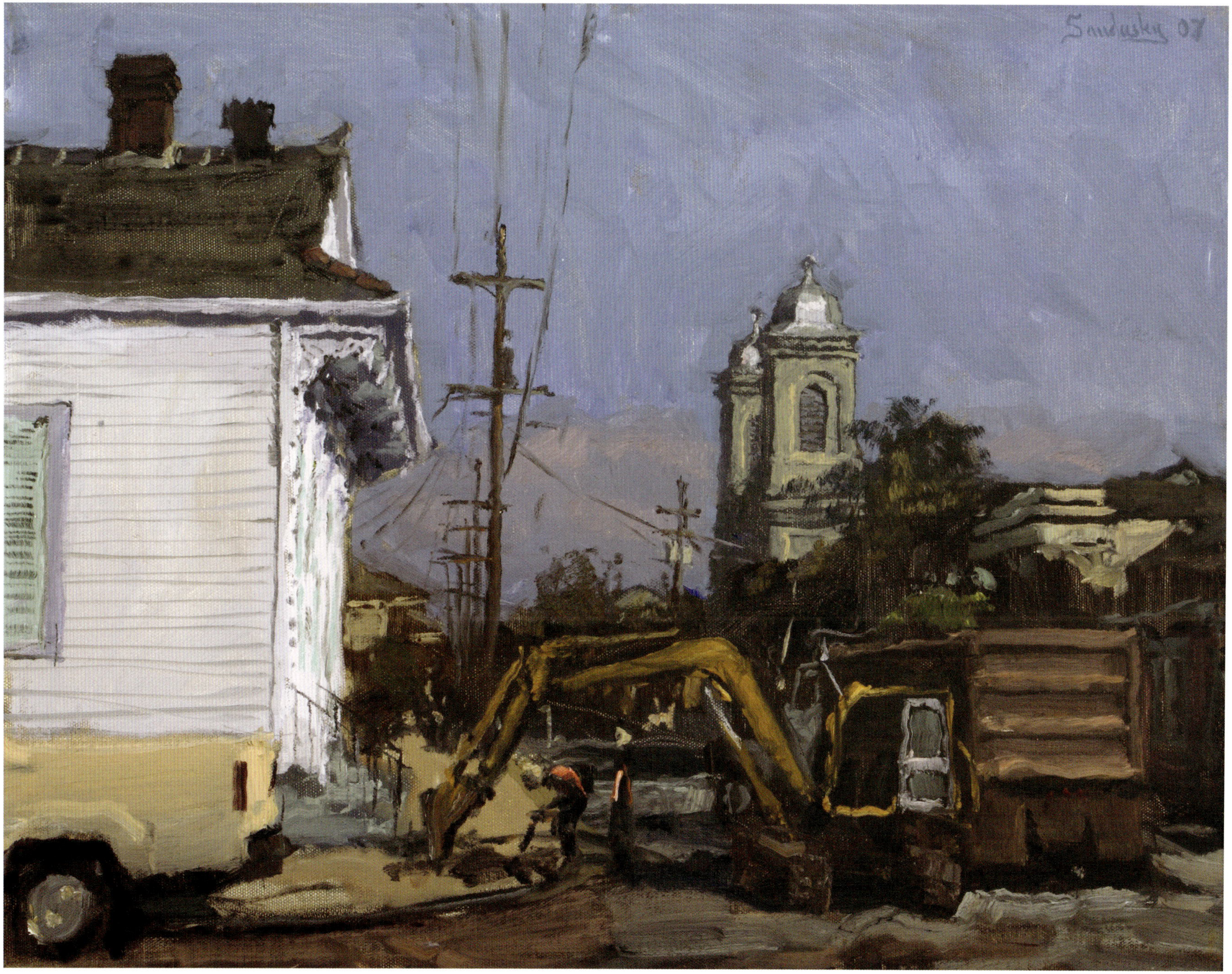

CONSTRUCTION WORK AT ST. FERDINAND AND ROYAL STREETS 16" X 20" THE CONSTRUCTION CREW AND EQUIPMENT ARRIVED AFTER I STARTED THE PAINTING. FORTUNATELY, I WAS ABLE TO WORK THEM INTO THE COMPOSITION.

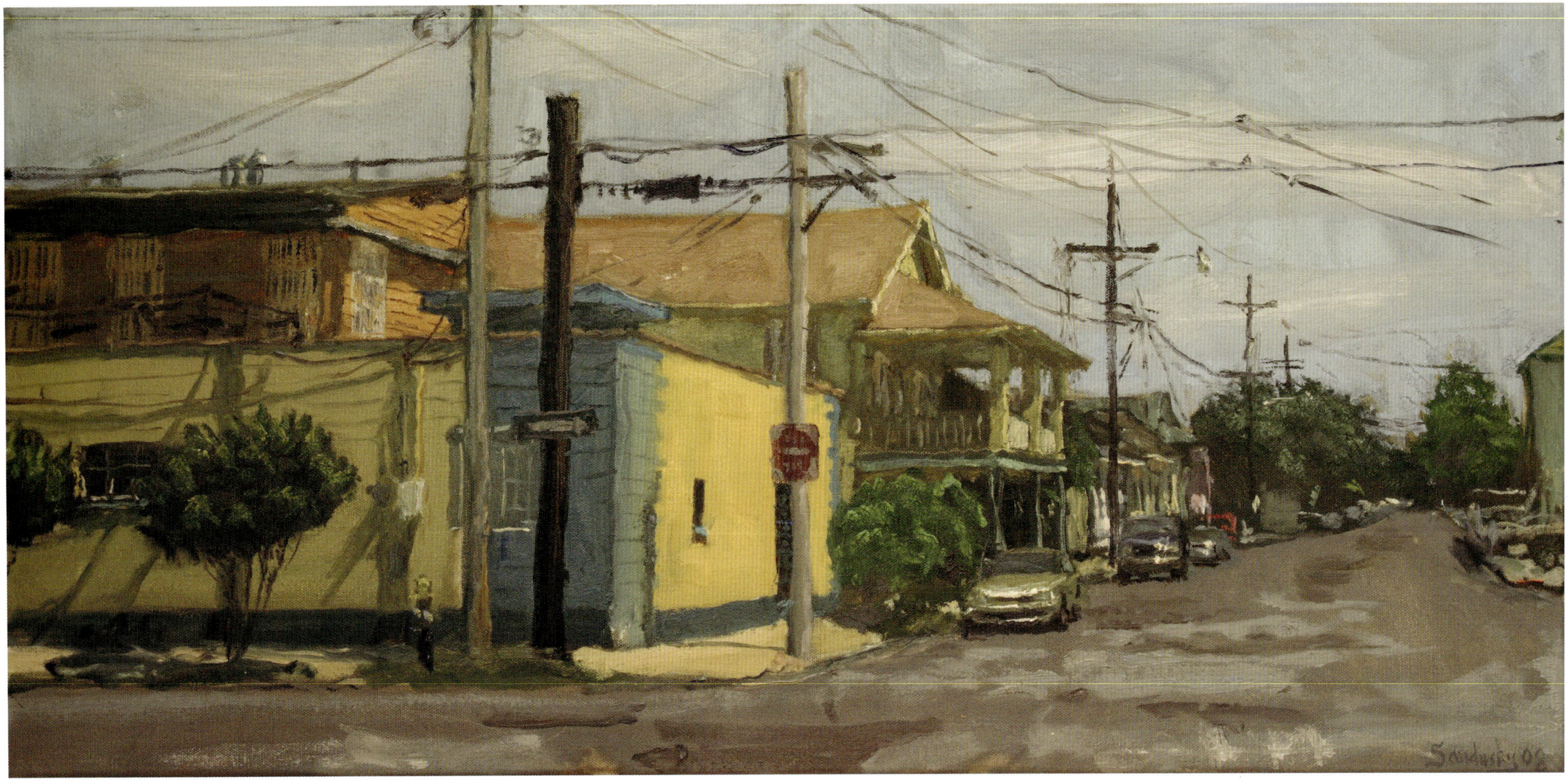

A MODERN REMODELING AT THE CORNER OF CHARTRES STREET AND FRANKLIN AVENUE 15" X 30"

white) and they were limited in the subtlety of the lighting effects that they could capture.

The utilitarian function of documentation had fostered huge numbers of professional artists over the centuries, from whom ascended the great painters that formed the cannons of art history. The work of these great artists transcended documentation to become aligned with human vision and communicate unique points of view. As photography became more popular, it began to usurp painting's role in documentation. Photography was better suited to documentation because of its objective accuracy, lower cost, and quick execution. Just as once had been the case with realistic painters, eventually there was such a large field of photographers that from their ranks also ascended a few whose work rose above mere documentation to communicate a point of view. But unlike painters, this new elite class of fine art photographers and photojournalists had to make the transcendental statement despite being bound to the objective image, having no more latitude than precisely reproducing it with the push of a button. Admittedly there were a few minor adjustments to the image that could be made in the dark room, and apertures could produce varying depths of field. But for the most part, photographers could only communicate a point of view through selection of subject matter, selection of a vantage point from which to photograph it, and composition (how to frame the subject in the view finder). Because our memories effect how we scan a view with our eyes, choosing what part of the visual field to align the camera's view finder could help communicate a point of view. To jar peoples' sensibilities, these elite photographers usually had to choose unusual subject matter and their compositions eventually became much more overtly interesting than those of academic painters, whose compositions were no less important but usually more subtle, having a hidden strength so as not to distract the viewer from what would

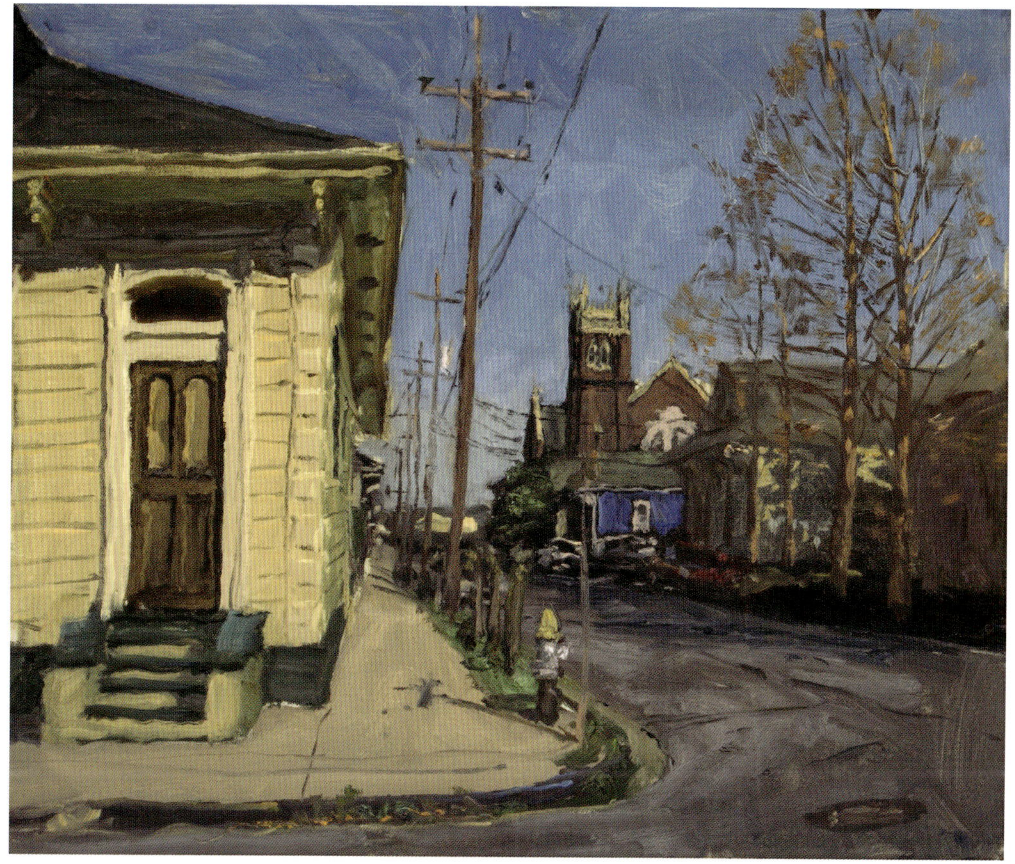

CORNER OF BURGUNDY AND FRANCE STREETS 20" X 20"

have been for the painter the greatly more important *rendering* of the subject.

One would imagine that the burgeoning of photography might have contributed to the mass exodus of painters from representation to abstraction, especially with color photography looming at the turn of the century. For the skeleton crew of representational painters who stood fast, a demon seed had been planted that they could not have seen. The appearance of photography was similar to that of traditional representational painting. They were both rectangular and two dimensional, and they both evoked many of the same sensory

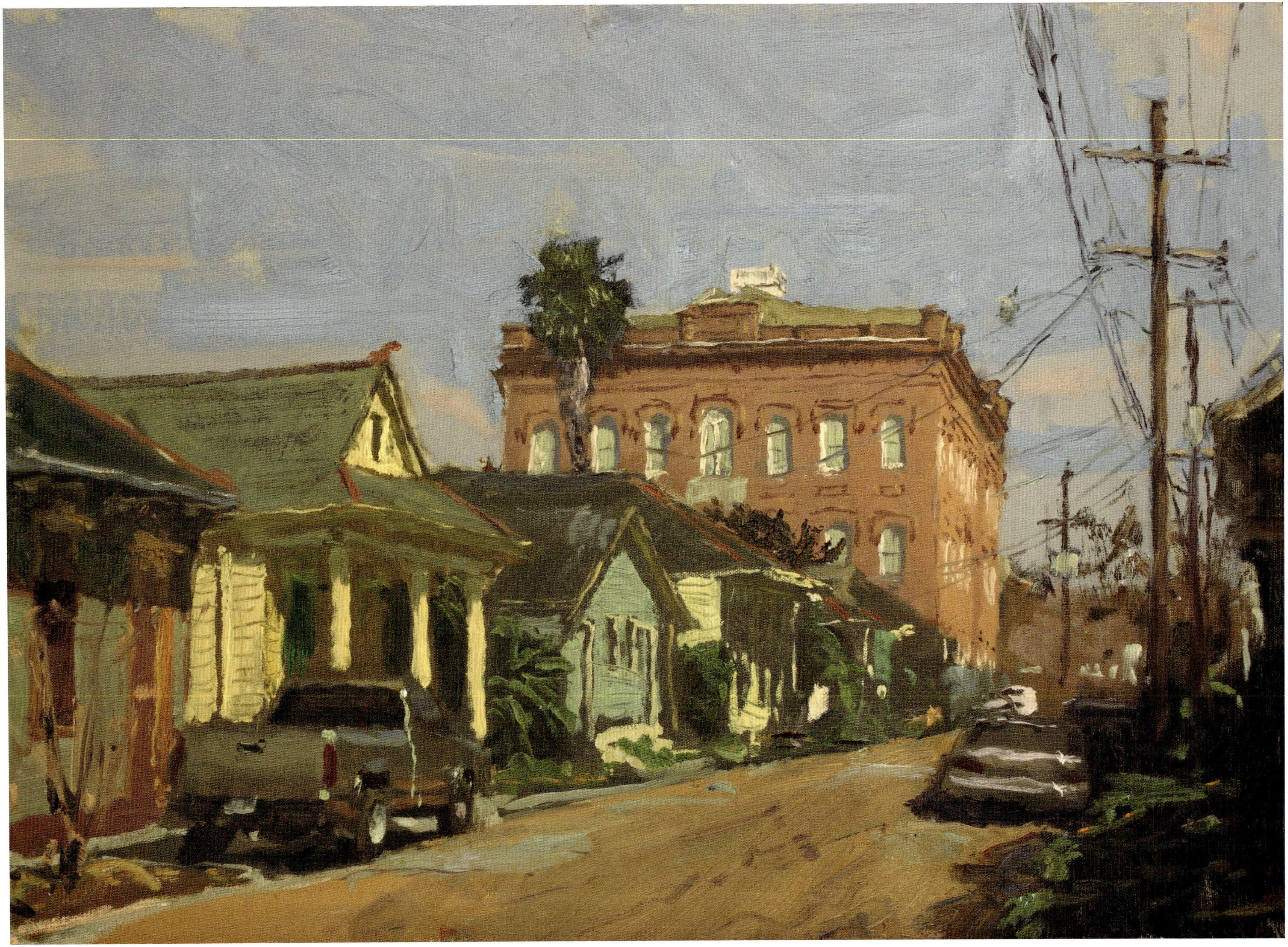

Looking down Congress Street from Burgundy Street 18" x 24"

evoked visual qualifiers. At first their similarity played to the advantage of painting. Few contested that representational painting was superior to photography, especially before the prominence of color photography. Viewers appreciated the qualities of the artist's poetic rendering of the subject over the starkness of photos, not to mention the more tangible advantage that paintings could be made large and in color. But eventually the increased innate quality of photography, the sheer numbers of photographs, and not least, quite a few brilliant accomplishments in the new medium, began to bend the esthetics of representational painting toward the esthetics of photography. All forms of representation of similar appearance were lumped into the same esthetic pot, and photography won out by sheer number. The newness of photography and its scientific advancement also played in its favor. Seeing and rendering the subject became less valuable to the art establishment, and composition and selection of subject matter became more valuable. This and the increased quality of photographic references would have greatly de-incentivized a younger generation of representational artists from investing the time and hard work necessary to become proficient in working from the live subject. The objective image, from which artists across the millennia borrowed to minimize the ambiguity of their statements, had taken a concrete form in the photograph, and would now demand payment in full, *with interest.*

Impervious to this foreclosure that the objective image would make upon representational art were those artists and their followers who would maintain for their own edification the soon-to-be unfashionable tradition of working *at least predominantly* from the live subject. Because they continued to communicate individual points of view more through rendering, it behooved them to continue painting from the same intimately familiar, common subjects that had always been used, such as the nude and the still life. Because the new representational esthetic greatly emphasized creativity with

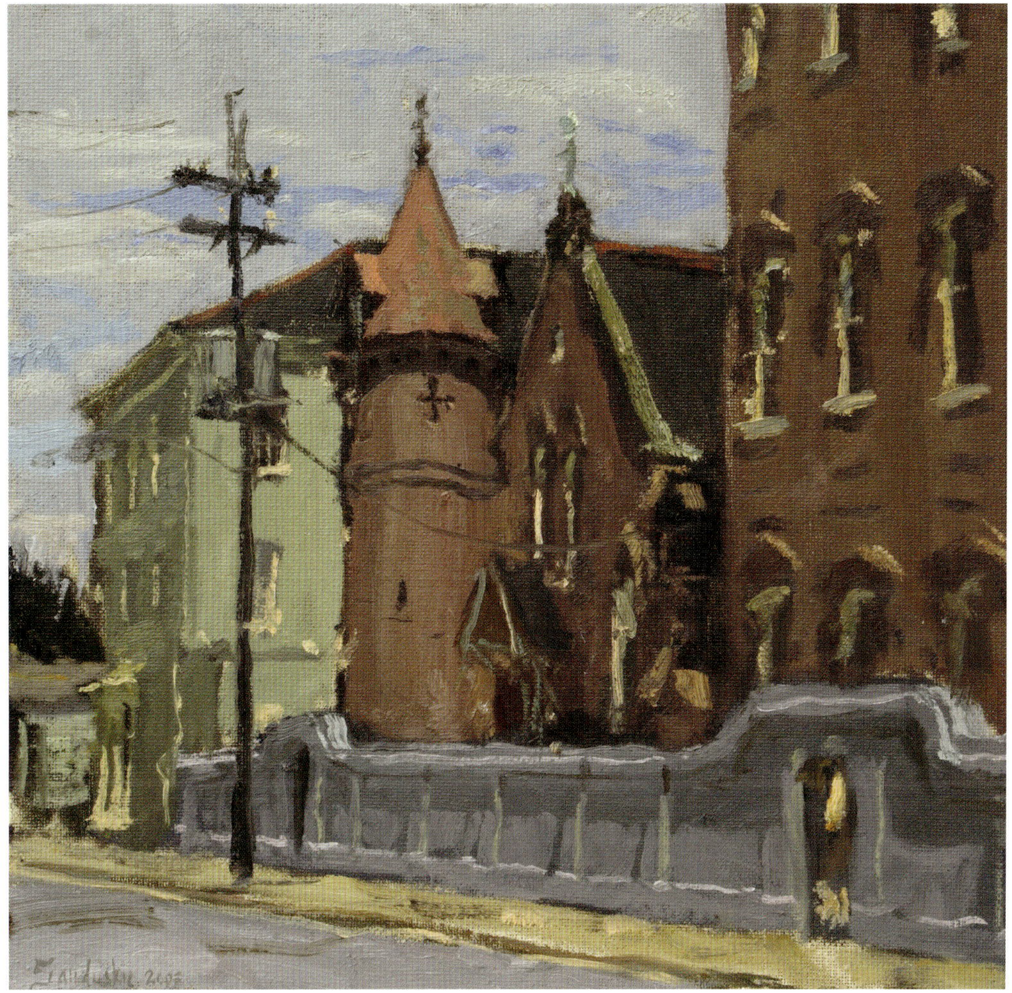

VIEW FROM THE INTERSECTION OF NORTH RAMPART AND CONGRESS STREETS 12" X 12" THIS AMAZING LITTLE CHAPEL IS NEXT TO THE LARGE RED BRICK BUILDING SHOWN IN THE PAINTING ON THE FACING PAGE.

subject matter, these stalwart traditional academic realists were scorned by the new art establishment for regurgitating what had already been done. They struggled on through the twentieth century in little enclaves, sheltering themselves from critical abuse and neglect, and have recently been able to safely re-emerge in the confusion of post-modernism.

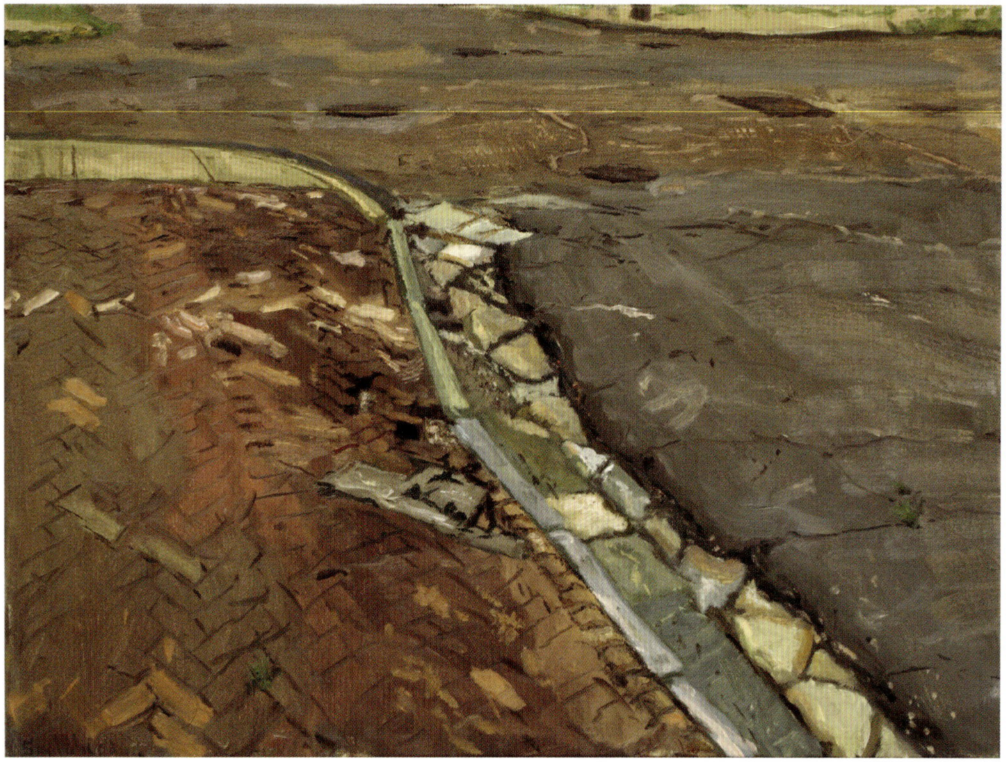

Asphalt over Cobblestones 18" x 24"

Representational painting could only find a niche in the new esthetic by exploring fantastical subjects that could not easily be broached by photography. Because the content of the representational painting was now deemed greatly more important than its rendering, a new lineage of representational artists who sought to remain in good favor with the new establishment would take the considerably easier path of copying photographic images onto their canvases rather than interpreting the firsthand subject through the lens of memory as they would have been forced to do in an earlier era. Whereas rendering exclusively with the tools of accuracy was impossible when working from a changeable live subject, it was quite easy when working from the still images of photos. Also the color contrast of the paint eclipsed that of the photo, enabling artists to *copy* the colors from the photos rather than having to understand how they resonate. But memory was not at first completely disengaged. Often artists would compile an image on the canvas from multiple photographic references utilizing knowledge of such things as perspective and light. When copying from a *single* photographic reference, they might have accentuated certain aspects of it to more strongly communicate a point of view. These new artists also admired the works of their pre-photography forefathers and occasionally tried to replicate their painterly effects, though without the underlying causes. All of these things engage memory *somewhat.* Yet, the artist's statement was quickly becoming calcified by the objective image.

The objective image obtained its entrée into the human mind through representational artists' need to learn from it to bring the sensory evoked qualifiers forward in their perceptions so that their statements would be unambiguous. It obtained its first and most powerful ally in its tangible earthly manifestation, the photograph. It acquired more allies in the similarity of its appearance to traditional academic painting, and in the gifted photographers who could tailor its concrete manifestation into a meaningful statement. But it had yet another ally that was hidden and more insidious.

In one of the popular Harry Potter novels written by J. K. Rowling, there is an enchanted mirror called the "Mirror of Erised." Anyone who looks into this mirror sees himself as he would like to be, not as he is. A young boy who lost his parents in infancy sees in the mirror a reflection of himself with his parents as he would imagine them to be, standing behind him and lovingly embracing him. The objective image has a close analogy in the Mirror of Erised. We each see the objective image differently. Because we all have different memories, we each have a different set of qualifiers and mandates evoked when we experience the same objective image. Except for the transient aspect of our vision, a photograph can pretty powerfully re-evoke each person's unique vision. And so

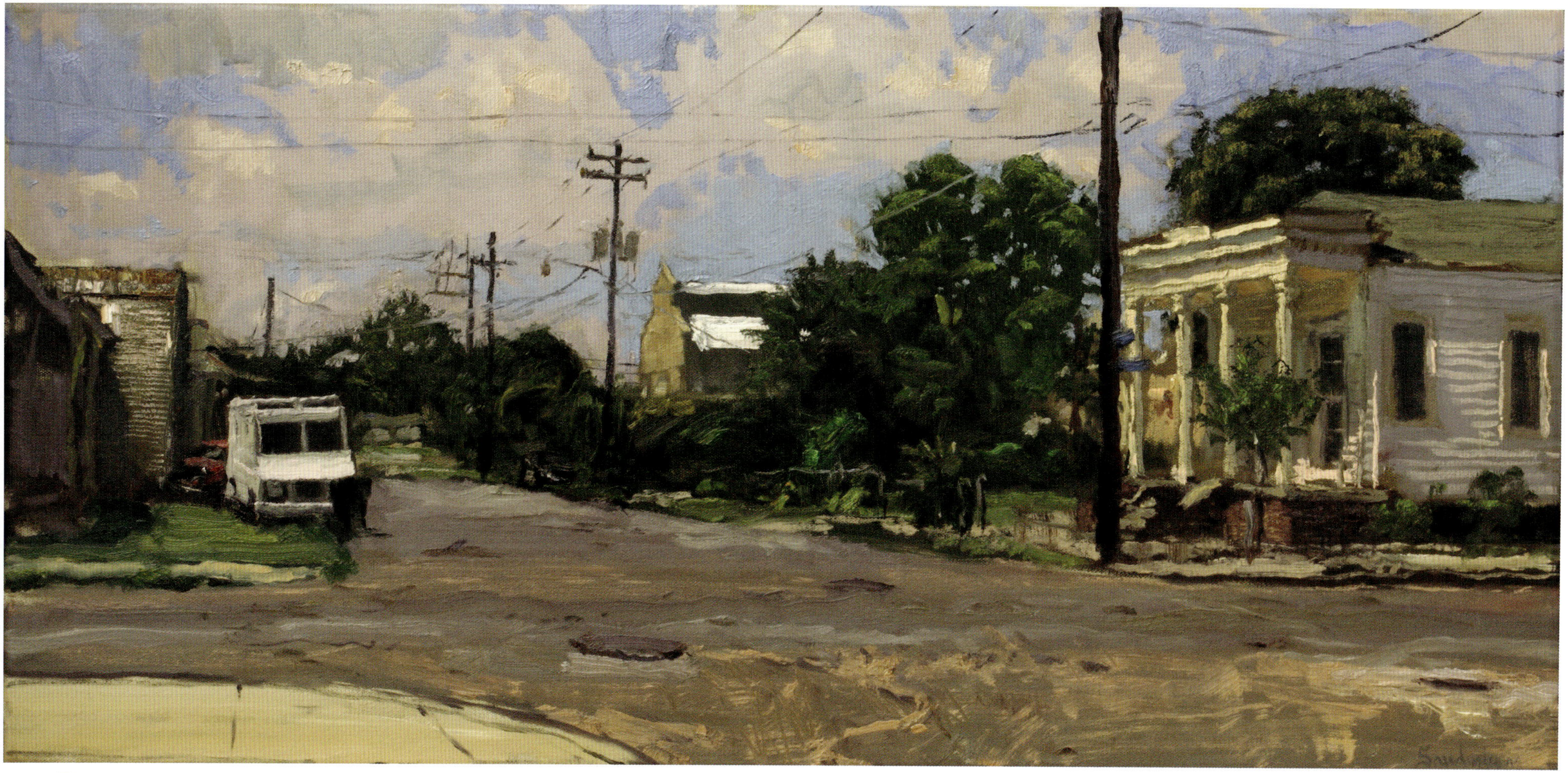

The intersection of Royal and Desire streets 15" x 30" If you look down from this view towards the ground you will see the view depicted on the previous page.

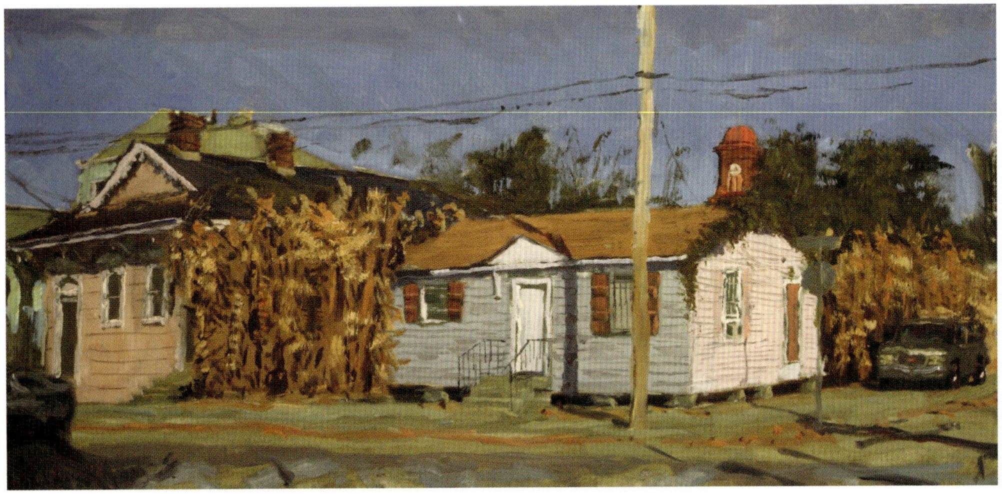

DEAD BANANA TREES AFTER A HARD FREEZE, CORNER OF CLOUET AND ROYAL STREETS 15" X 30"

this new, nontraditional, representational artist who has faithfully copied the objective image looks at what he's done as one looking into the Mirror of Erised, seeing the beauty or the qualities that compelled him to make this painting, but not realizing that each different person who looks at his painting will see something different. This ill effect is felt by the artist through unexpected lukewarm feedback from the viewers of his work, and though he does not understand it, it is minimized as he gravitates to subjects more alien to his audience. Fine art photographers had been down this road before. The subtle differences in individual points of view that cannot be communicated with an objective image are *accentuated* with ordinary subjects. Unusual subjects *de-accentuate* those differences. And the new representational esthetic had been adjusted to accommodate this newfound importance in subject matter. Entranced by this *Erised effect,* which had become fortified by choice of subject, artists became less inclined to augment aspects of the photographic image from which they worked to better communicate their point of view. Eventually, aside from his skill as a photographer in creating the photographic reference from which he worked, the charm of handcraft—the artists' simple lack of perfect proficiency in copying the image—became the only thin line of communication from his process of rendering to the rest of his mind.

All that remained would be to cut off this last thin line of communication to the mind. Earlier we saw that the easiest way to accurately render the objective image is to make the subject unfamiliar. When the subject becomes unfamiliar, the sensory evoked qualifiers come forward in your perception because there are fewer memory associations. You can then easily recreate a set of forms on paper that re-evoke those sensory evoked qualifiers. We have seen that with no art instruction, one can accurately draw from a photograph that has been turned upside-down. This is the principle that photorealism employed to bring the strictly objective path to its perfect form. A very fine grid is superimposed upon a large photographic print. The grid is so fine that if you were to look into any single incremental box within the grid there would be nothing but meaningless abstract patterns. In fact, quite often there would be nothing but solid colors, perhaps with only a slight gradient in value or texture. The photorealist then recreates this grid, usually larger in scale, on the canvas. Then using paint, sometimes starting with a pencil outline, he separately transfers to the canvas the content of each box on the photograph, carefully mixing colors to perfectly match each spot of color on the photo. Thus the objective image has been accurately rendered, bypassing any part of the artist's mind that could augment it through the lens of memory or perception. Only the tiny part of the mind that contains this easy-to-learn procedure has been engaged. There is an alternate procedure that involves projecting the photographic image onto the canvas and faithfully tracing it.

Photorealism sprang from the Pop Art movement of the mid-twentieth century, thriving to present, amassing a large following. It has also been referred to as Superrealism

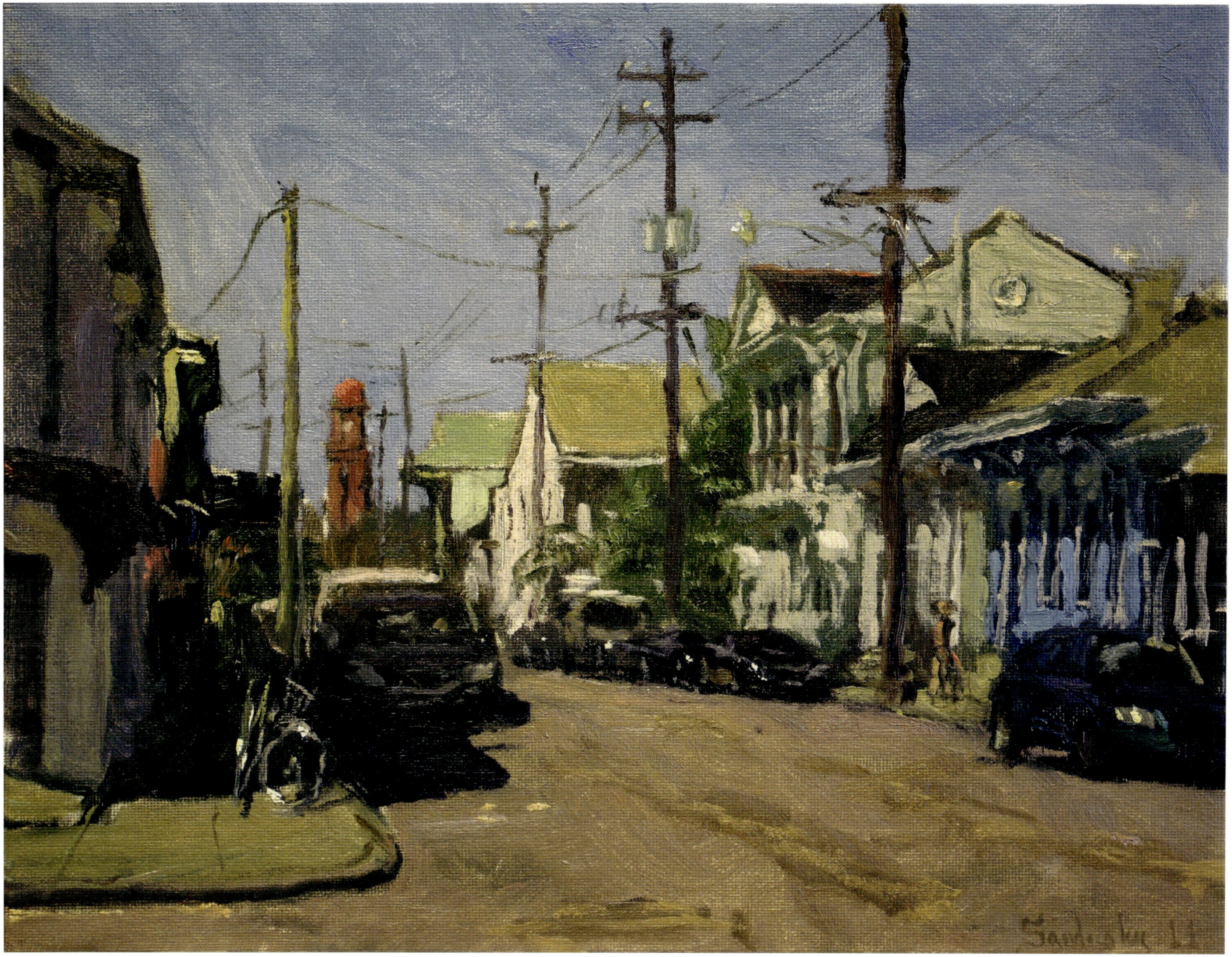

LOOKING UP DAUPHINE STREET FROM PIETY STREET 11" x 14"

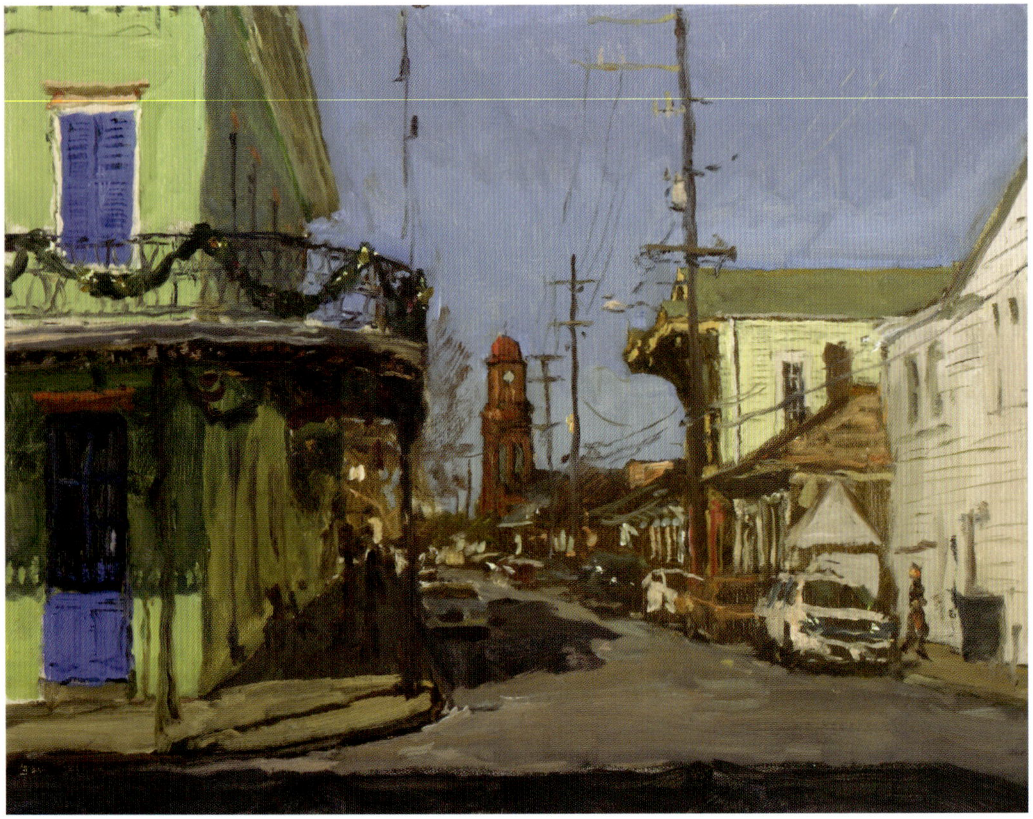

LOOKING UP DAUPHINE STREET FROM LOUISA STREET 16" X 20" THE BELL TOWER IN THE DISTANCE IS THAT OF ST. VINCENT DE PAUL CATHOLIC CHURCH.

and Hyperrealism to reflect the increasing quality of the photographic references upon which it depends. These artists have said that their objective is to perfectly reproduce the photographic image. Why would they not just use the photographic reference as the finished product? Why spend weeks and sometimes months manually transferring the photograph when there are machines that can do it better, quicker, and cheaper? And why do collectors buy these paintings?

First, we cannot discount the photorealist painter's skill as a photographer. The photograph that he has taken is beautiful and communicates his point of view as well as any photograph. But the only explanation for his mindless, time consuming, manual transfer of the photograph to canvas lies in the objective image's greatest ally, our lack of understanding of vision. The photorealist painter labors under the common misconception that the objective image is our perfect vision, unsullied by the human mind. He believes that when the camera was invented, our perfect uncorrupted vision was given its earthly embodiment as a photograph. He cannot improve upon it but can only adorn it by tirelessly transferring each little spot of color in each grid, disconnected from human imperfection, as a worshiper prostrating himself to his deity.

As to why collectors buy photorealist paintings, aside from being pleasing to the eye in their capacity as reproductions of nice photographs, in the art world value can be assigned based upon the amount of work as well as upon rarity of skill. Even though the photorealist technique is very easily learned and applied, its execution takes a tremendous amount of time. Perhaps photorealist painters can be thought of as the medieval scribes of our modern era. One approaches a photorealist painting with reading glasses and is impressed that a human being took the time to paint every minute line of grout in the rendering of a brick wall in the background. Of course the artist *might* not have known that he was painting a brick wall, and the viewer must be informed that he is looking at a painting instead of a photograph.

(Concluded on page 111)

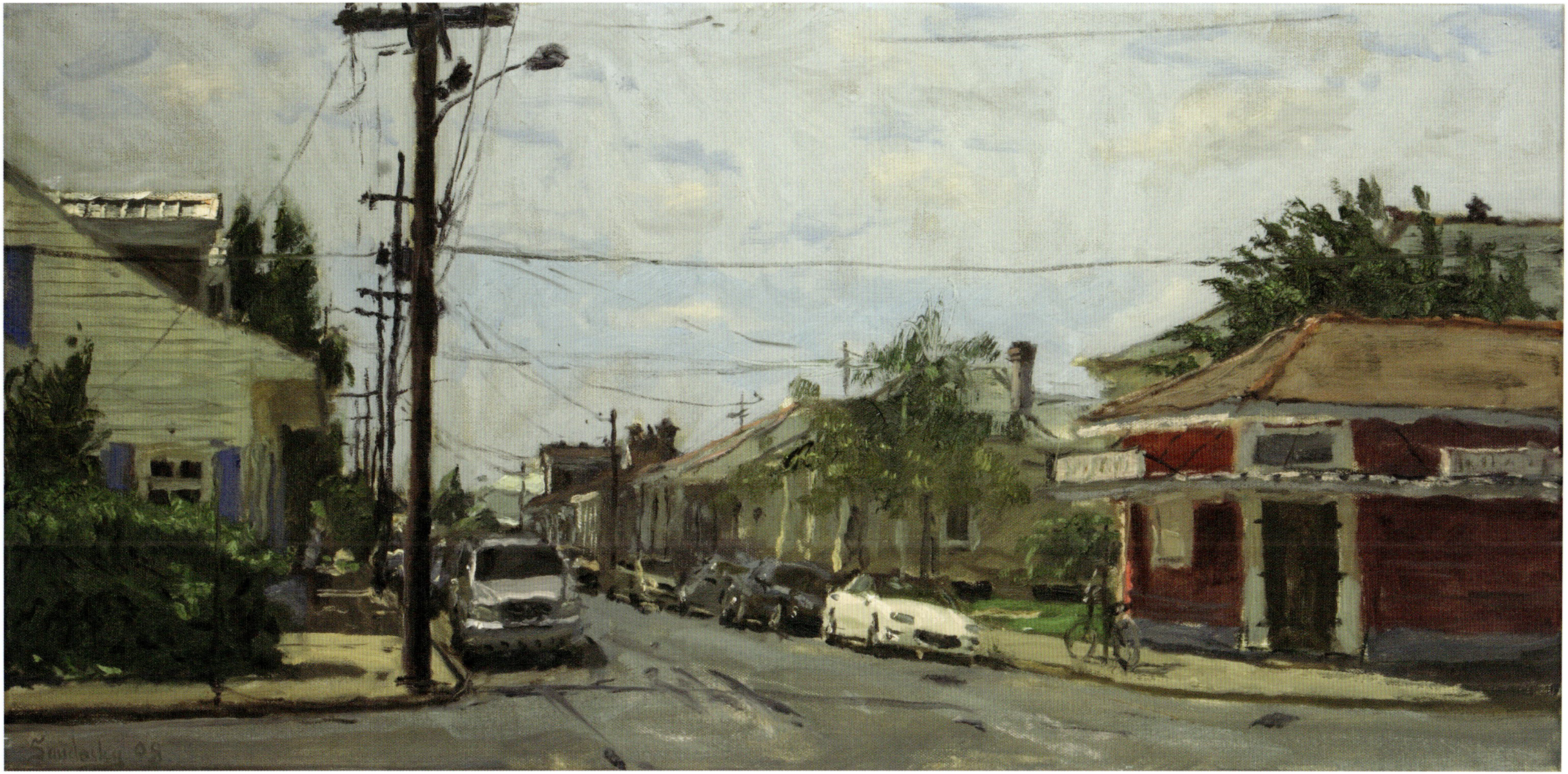

Markey's Bar, corner of Louisa and Royal streets 15" x 30"

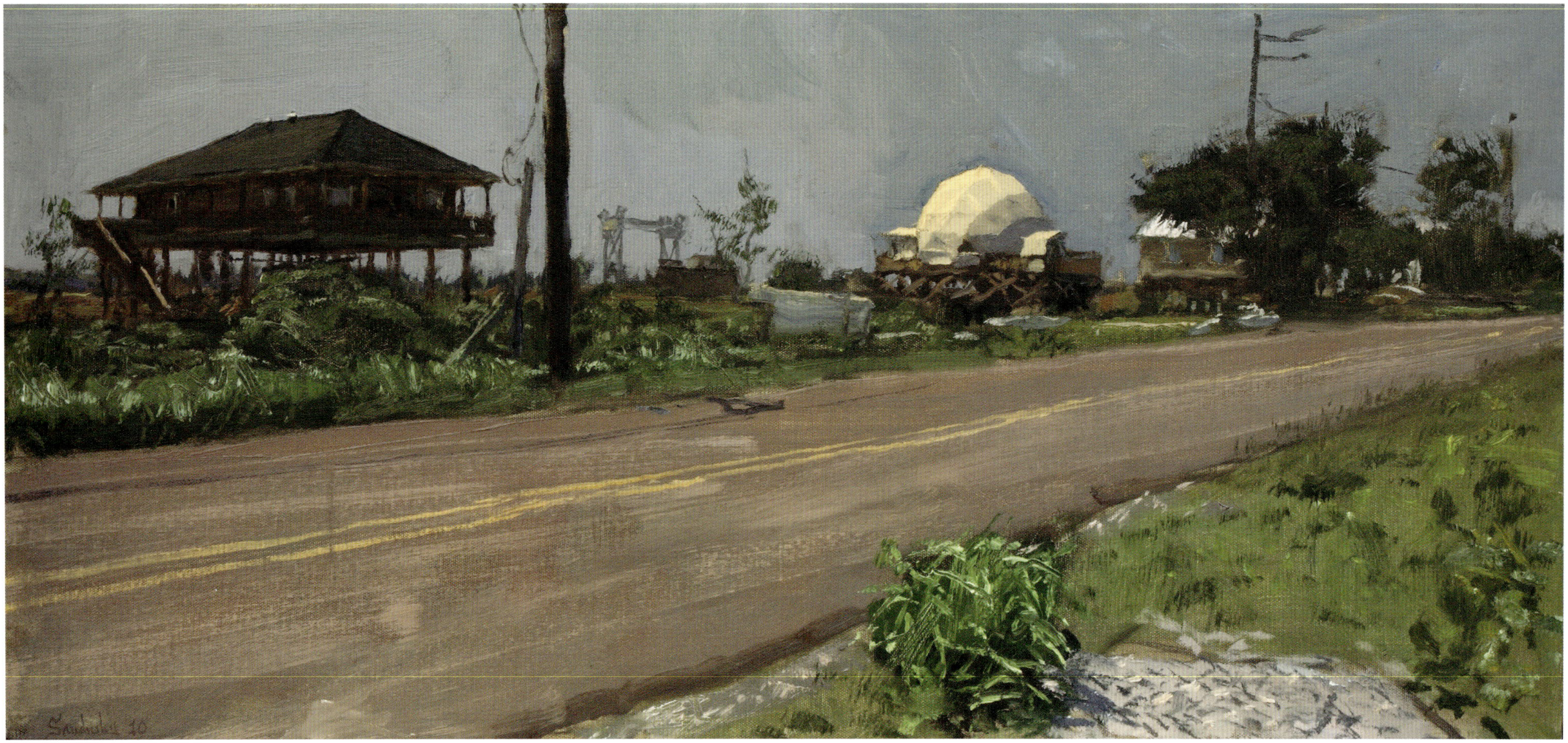

The next fourteen paintings were done in Lower St. Bernard Parish. This painting (15" x 30") is of residences along the Yscloskey Highway in Yscloskey.

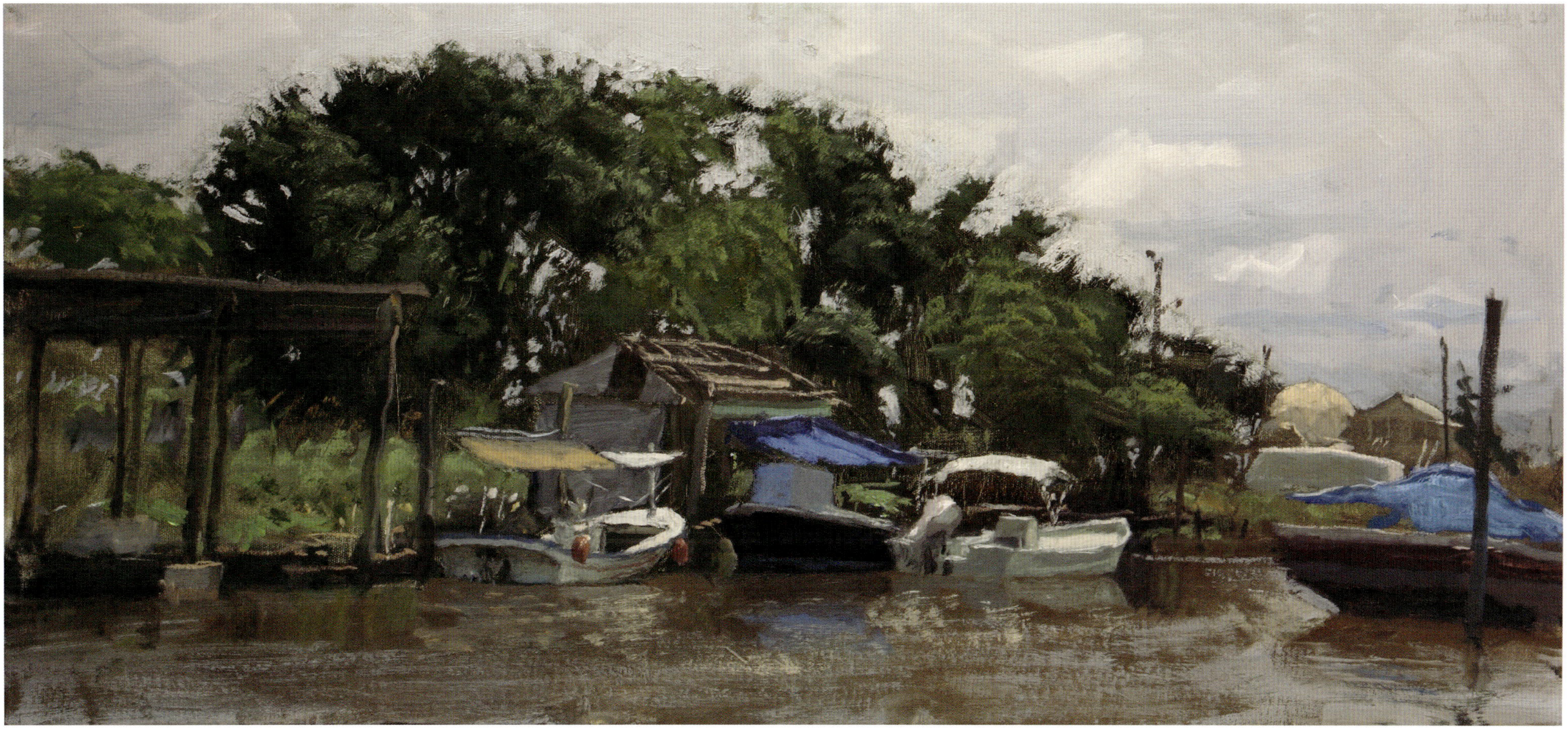

Small boats docked in Ycloskey 15" x 30"

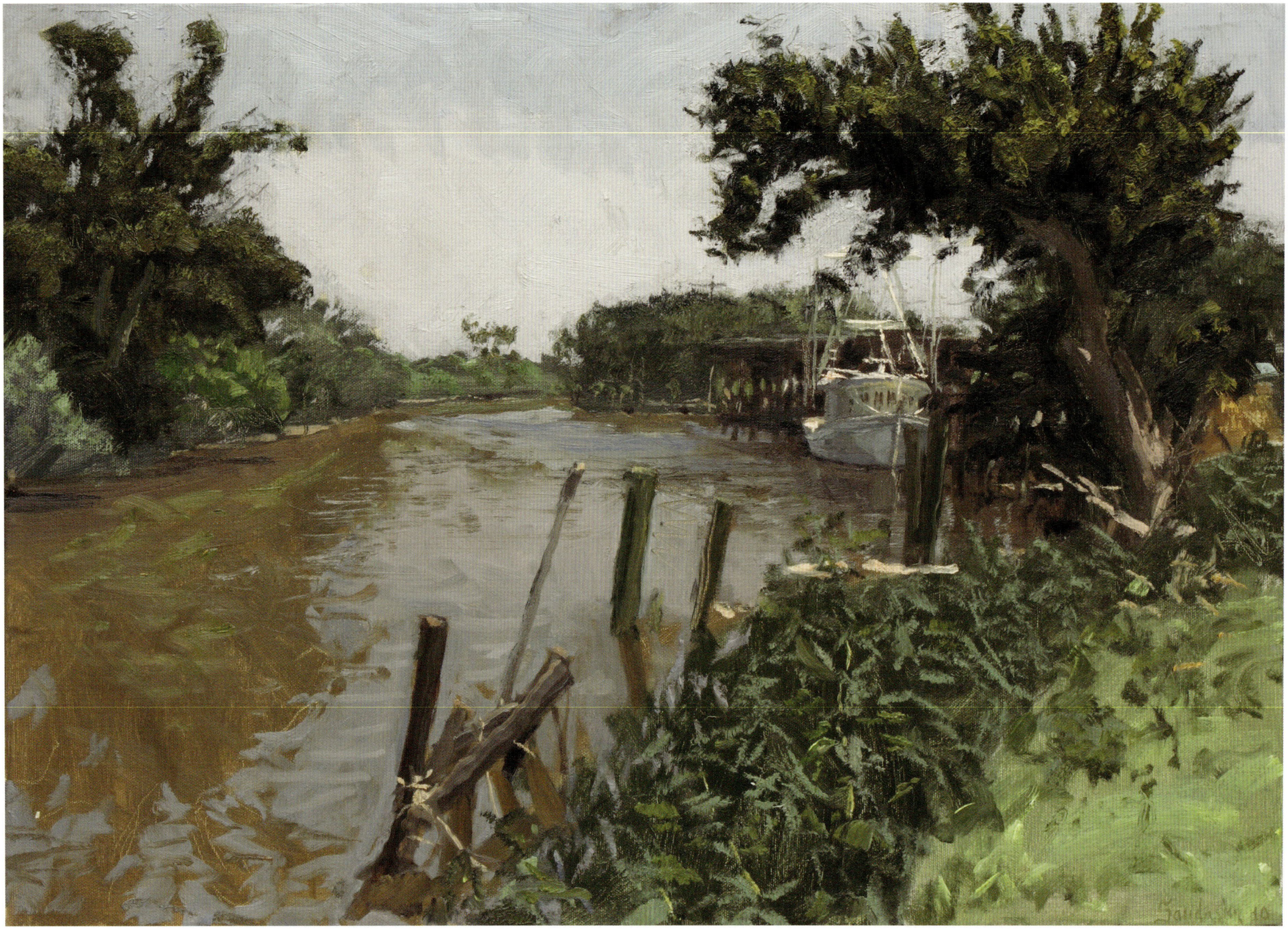

LONE DOCKED SHRIMP BOAT IN YSCLOSKEY 18" X 24"

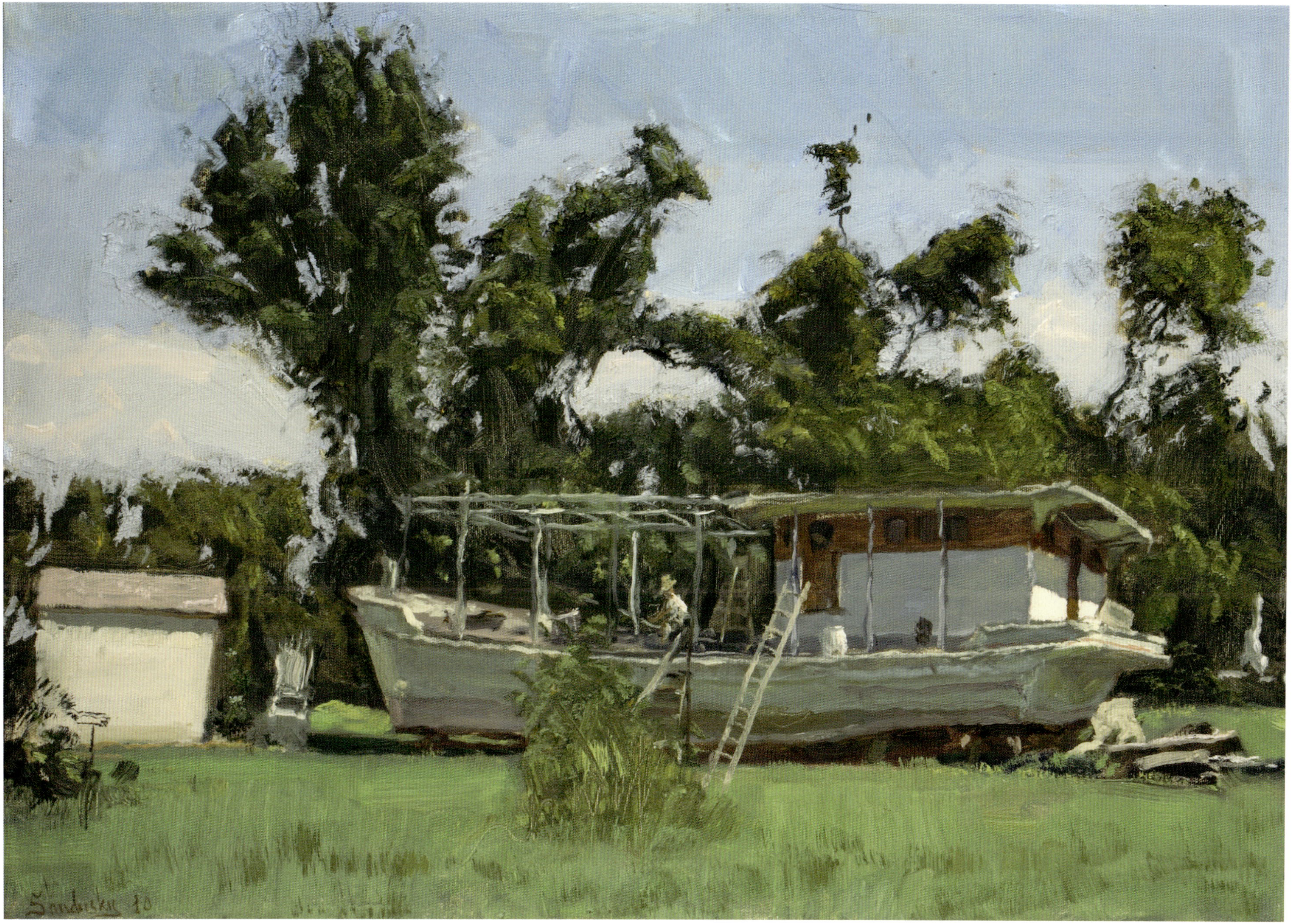

Boat under construction 18" x 24" Representative of the pioneer spirit of the people who live in Lower St. Bernard Parish, an eighty-two-year-old man was single-handedly building this boat in the August heat. He alternated work outside and rest indoors in the air conditioning each half hour.

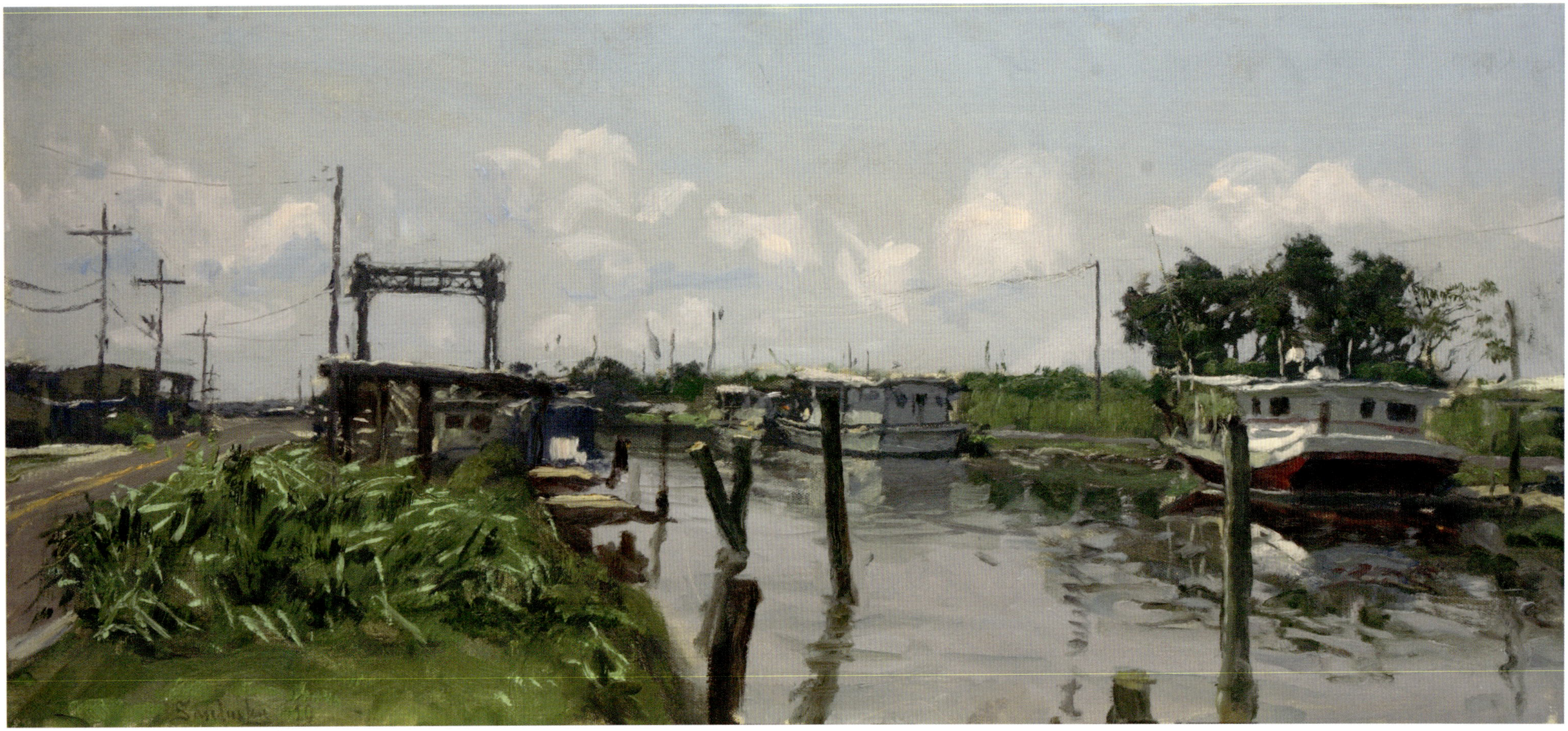

The drawbridge in Yscloskey 15" x 30"

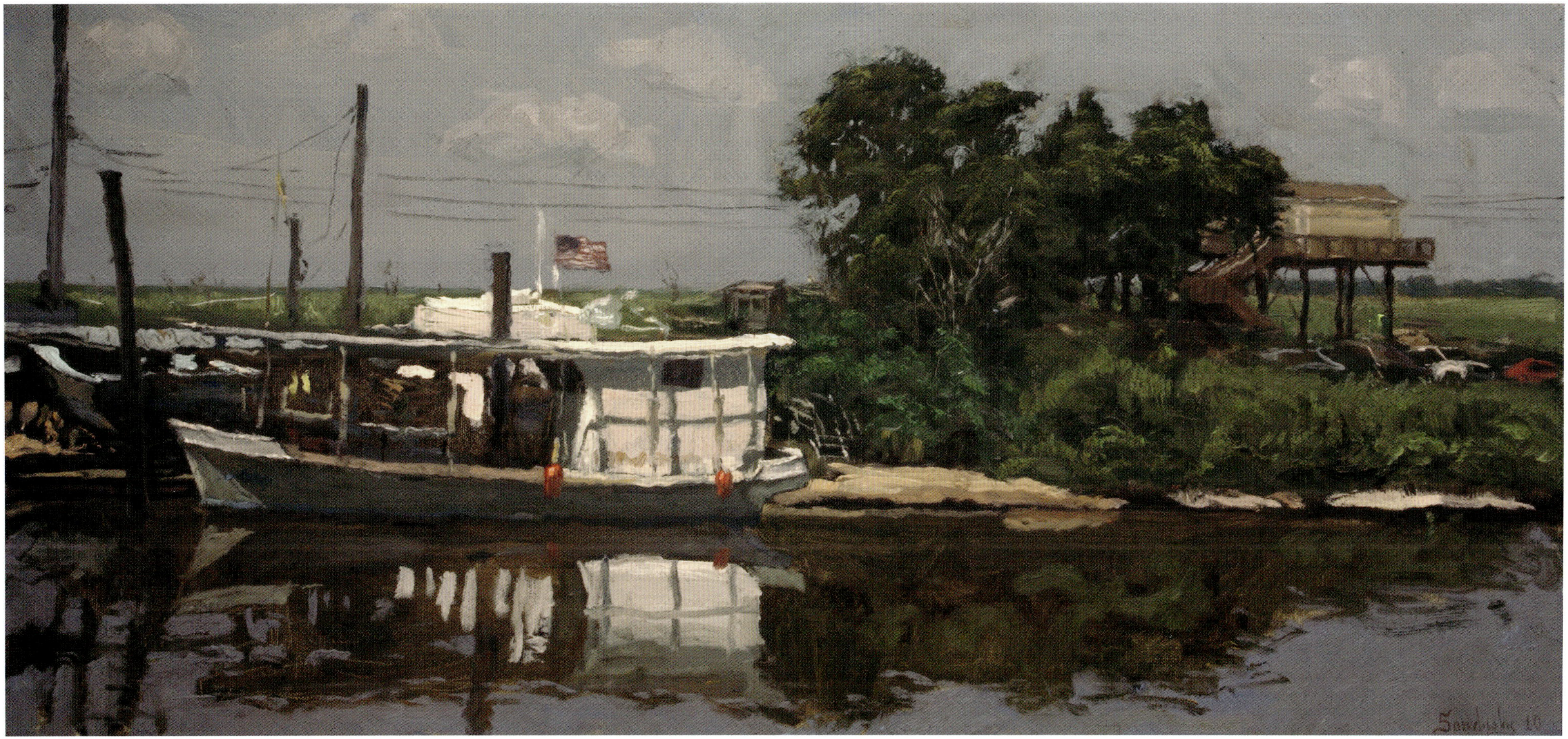

View out across the marsh in Yscloskey 15" x 30"

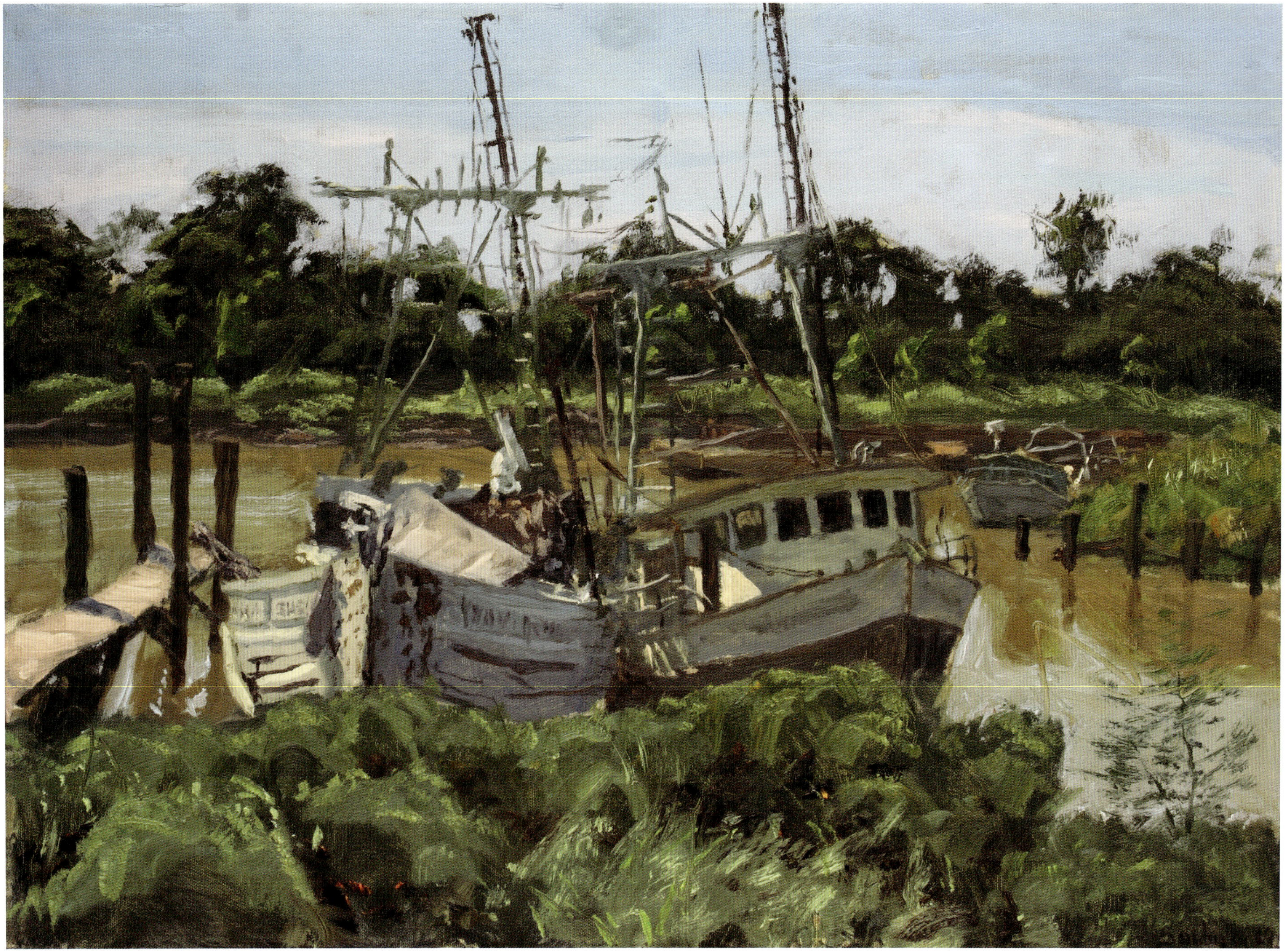

Derelicts 18" x 24" This and the painting on the following page were done in Violet, a small hamlet in Lower St. Bernard Parish.

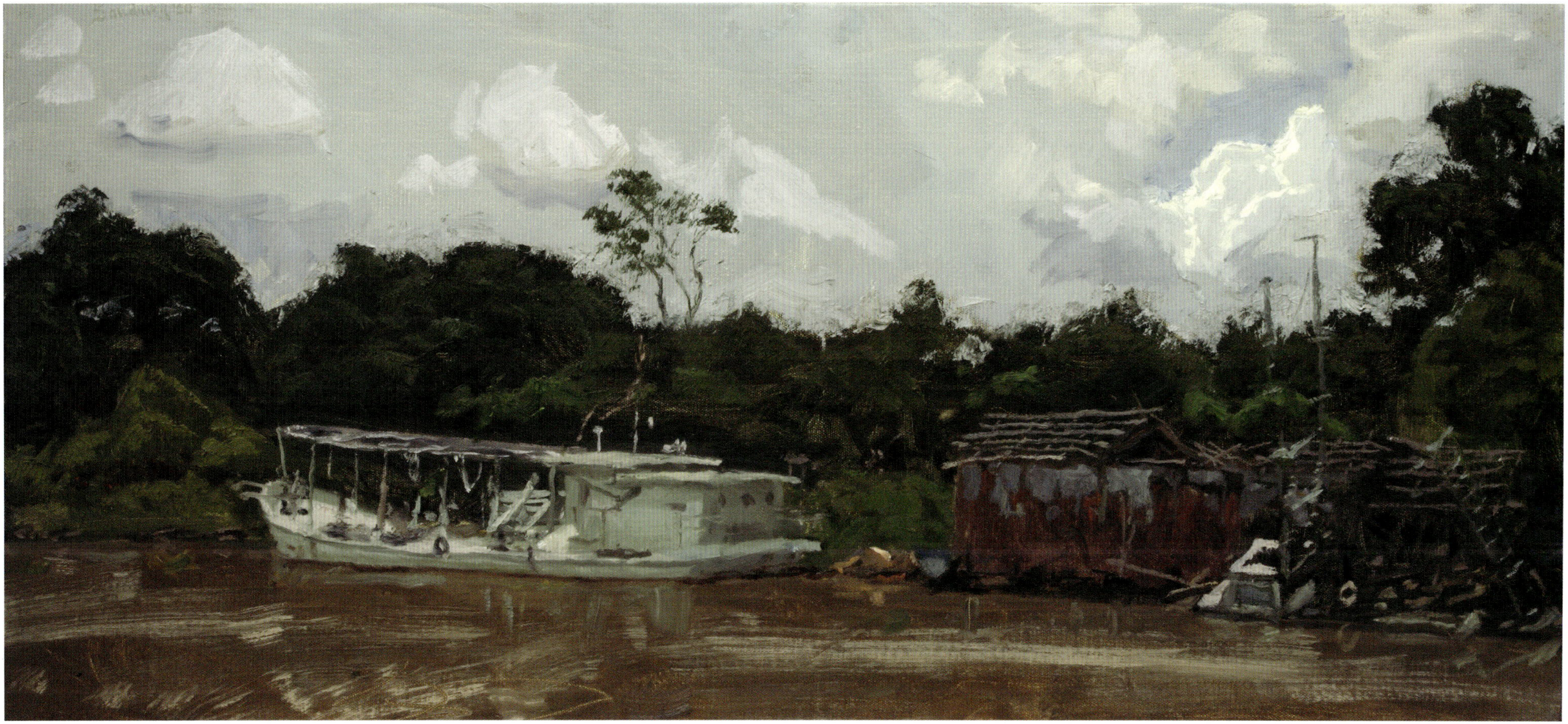

ABANDONED OYSTER BOAT 15" X 30"

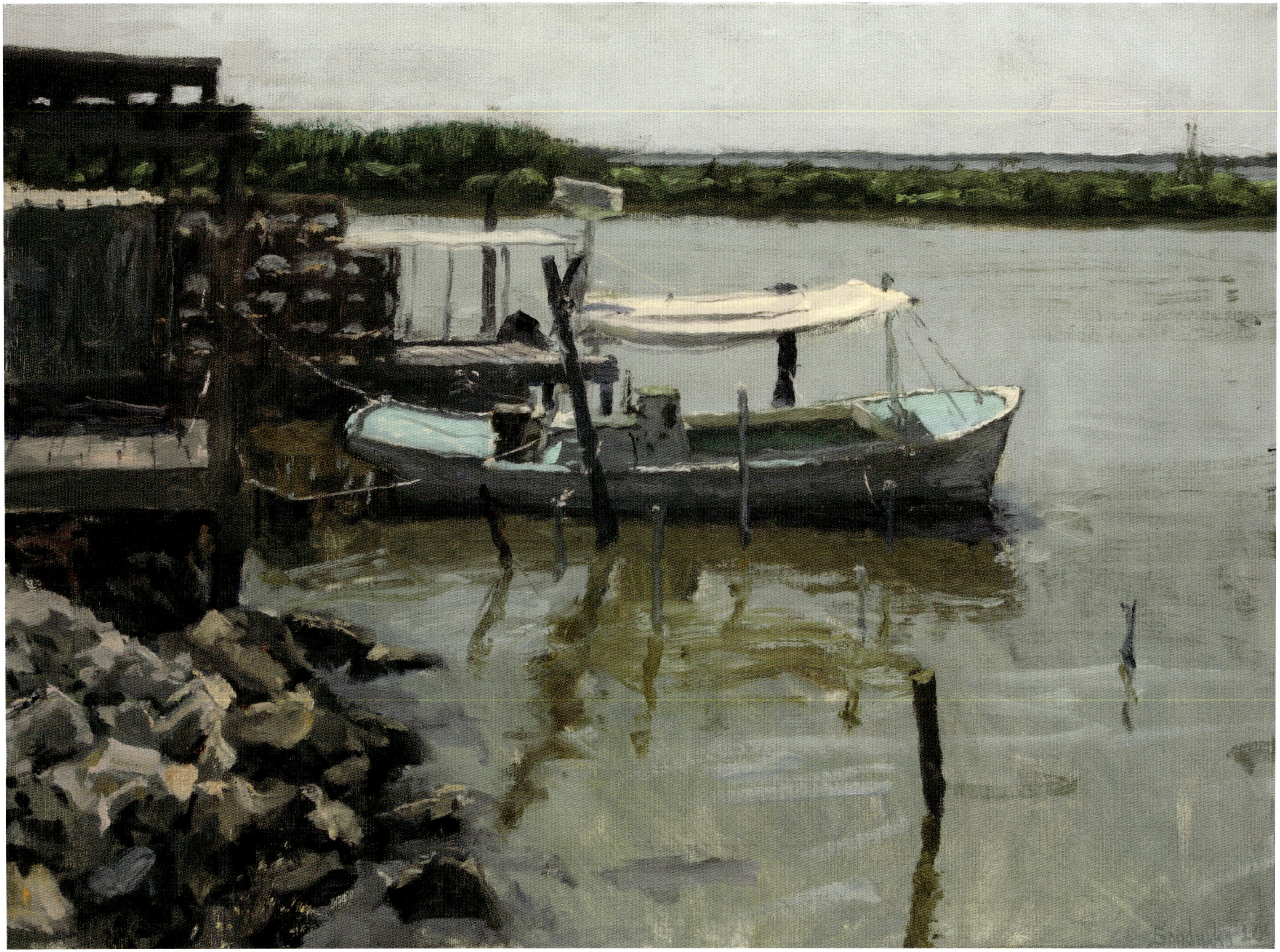

Blue-green skiff 18" x 24" This and the next five paintings were done in and around Delacroix.

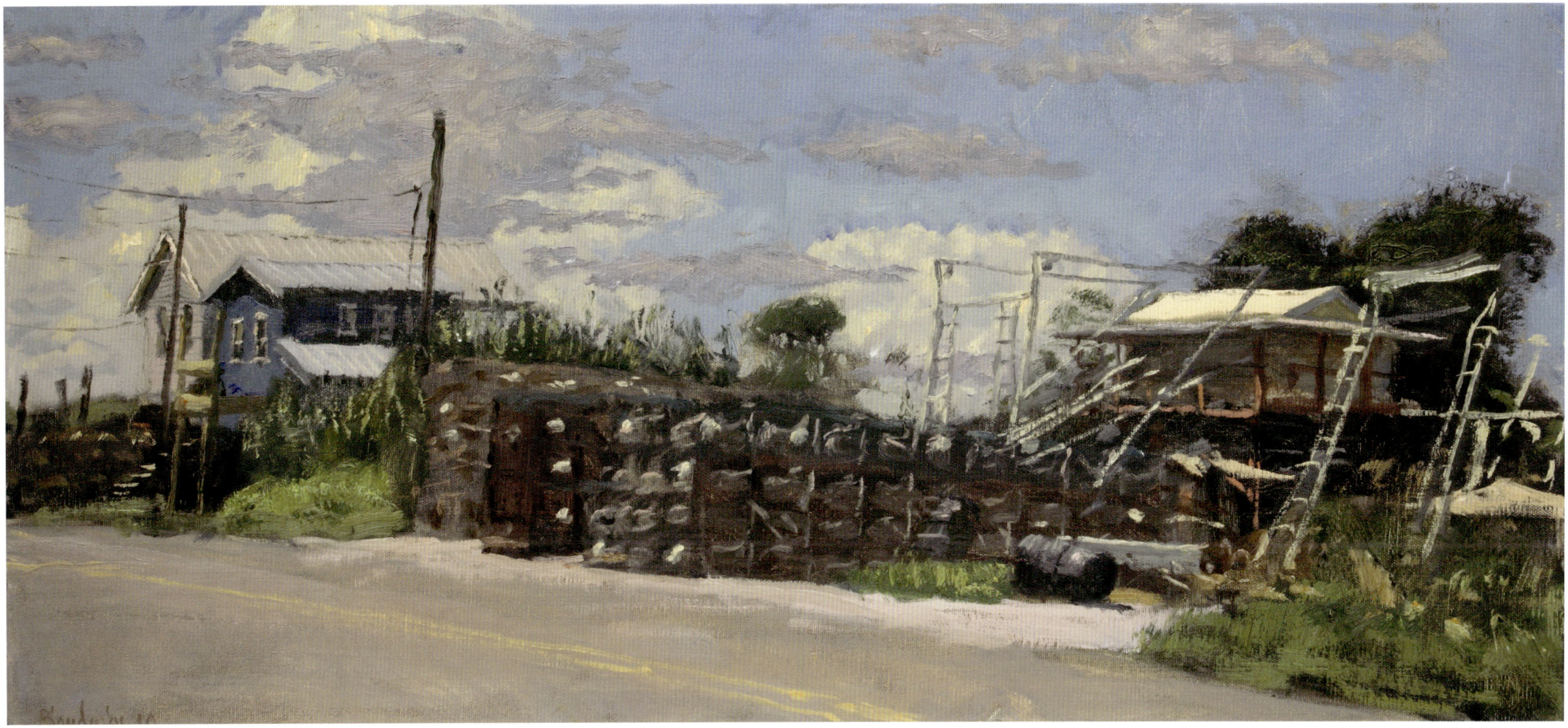

Crab traps 15" x 30"

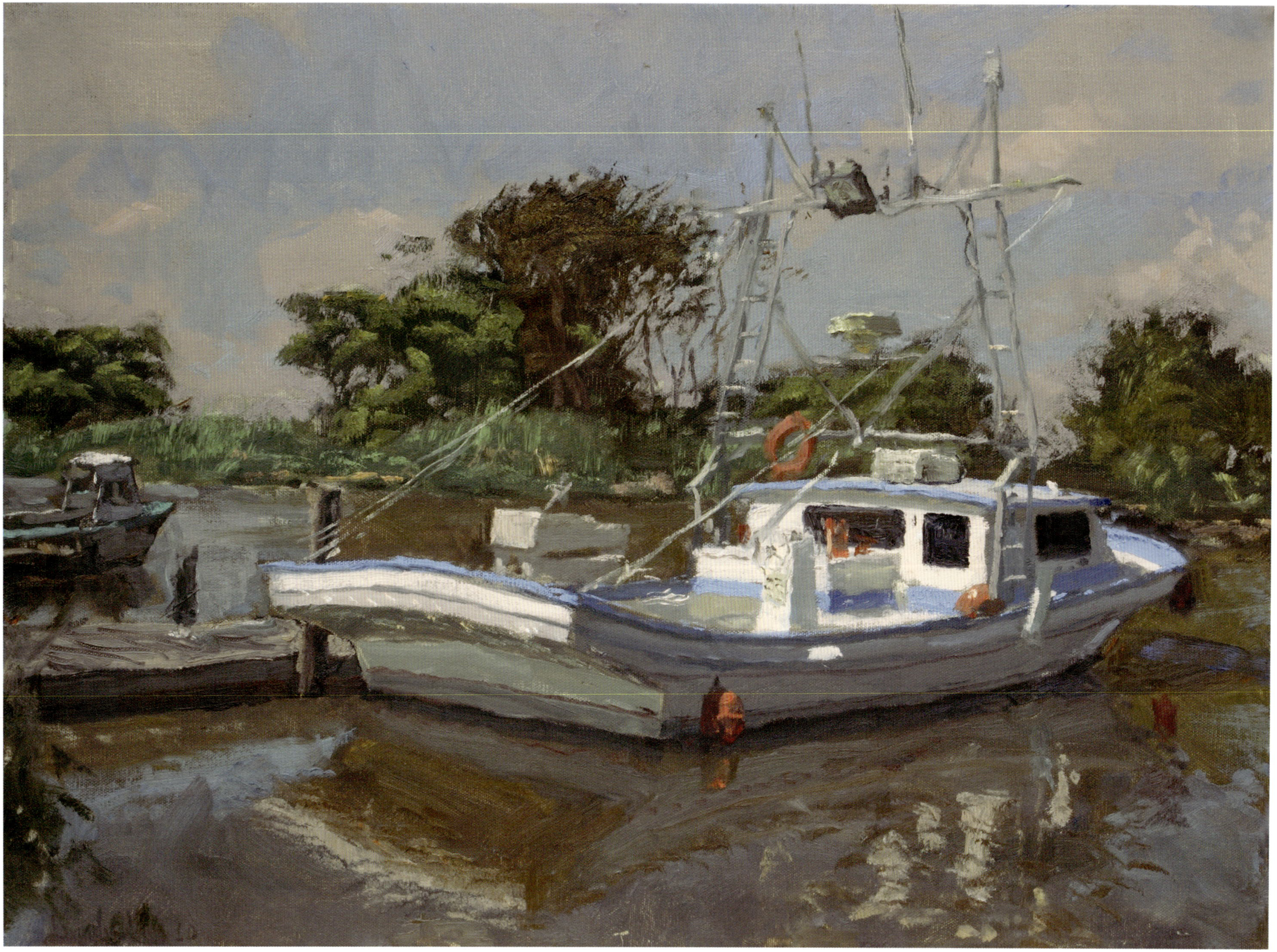

Fishing boat right outside of Delacroix 18" x 24"

Conclusion

I am considered an ideologue by some of my colleagues for refusing to work from photos. Perhaps they have a point, considering that some very fine academic artists in the last century have used them, and on rare occasion there have even been some first-rate representational artists who have worked *exclusively* from photos. But I believe that in general academic painting has not been improved through the use of photography. A photographic reference has two sides, one as a *memory aid,* and the other as a *memory crutch.* You can't take one without the other. The limitations of working from life not only align the artist's statement with vision, but they strengthen the representational artist in all of the ways that he must be strong.

We academic artists believe that we should be able to communicate better with paint than with words. I have tried to demonstrate with my life's work what can be accomplished when working exclusively from the live subject. But, as much as I have tried to enlighten the viewers of my work about the difference between vision and the objective image, the appearance of painting (vision's stand in) and that of photography (the image's stand in) are so similar that the best paintings have only made this distinction subtly and intuitively, and perhaps not well enough in many cases to overpower new twentieth-century biases. In this essay I have shined a light sideways on the distinction between the image and what we see, weaving together bits of science rather than paint to portray our vision. Many people are averse to scientific explanations of vision and the artistic process. Science seems to put things into a box, replacing intuition with cold rationality. But in this case we have used science to *remove* our voluptuous multifaceted vision from a tiny, thin box into which it has been stuffed, so that we can more fully appreciate it and how good representational painting has responded to it and conveyed it.

Many are disheartened when they compare representational art of today with the work of great representational painters of the past. They consider that perhaps representational painting has passed its prime. But the great artists of the past didn't understand vision any better than artists of today. They were just forced to align their statement with vision because of the limitations of working from life. When the camera removed those limitations and there was no increase in understanding of vision to compensate, many representational painters were conquered by the very tool that freed them. We can see the embers of greatness still alive today in those who have worked from life. But imagine what can be done when the artist's accomplishment is born from an *understanding* of vision rather than merely serendipitously permitted by the limitations of a process. I believe that when a good visceral understanding of vision permeates the world, art will escape from the postmodern quagmire and leave the old masters so far behind that their work will seem to our descendents as ancient hieroglyphs seem to us.

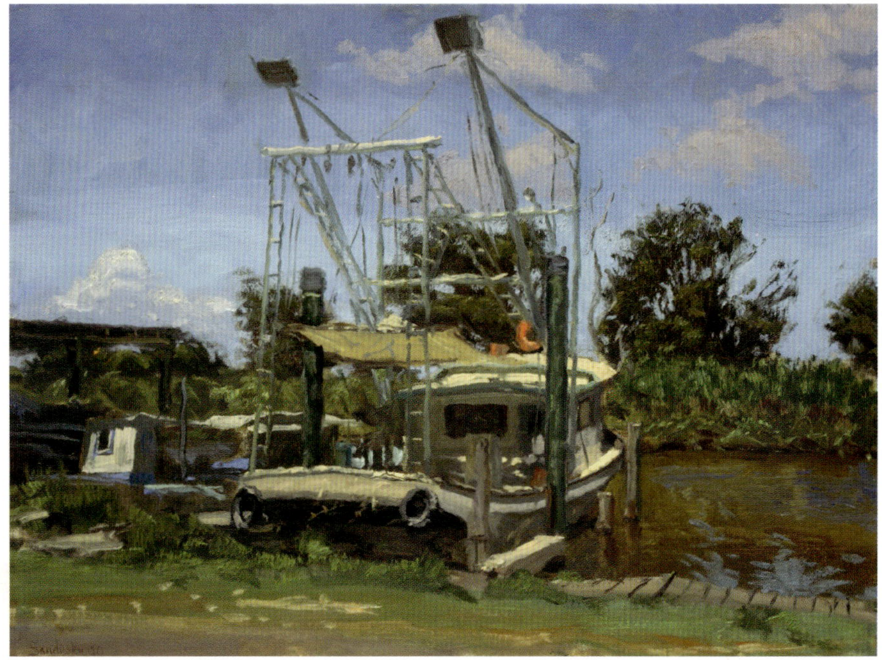

Stern of Trawler 18" x 24"

Until then we will have monk scribes cloistered in the monastery of the image. And every tiny spot of paint that they carefully place into the grid is a parcel of penance that we must pay for failing to understand our vision.

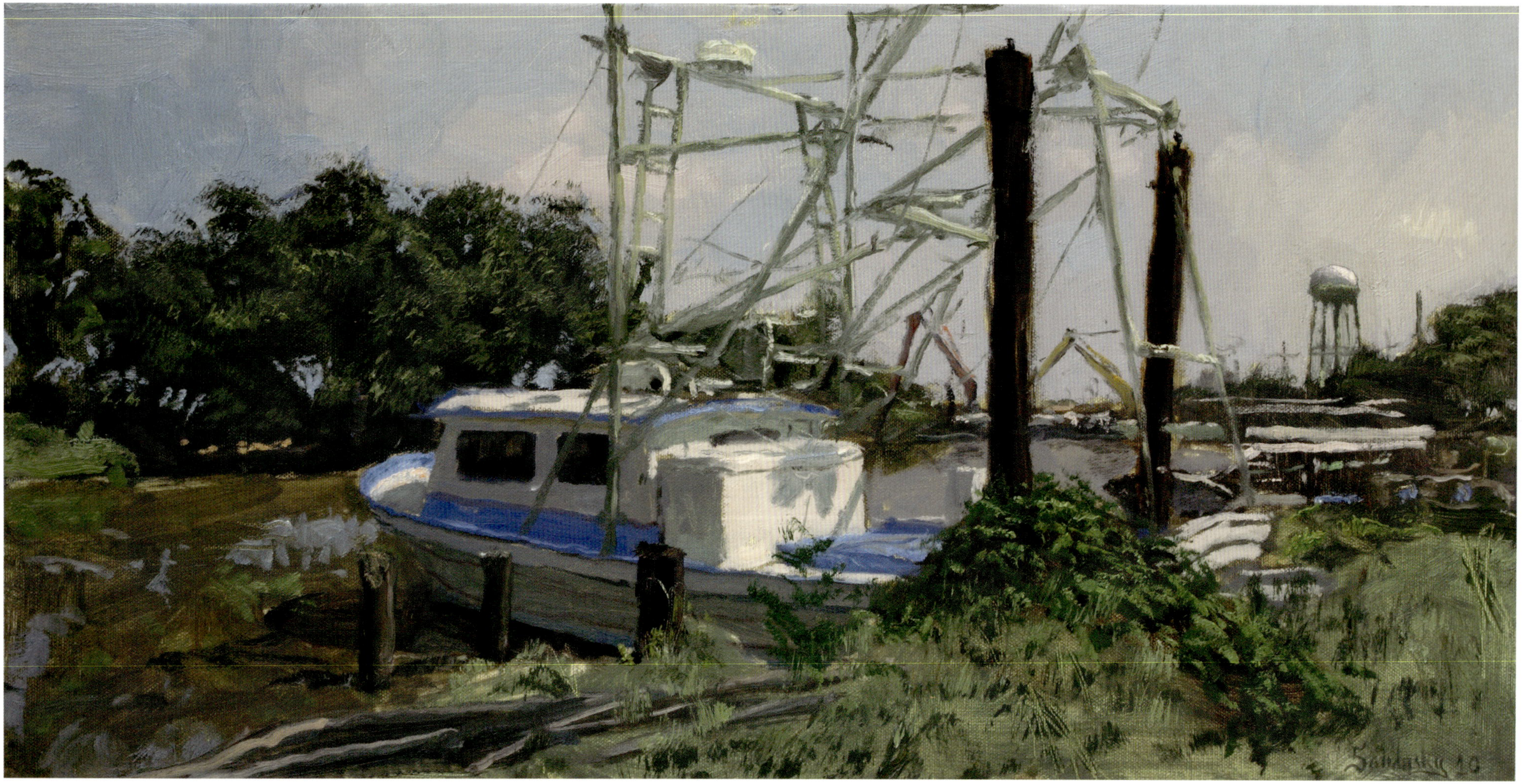

DOCKED TRAWLER AND WATER TOWER 12" x 24"

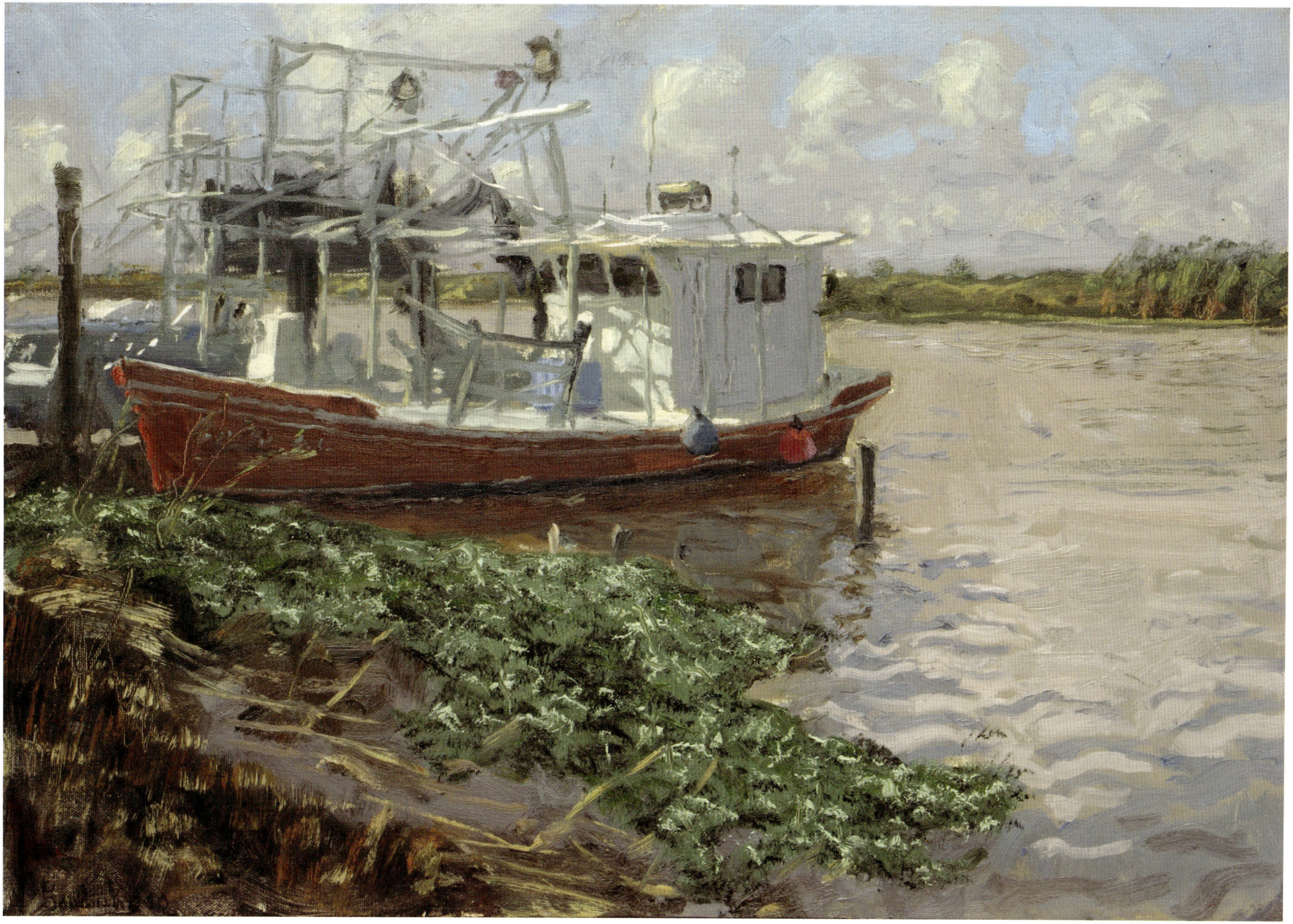

RED TRAWLER AND WATER HYACINTHS 18" X 24"

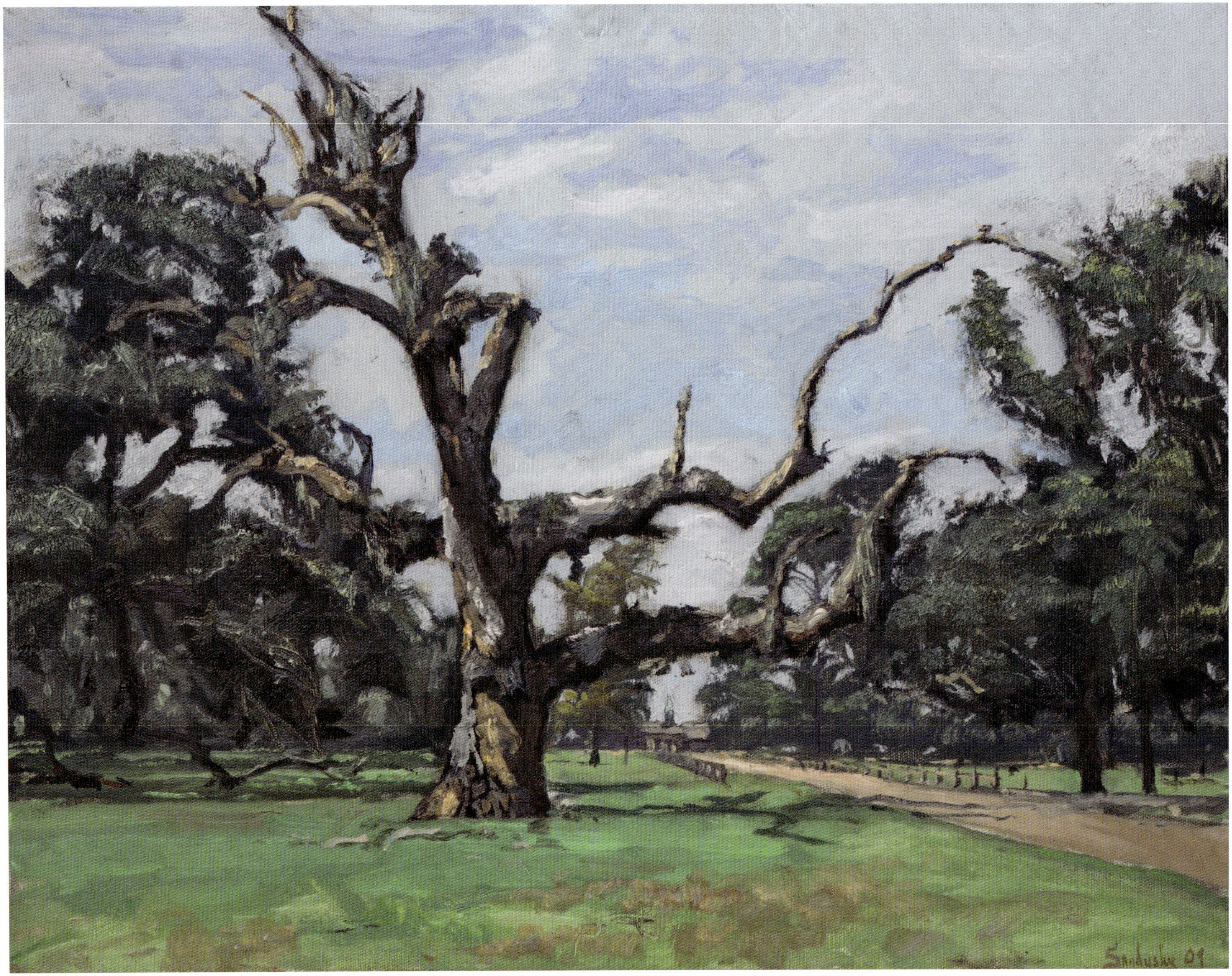

Dead live oak in Fontainebleau Park 16" x 20" This and the next several paintings were done on the North Shore (of Lake Pontchartrain) in Fontainebleau State Park and Abita Springs.

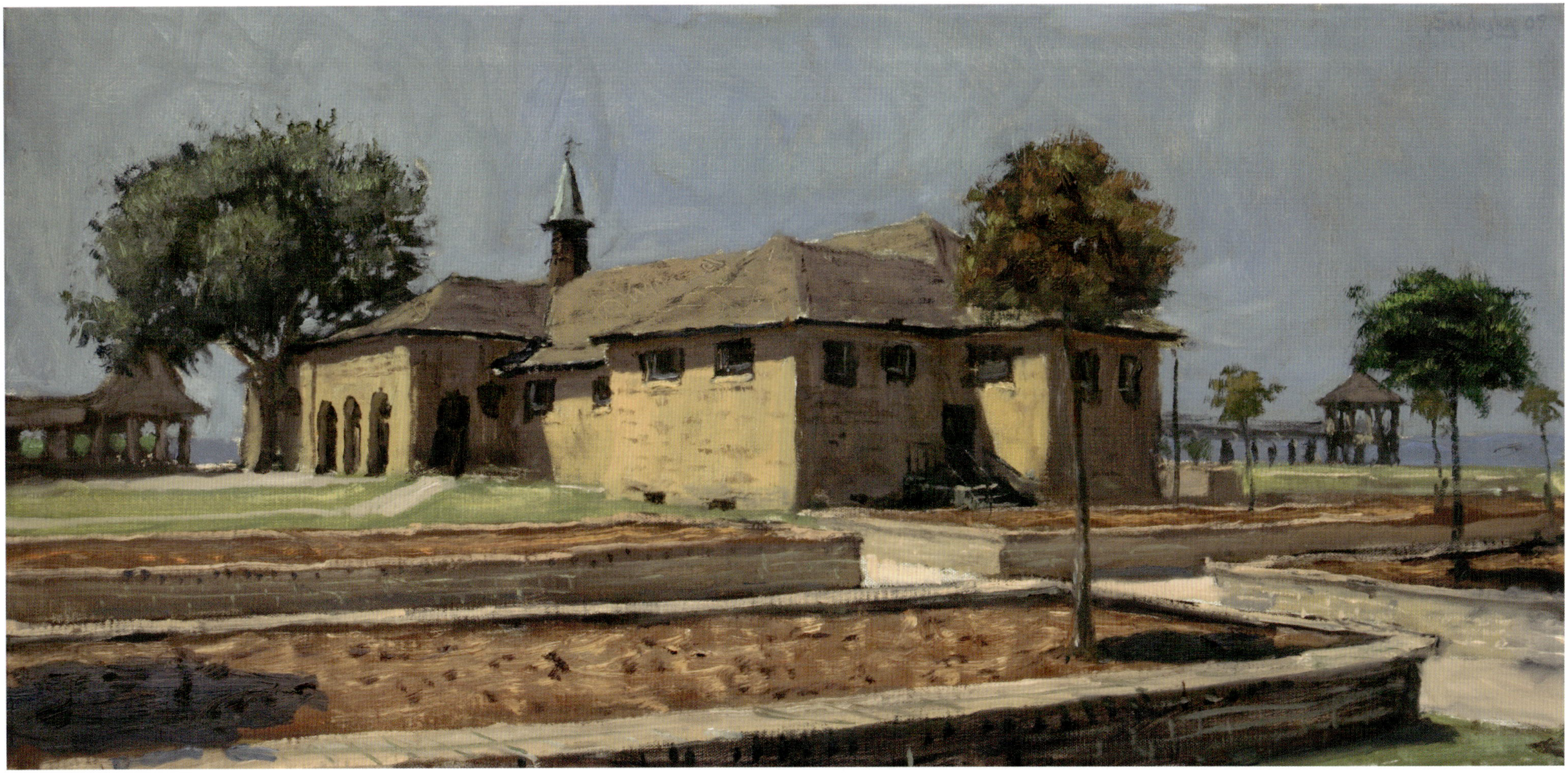

The historic bathhouse in Fontainebleau Park 15" x 30"

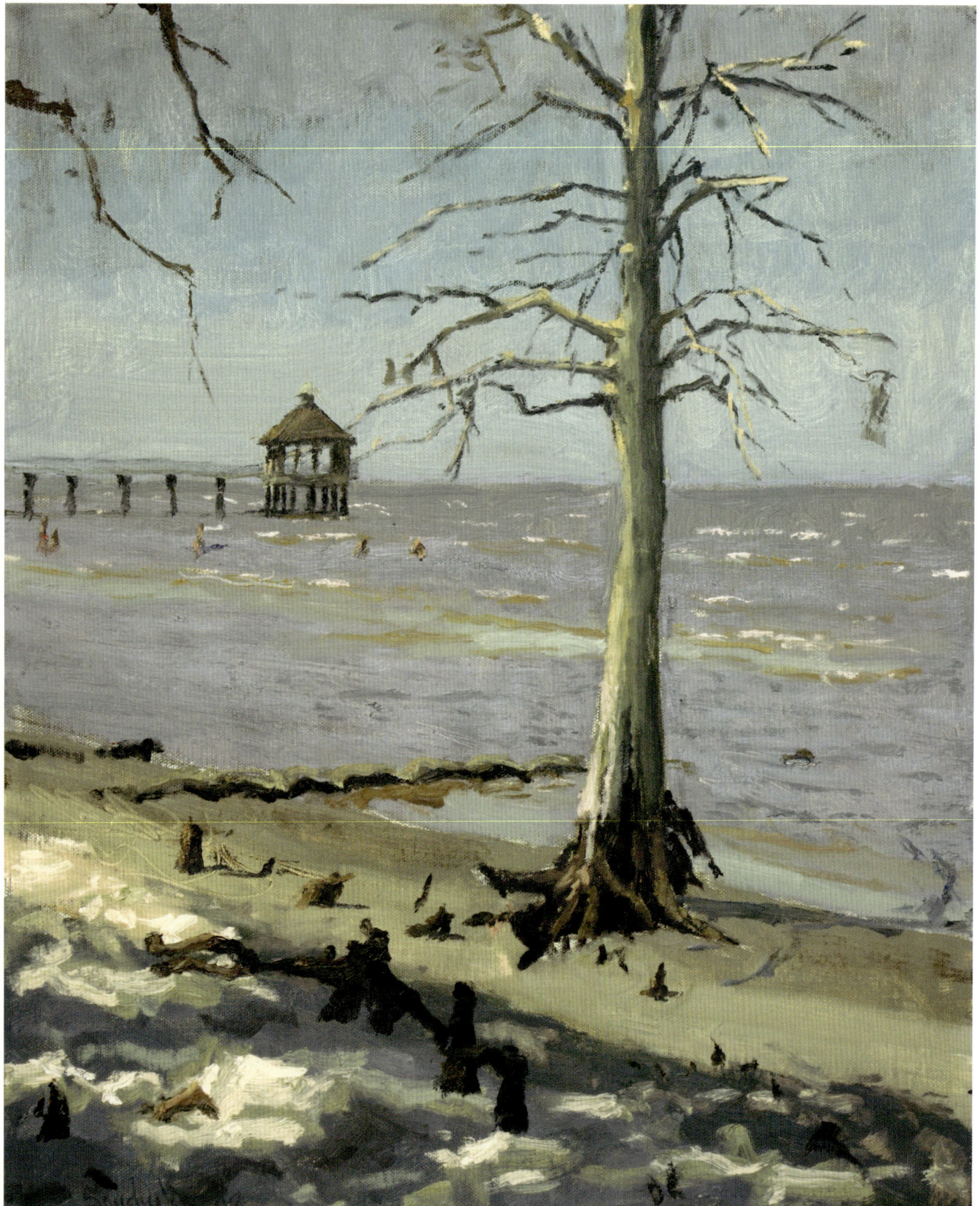

Cypress in the sand, Fontainebleau Park
20" x 16"

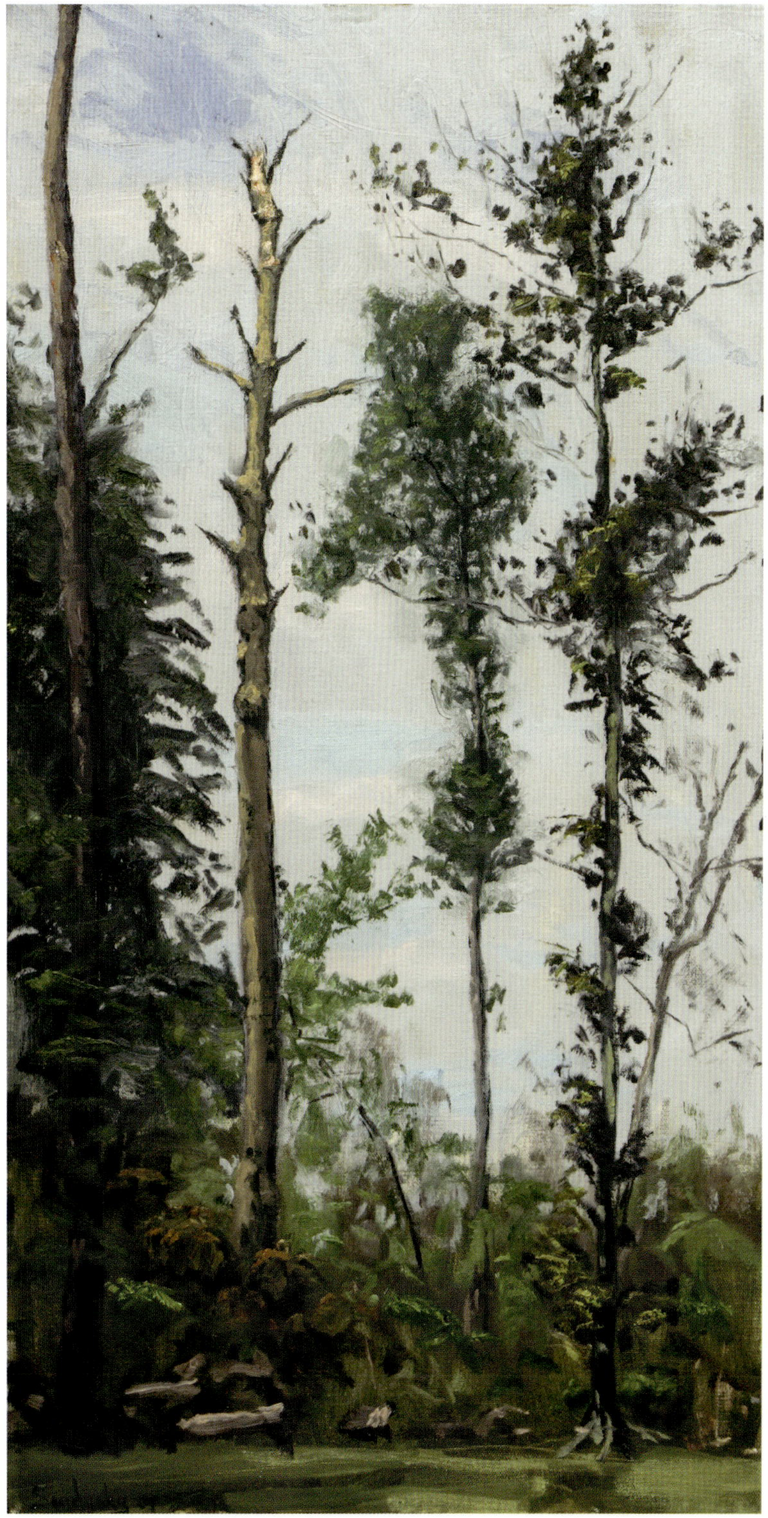

Wild wood, Abita Springs 30" x 15"

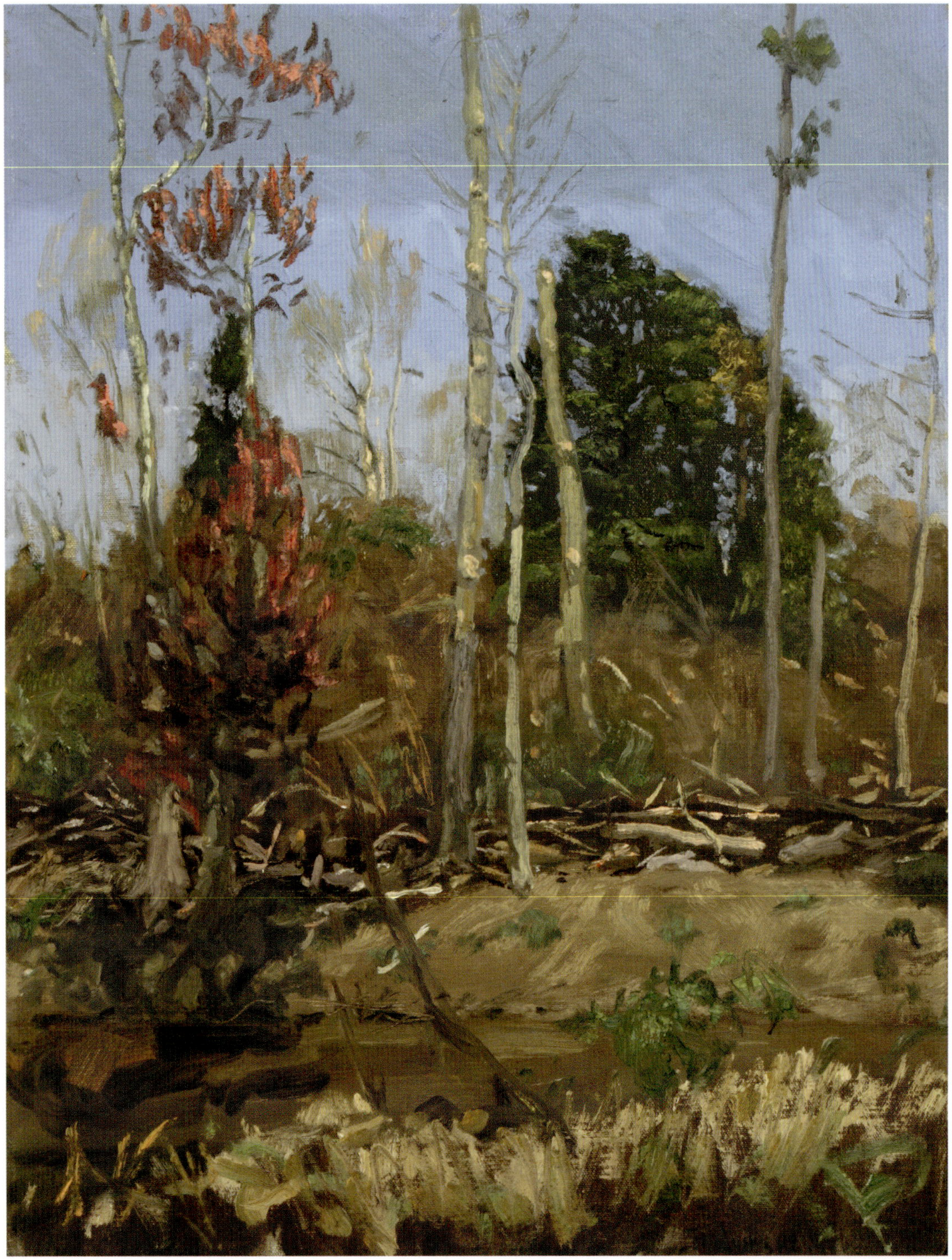

DEAD WOOD, ABITA SPRINGS 24" X 18"

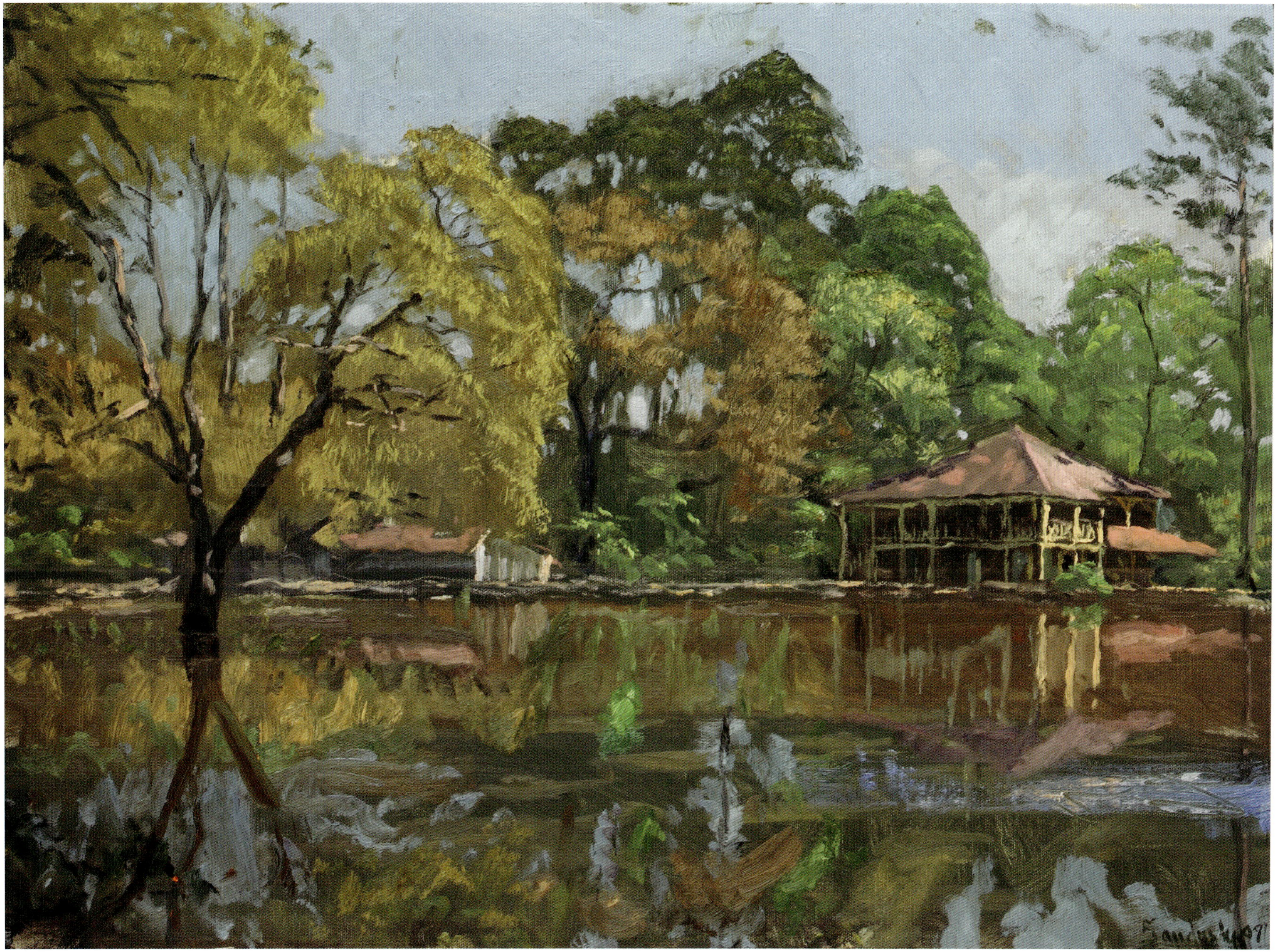

Bathhouse and receding floodwater on the Elander property, Abita Springs 18" x 24"

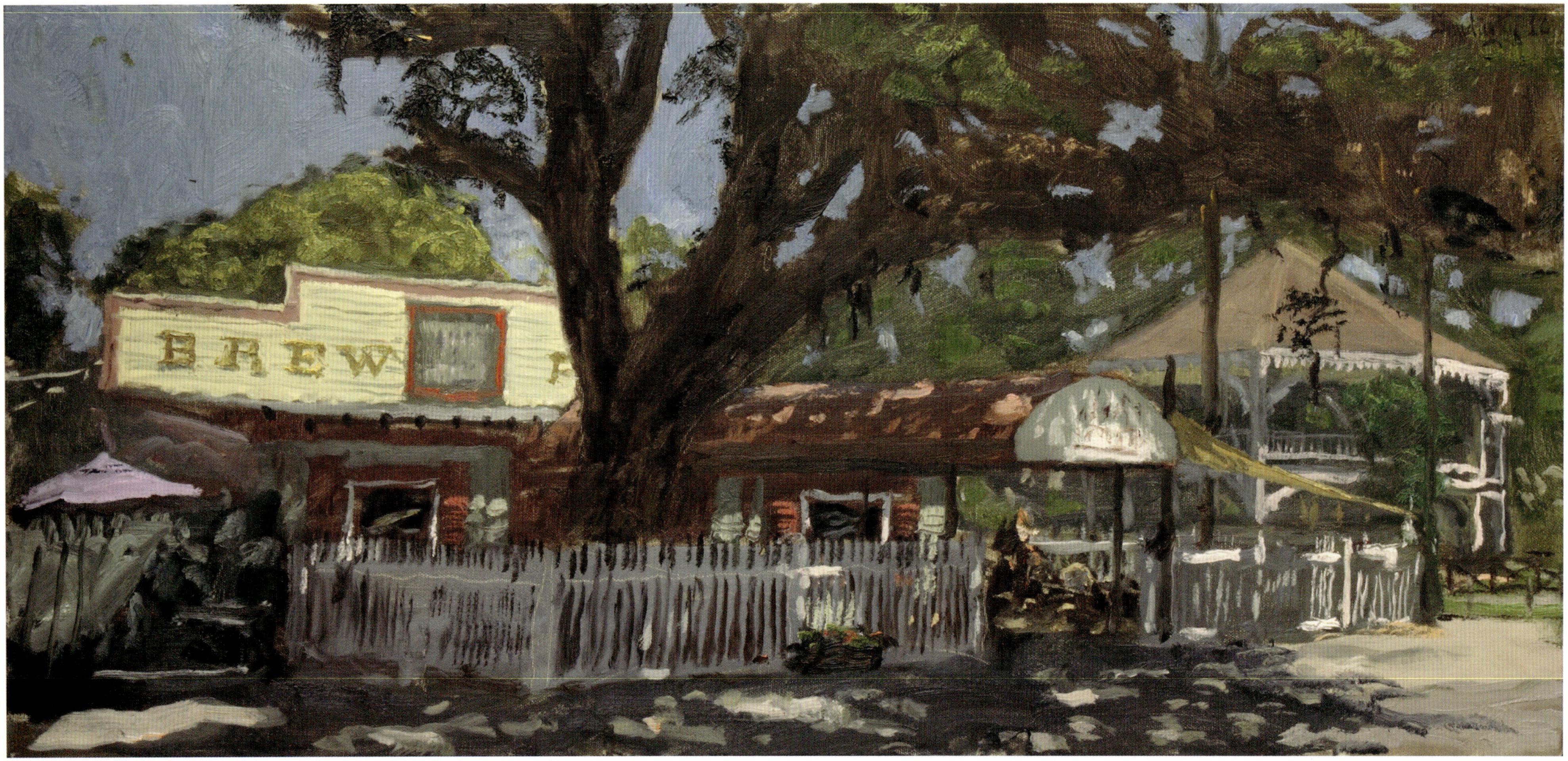

Abita Brewpub 15" x 30"

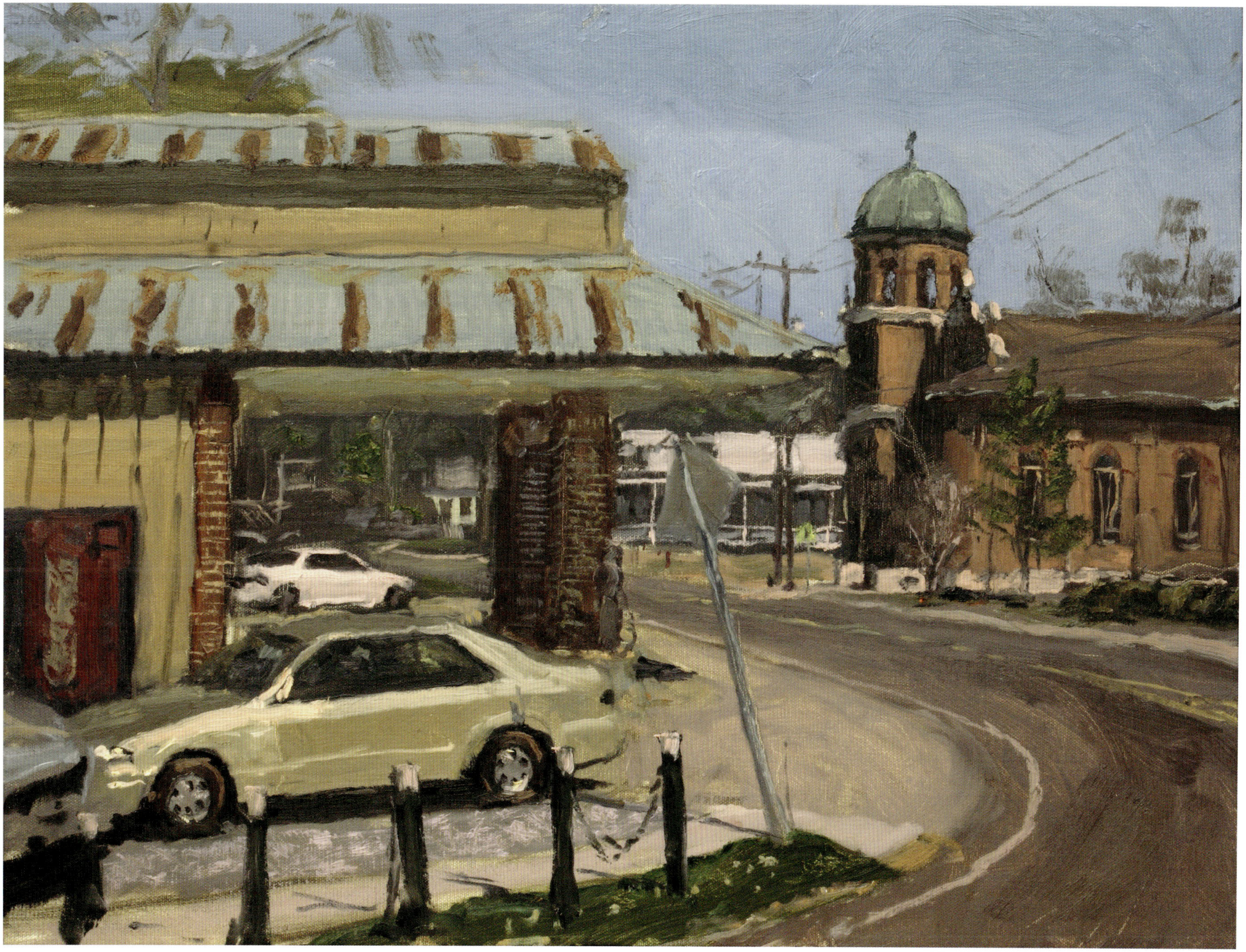

SERVICE STATION AND CHURCH, ABITA SPRINGS 18" X 24"

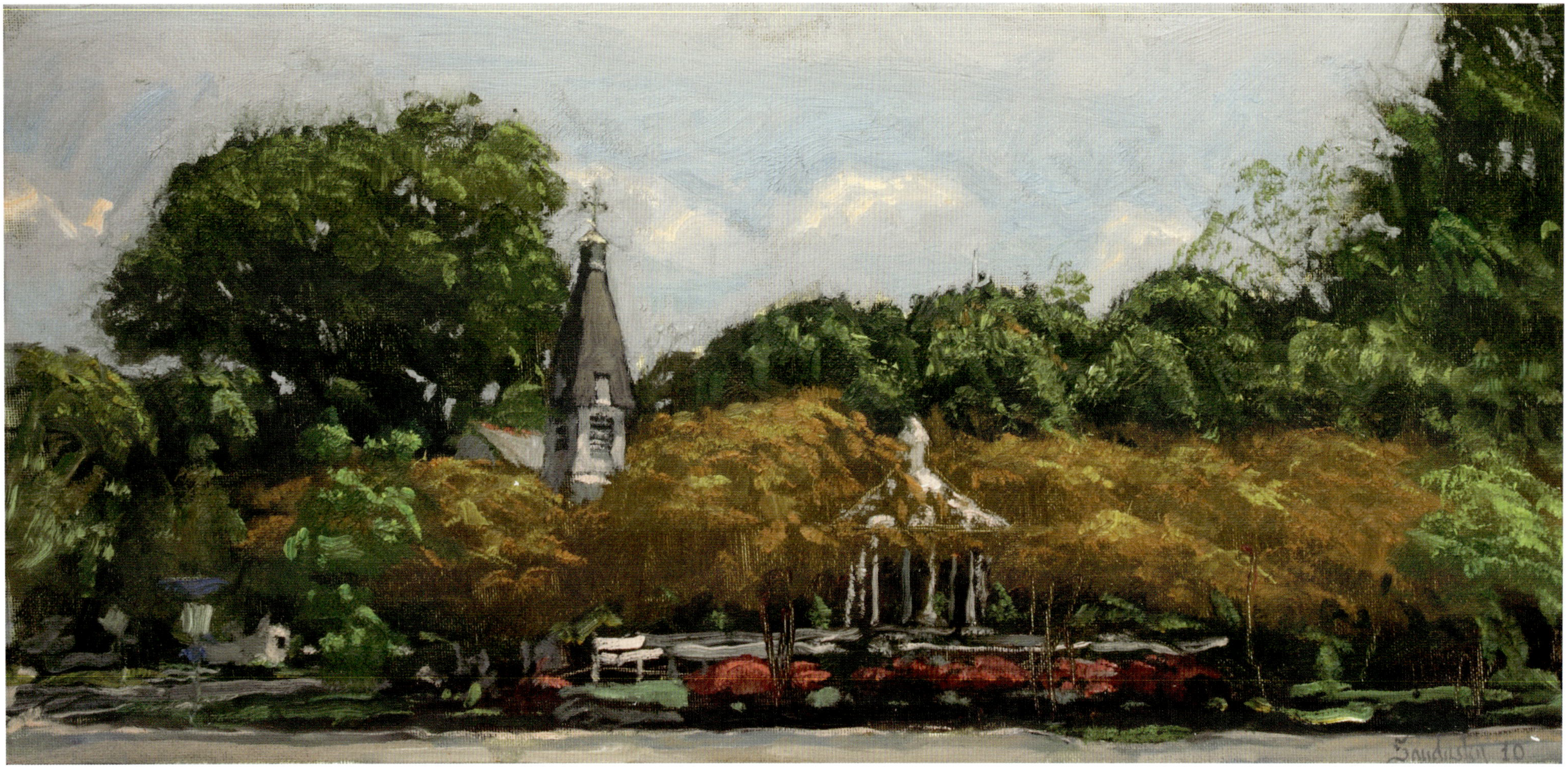

GAZEBO, ABITA SPRINGS 10" X 20"

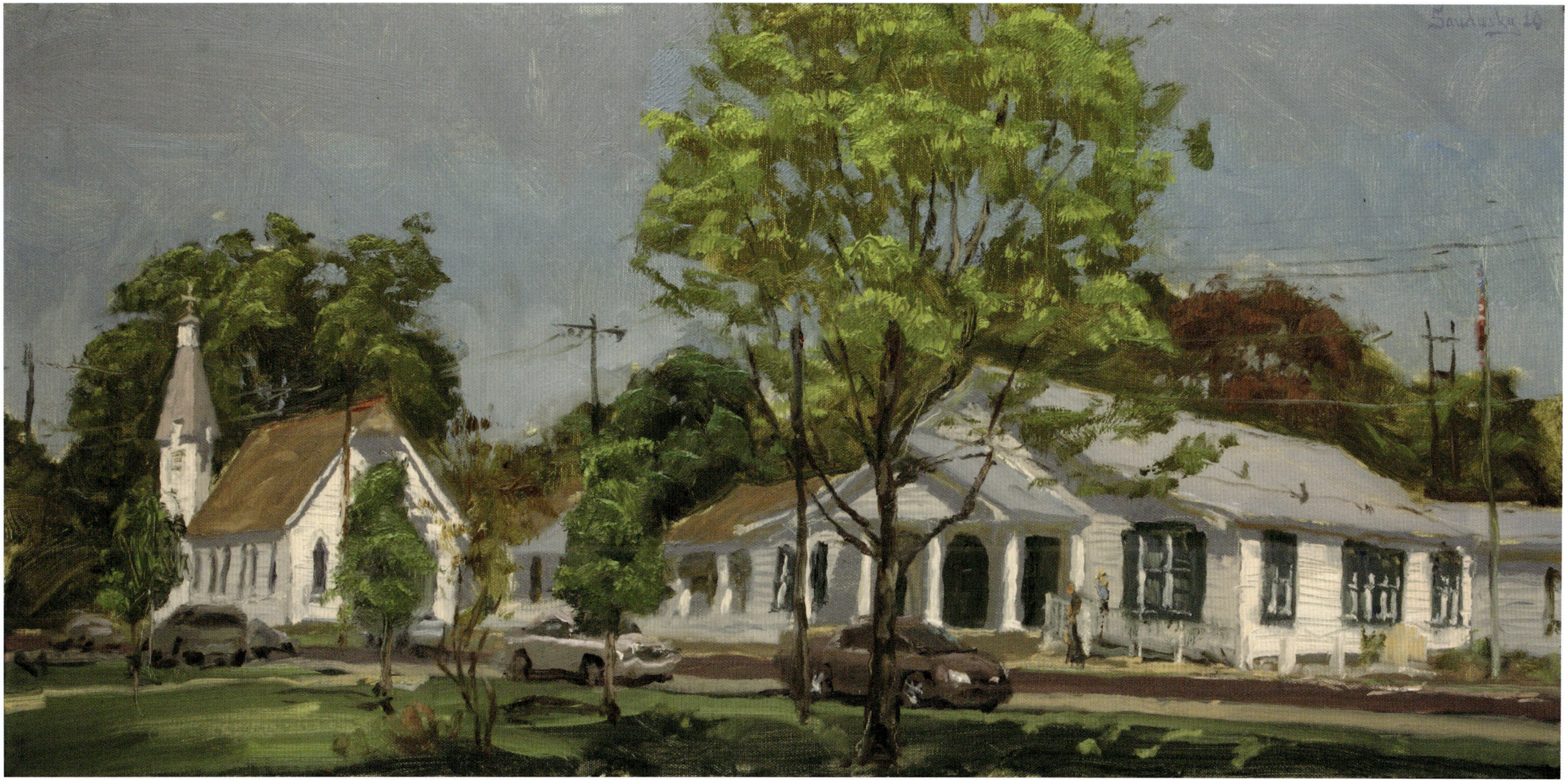

Abita Town Hall 15" x 30"

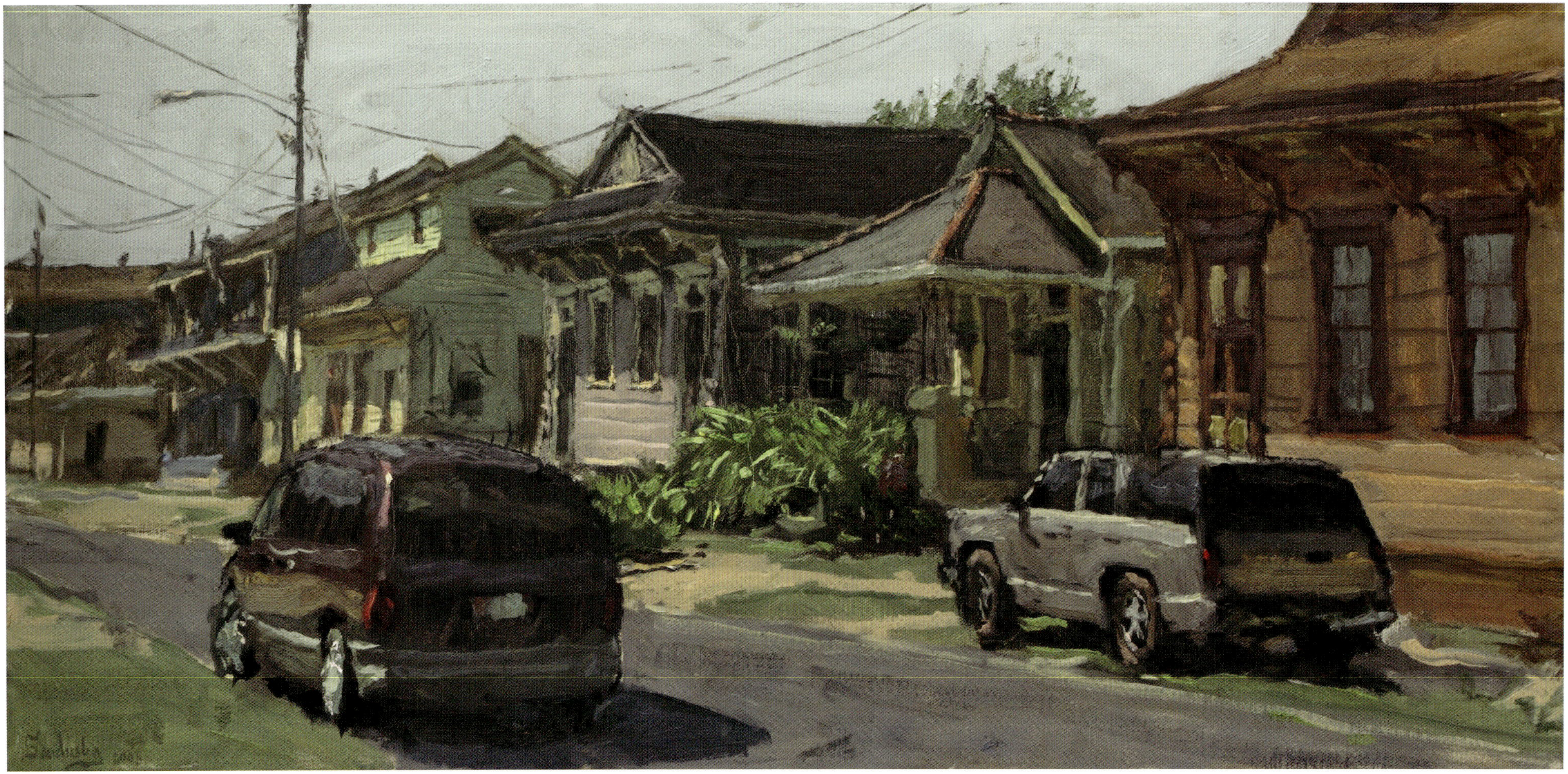

LAPEYROUSE STREET AT NORTH JOHNSON STREET 15" X 30" RETURNING TO NEW ORLEANS, THE NEXT FEW PAINTINGS WERE DONE ALONG THE ESPLANADE RIDGE AND BAYOU ST. JOHN.

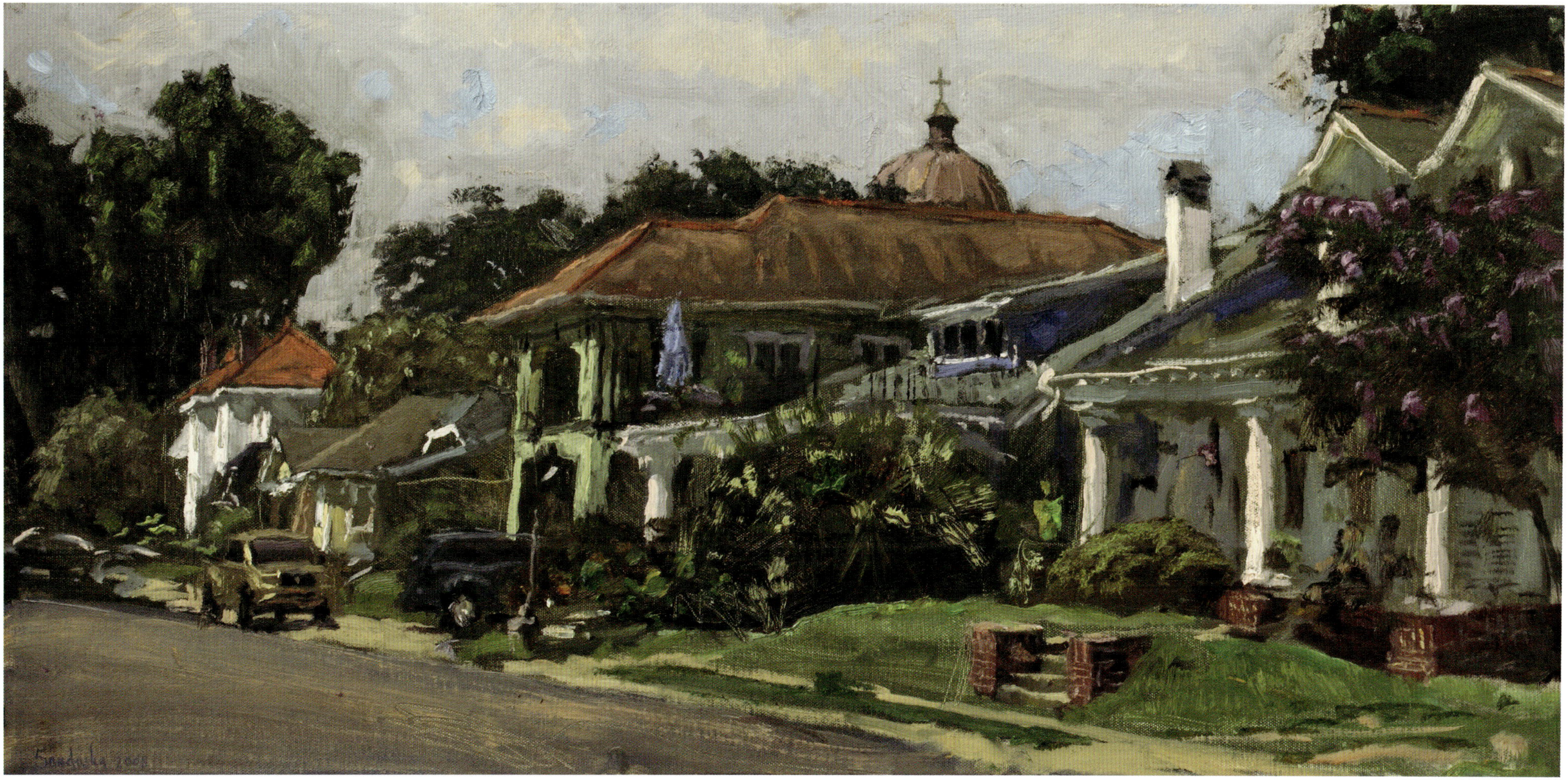

VERNA STREET NEAR MARIE STREET 15" X 30"

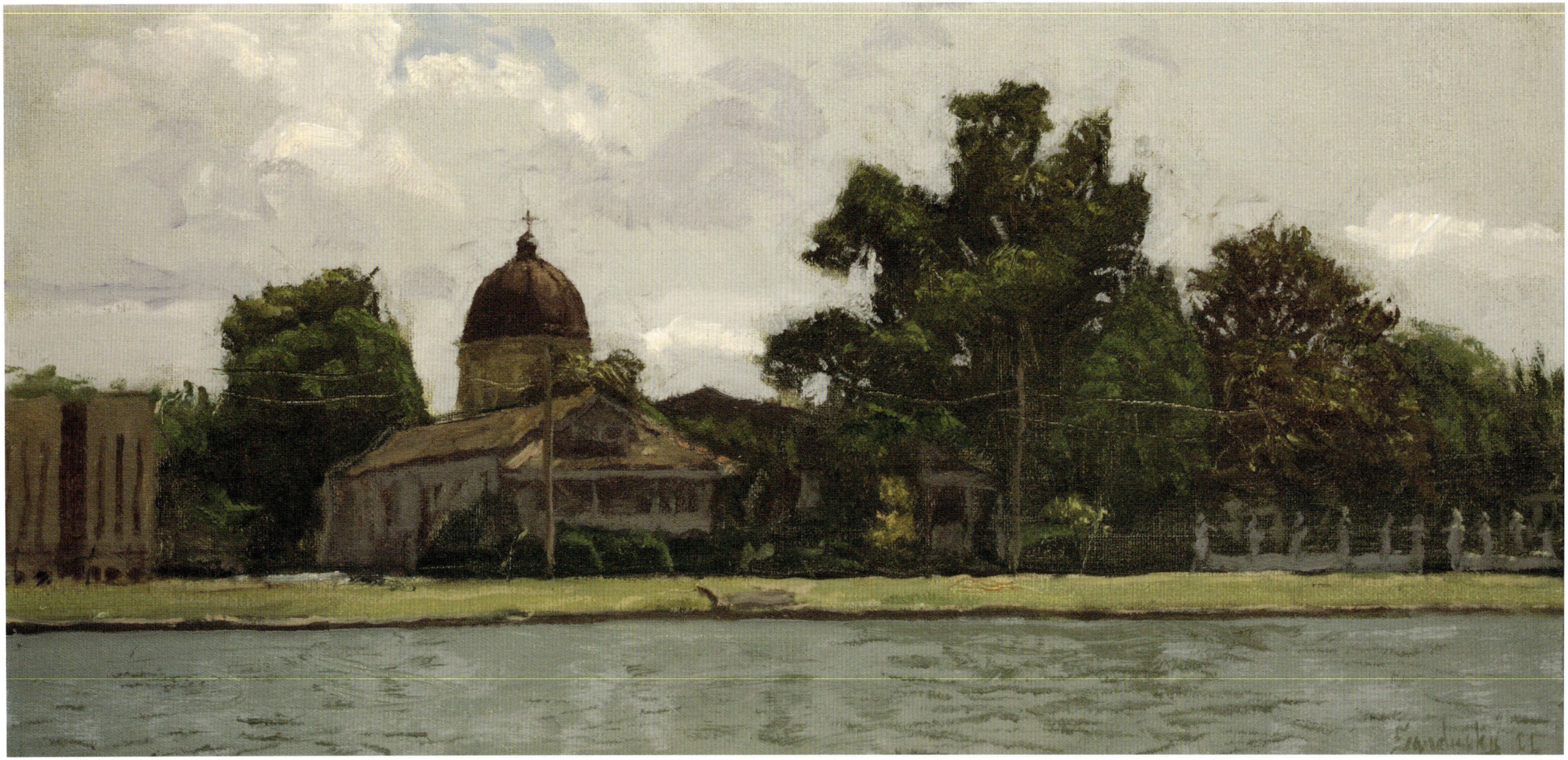

Bayou St. John on a cloudy day, viewed from Moss Street and Harding Drive 10" x 20"

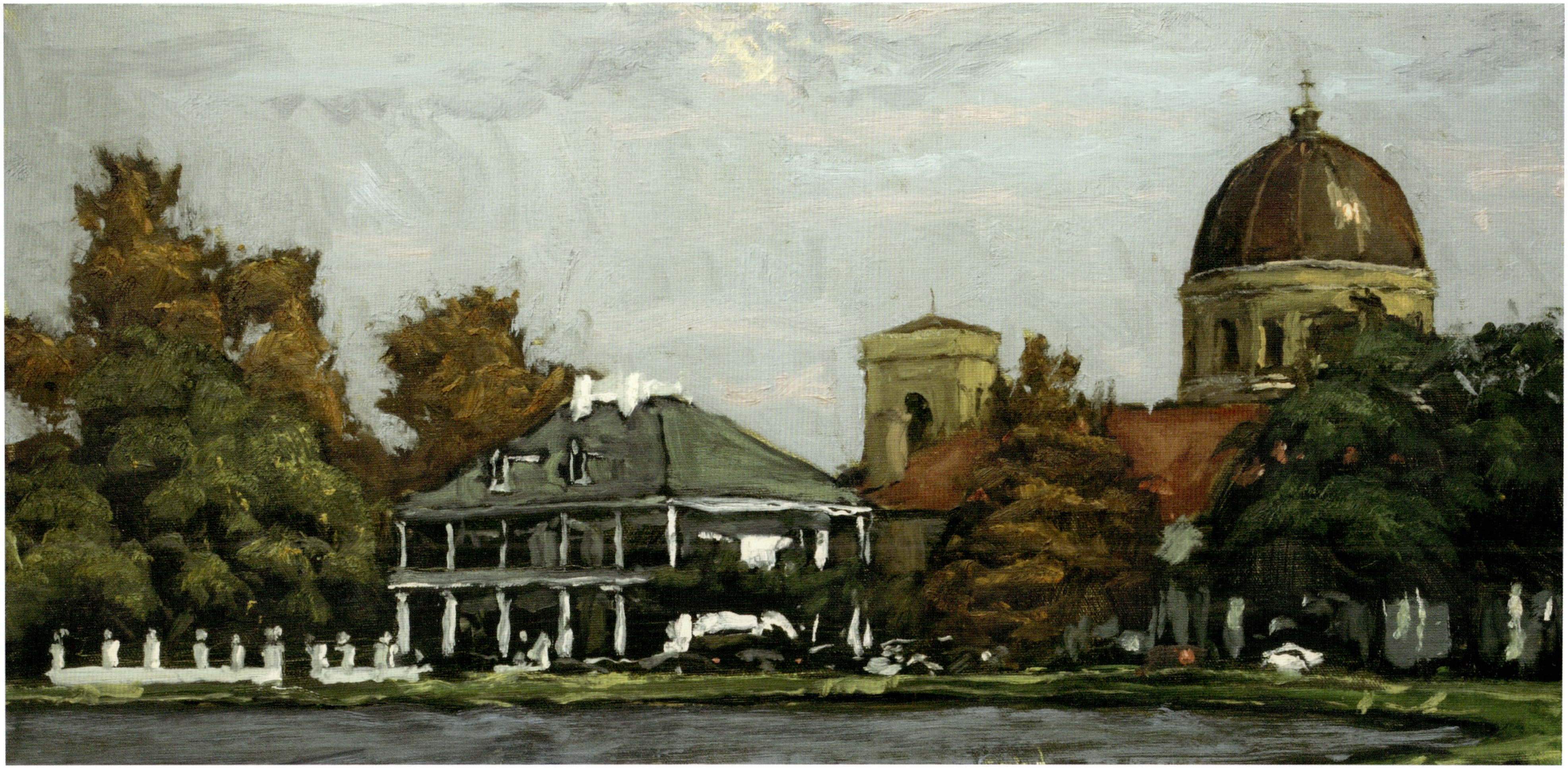

MONTESSORI SCHOOL AND OUR LADY OF THE ROSARY CHURCH 12" x 24"

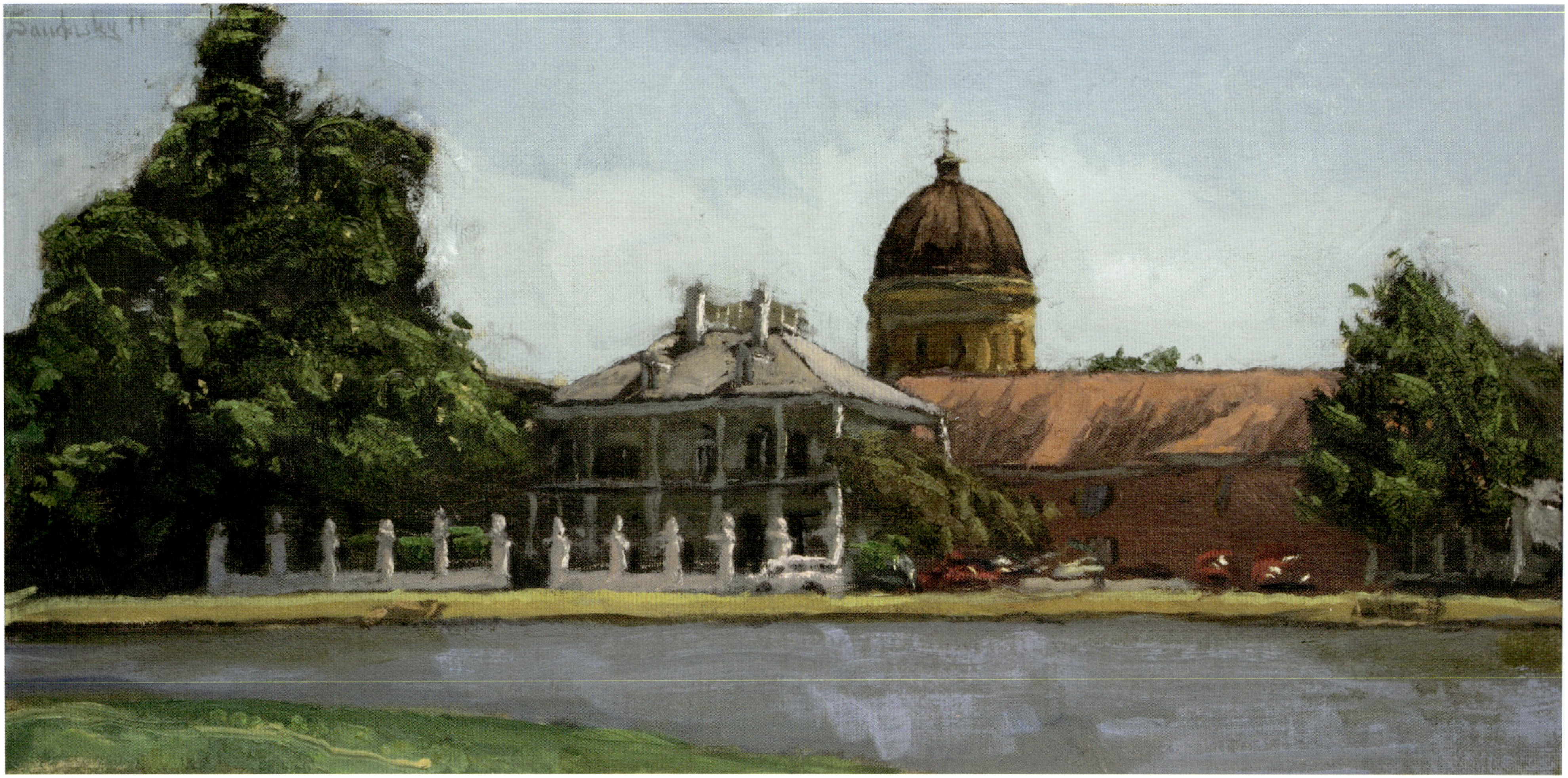

MONTESSORI SCHOOL AND OUR LADY OF THE ROSARY CHURCH, LATE SPRING 2011 10" X 20"

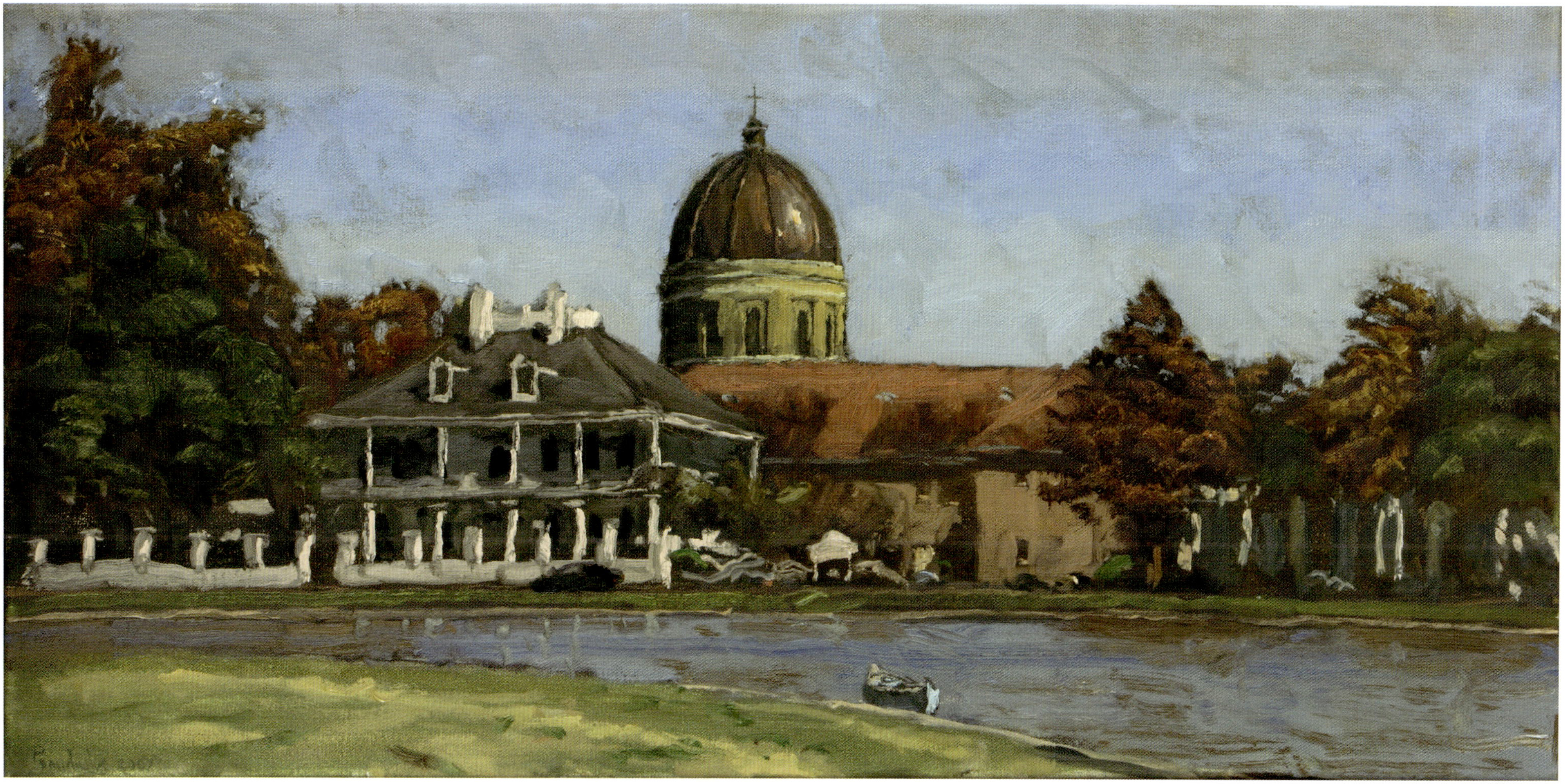

MONTESSORI SCHOOL AND OUR LADY OF THE ROSARY CHURCH, LATE FALL 2007 15" X 30"

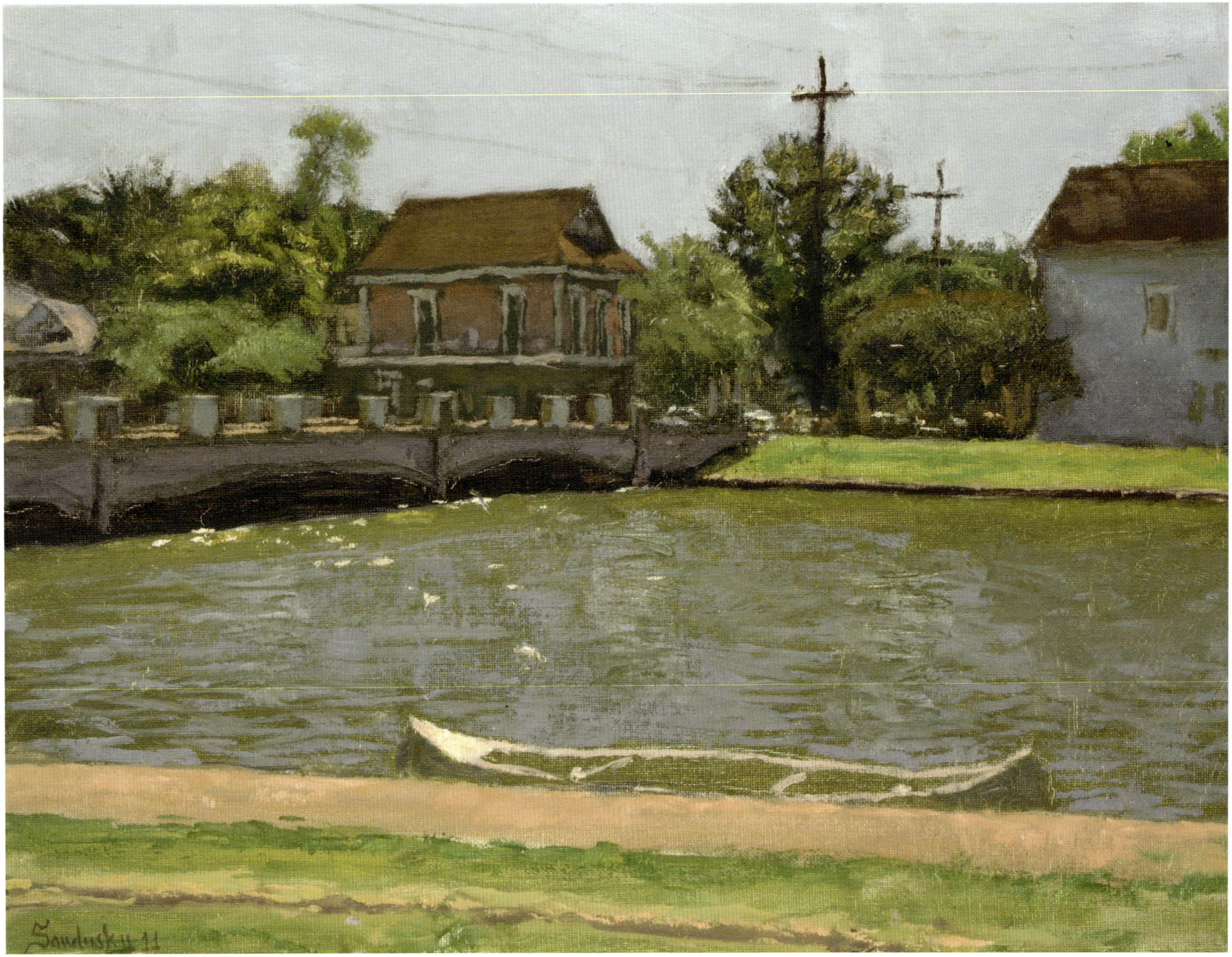

Dumaine Street Bridge 14" x 18"

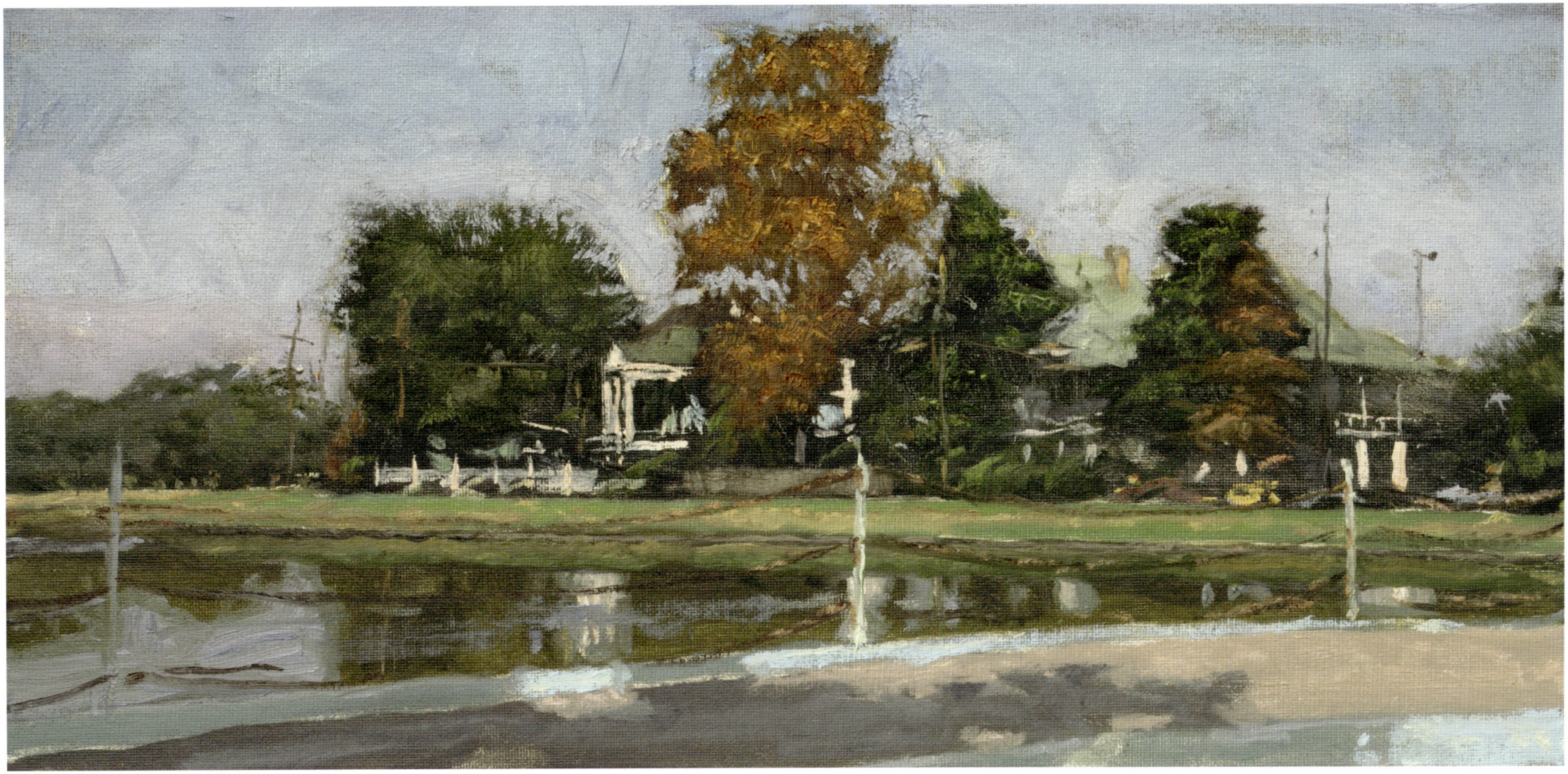

Pitot House seen from Moss Street at Harding Drive 10" x 20"

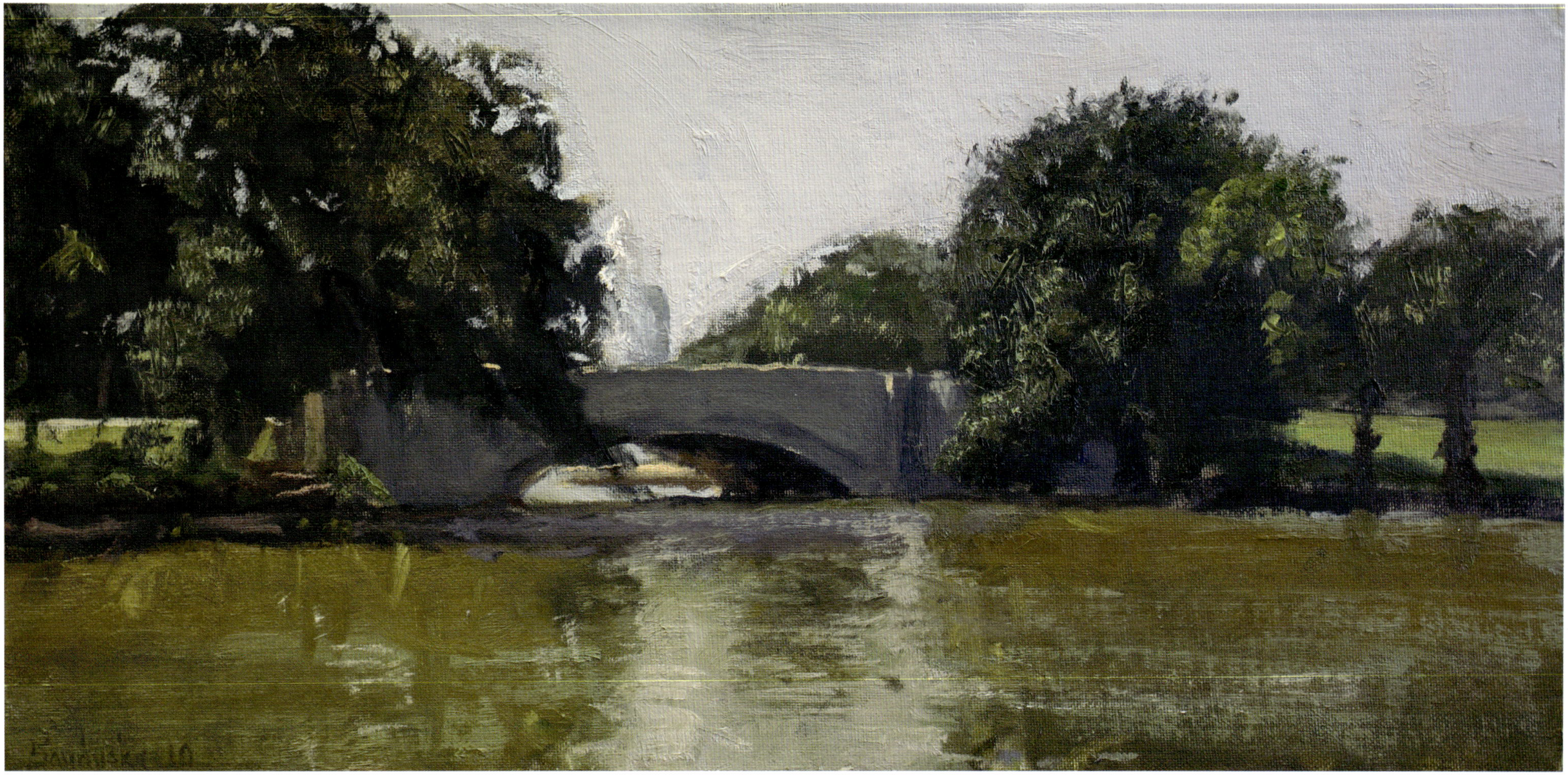

Enrique Alferez Drive bridge in City Park 10" x 20"

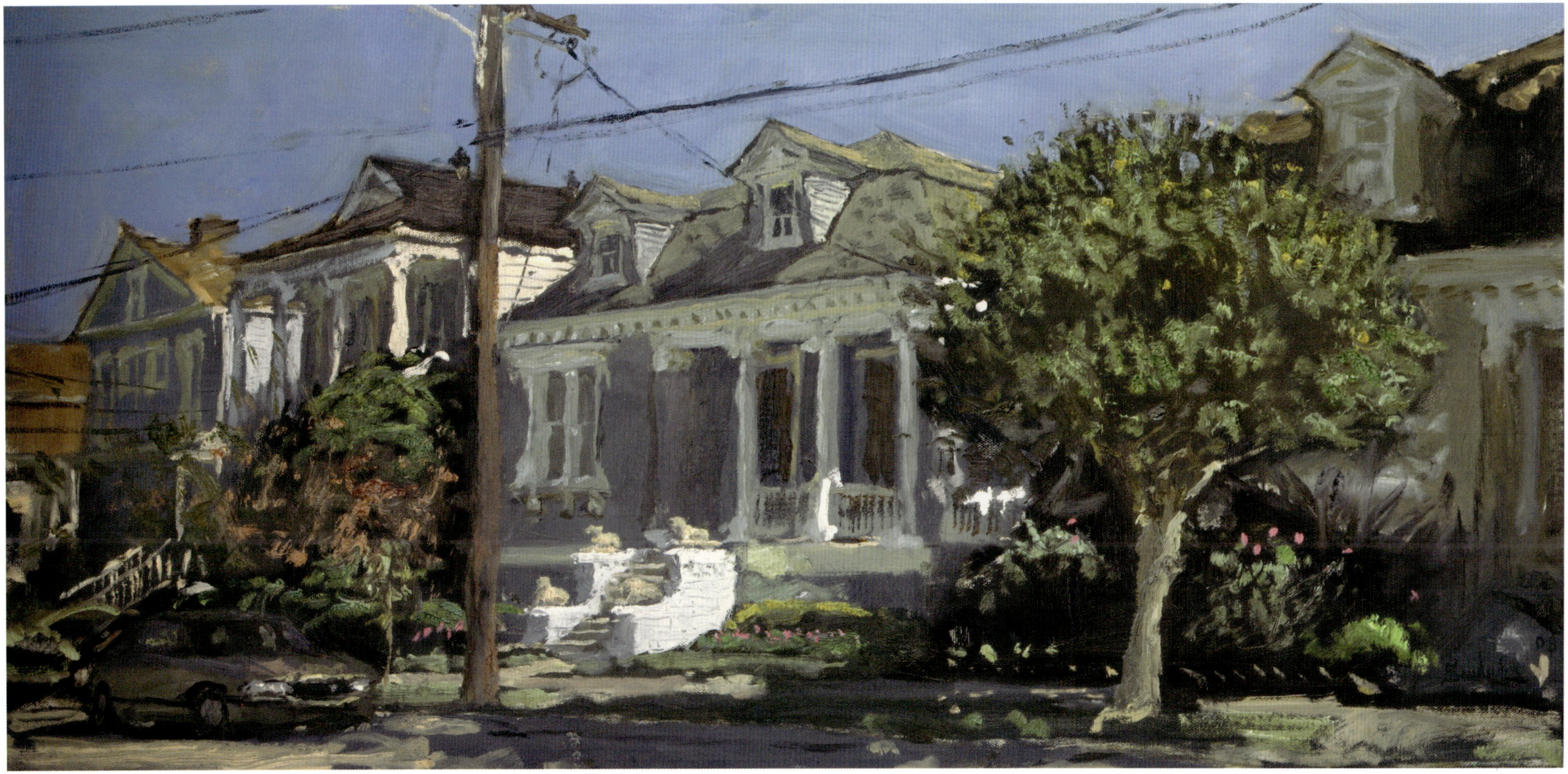

HOUSES ON GENERAL PERSHING STREET NEAR CARONDELET STREET 15" X 30"

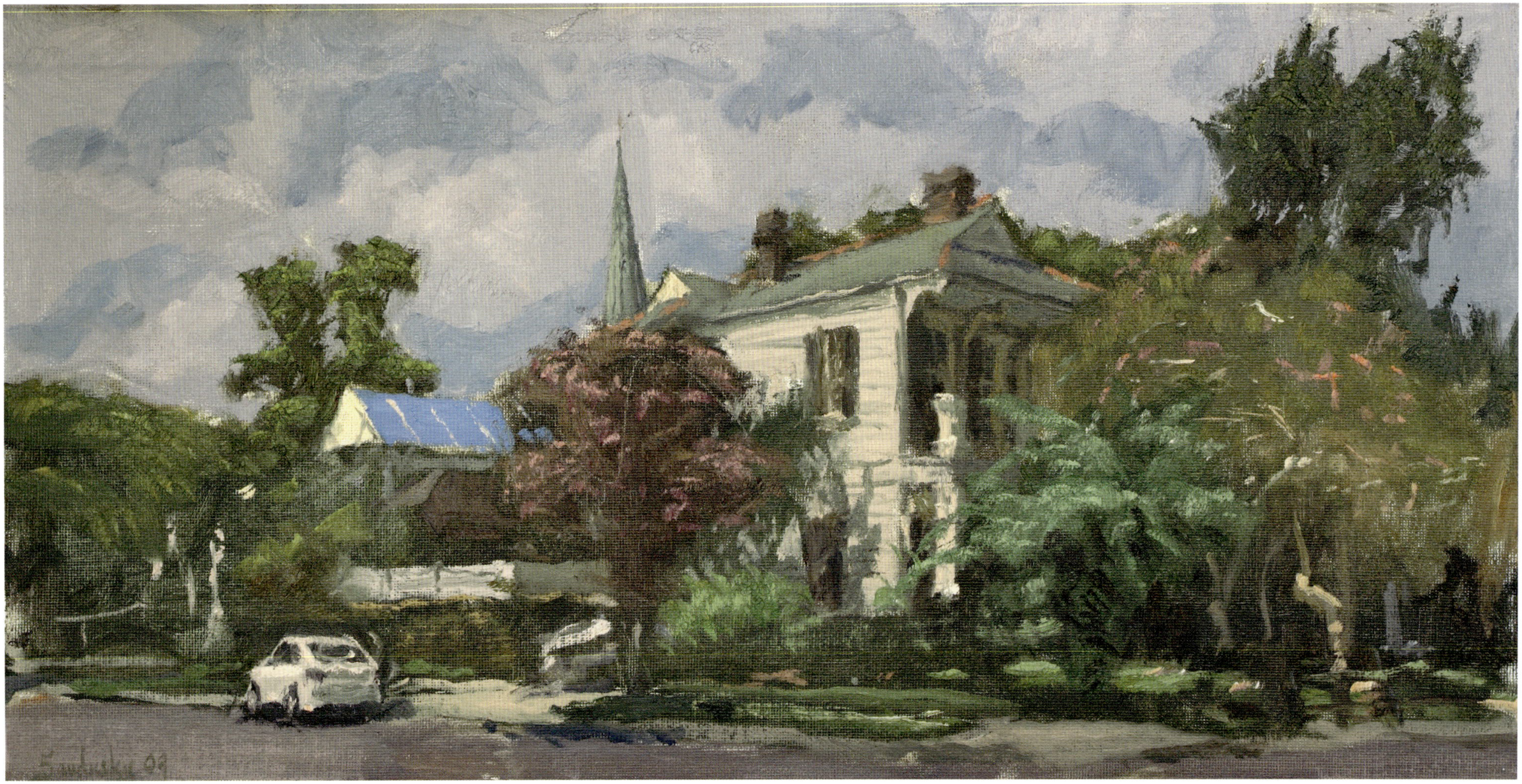

View from the corner of General Pershing and Coliseum streets 10" x 20"

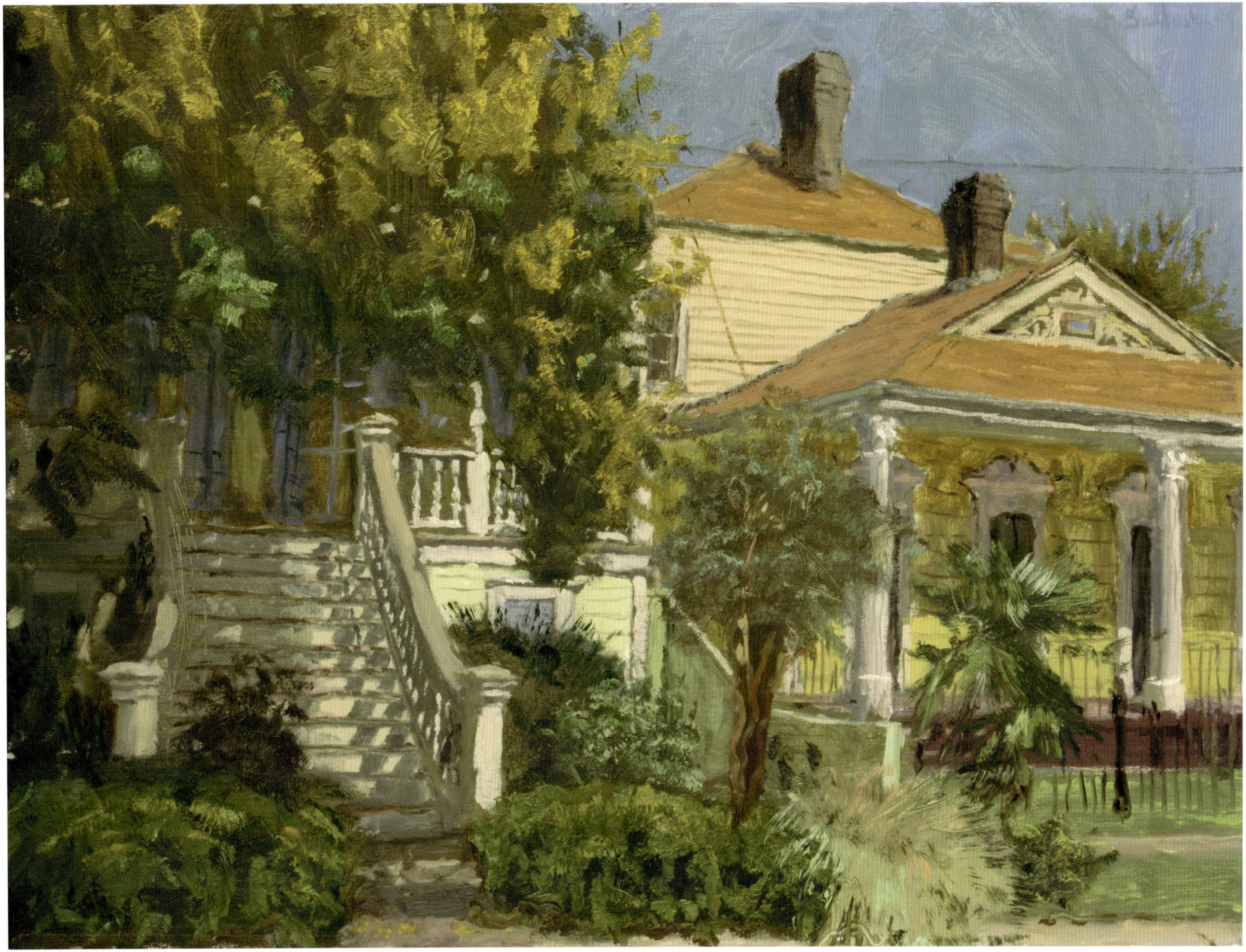

Golden rain tree on Chestnut Street near General Taylor Street 18" x 24"

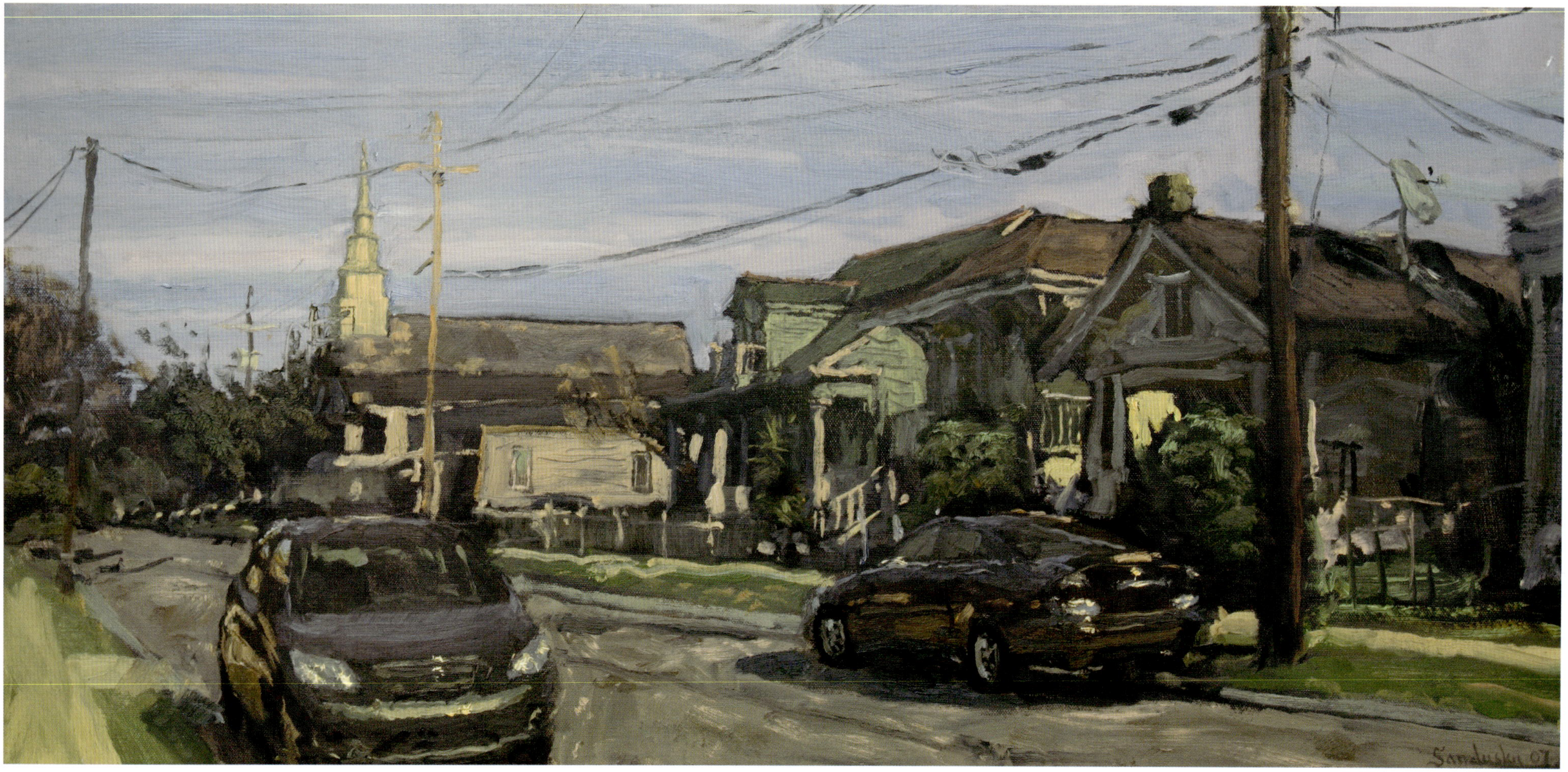

Looking down Austerlitz Street from a position between Constance and Laurel streets 15" x 30"

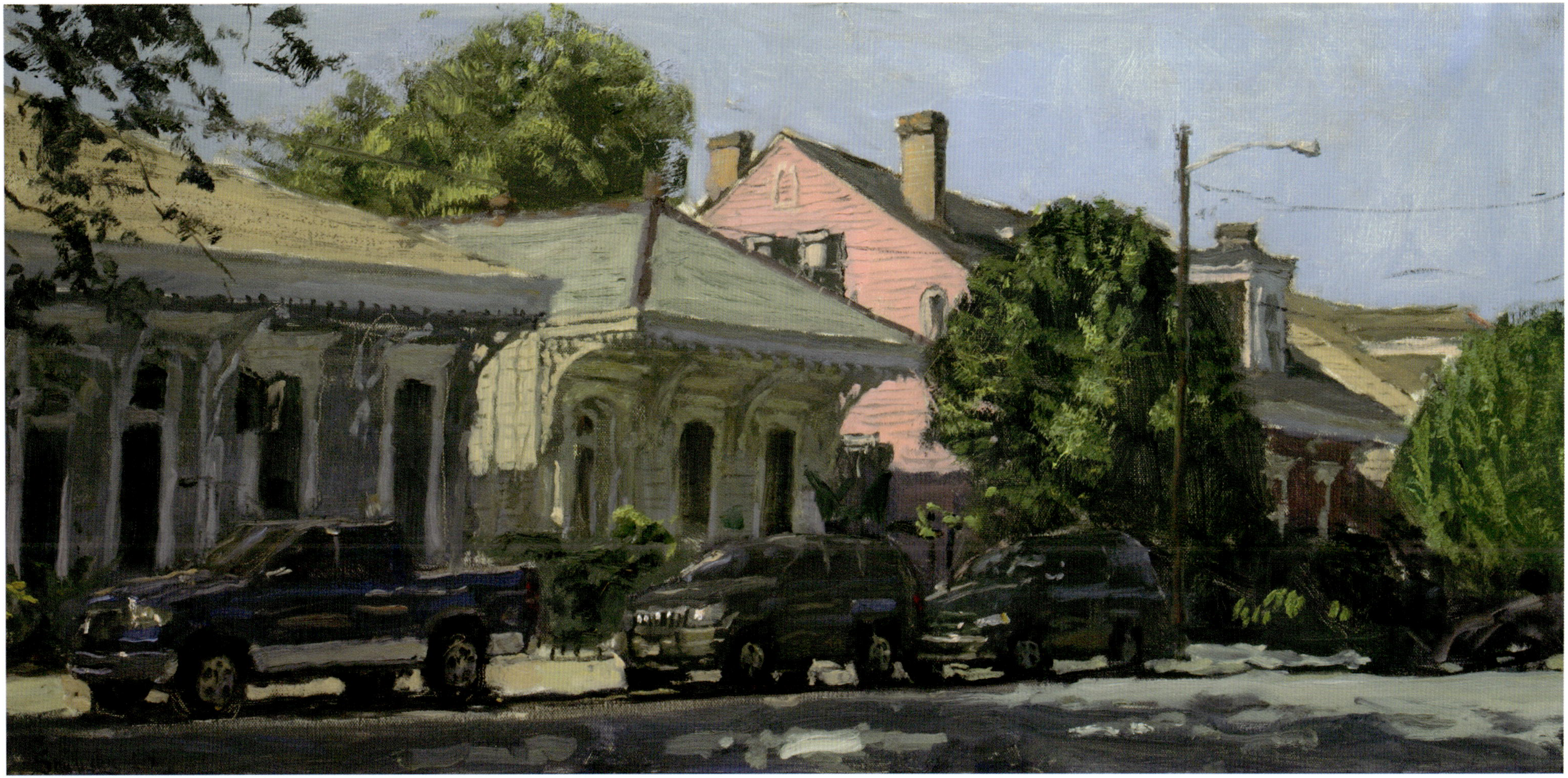

Houses on Harmony Street near Chestnut Street seen from the Ninth Street and Harmony split 15" x 30"

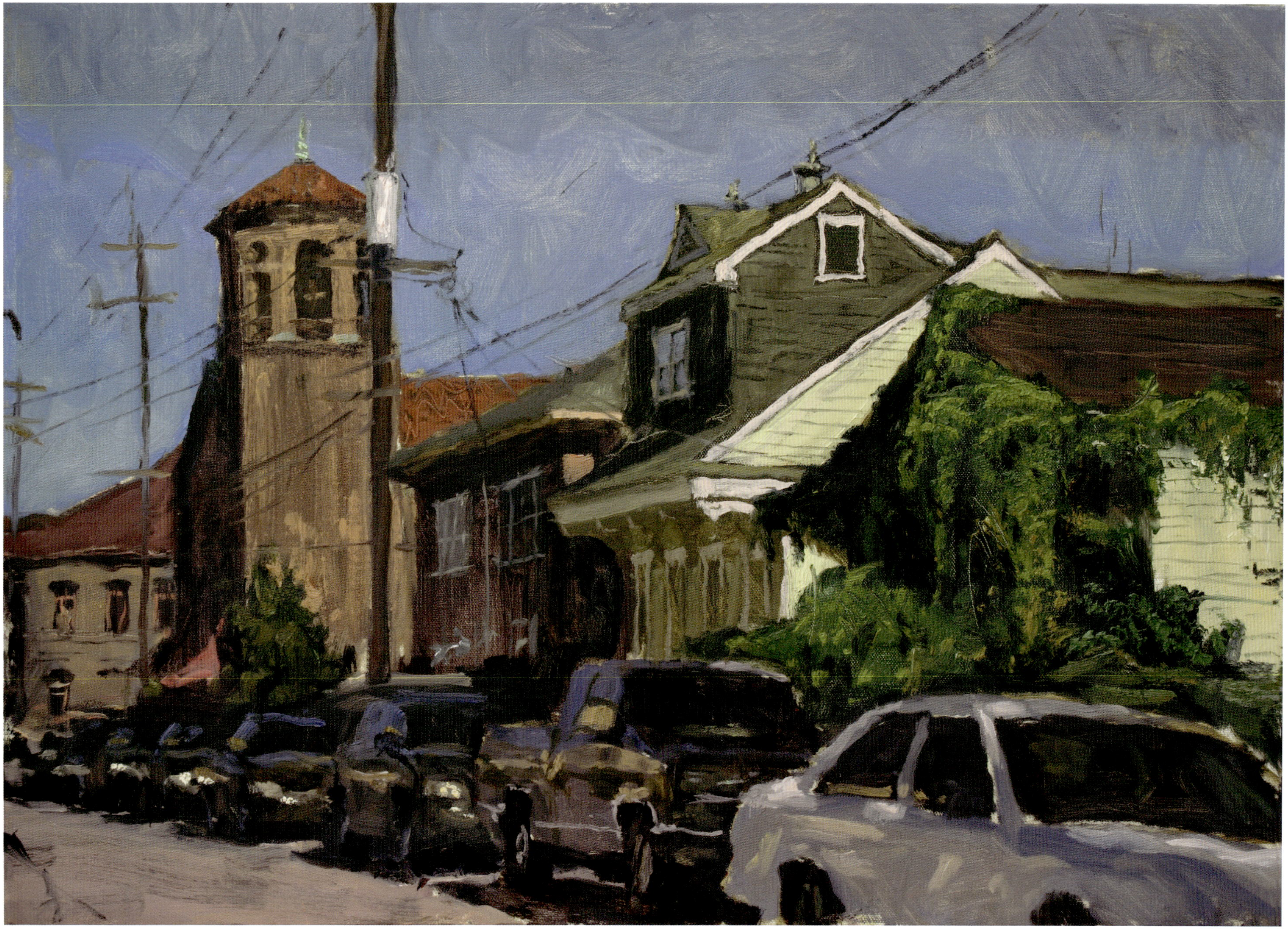

St. Henry's Catholic Church seen from General Pershing Street close to Laurel Street 18" x 24"

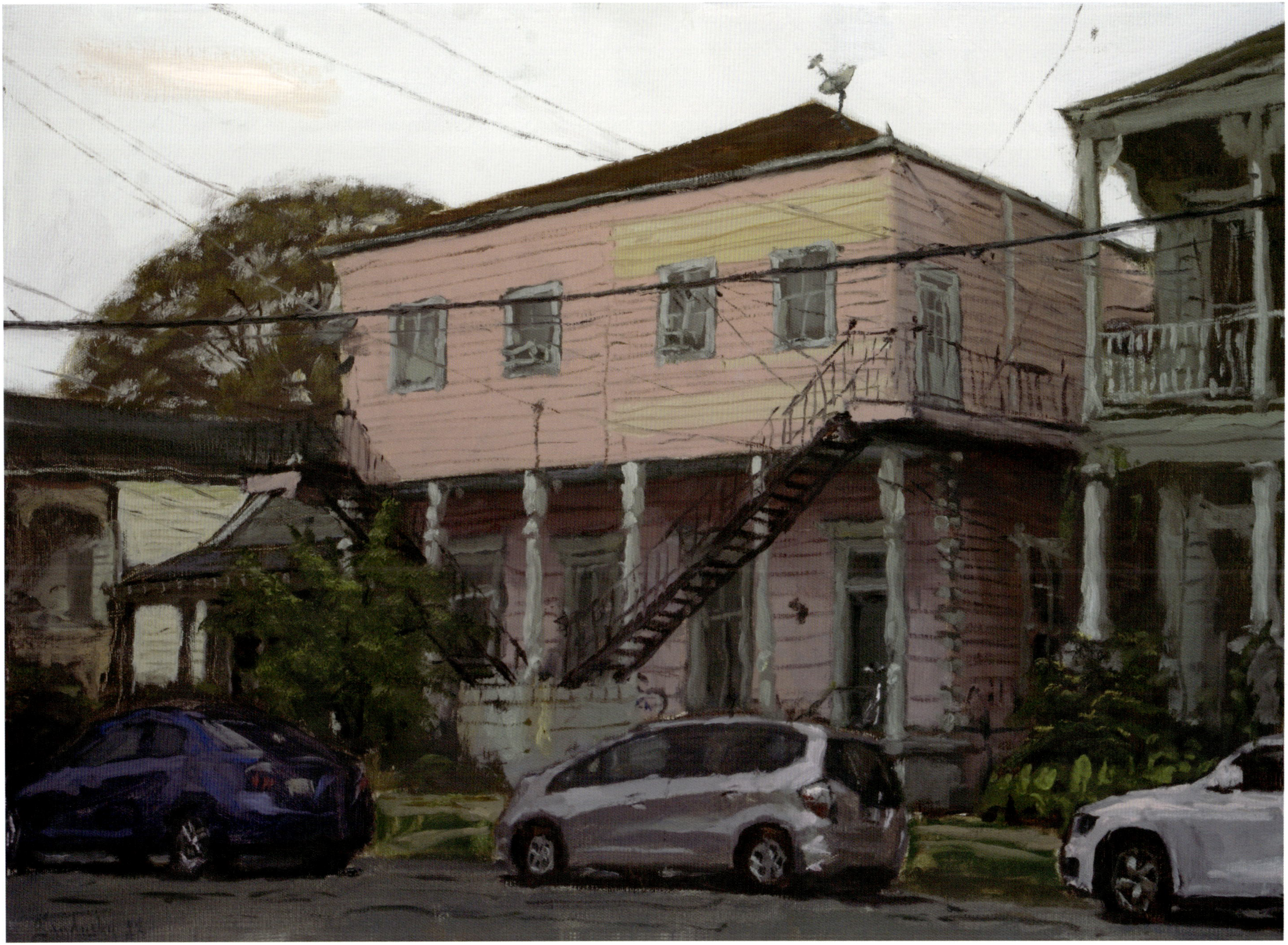

Apartments seen from Camp and Upperline streets 18" x 24"

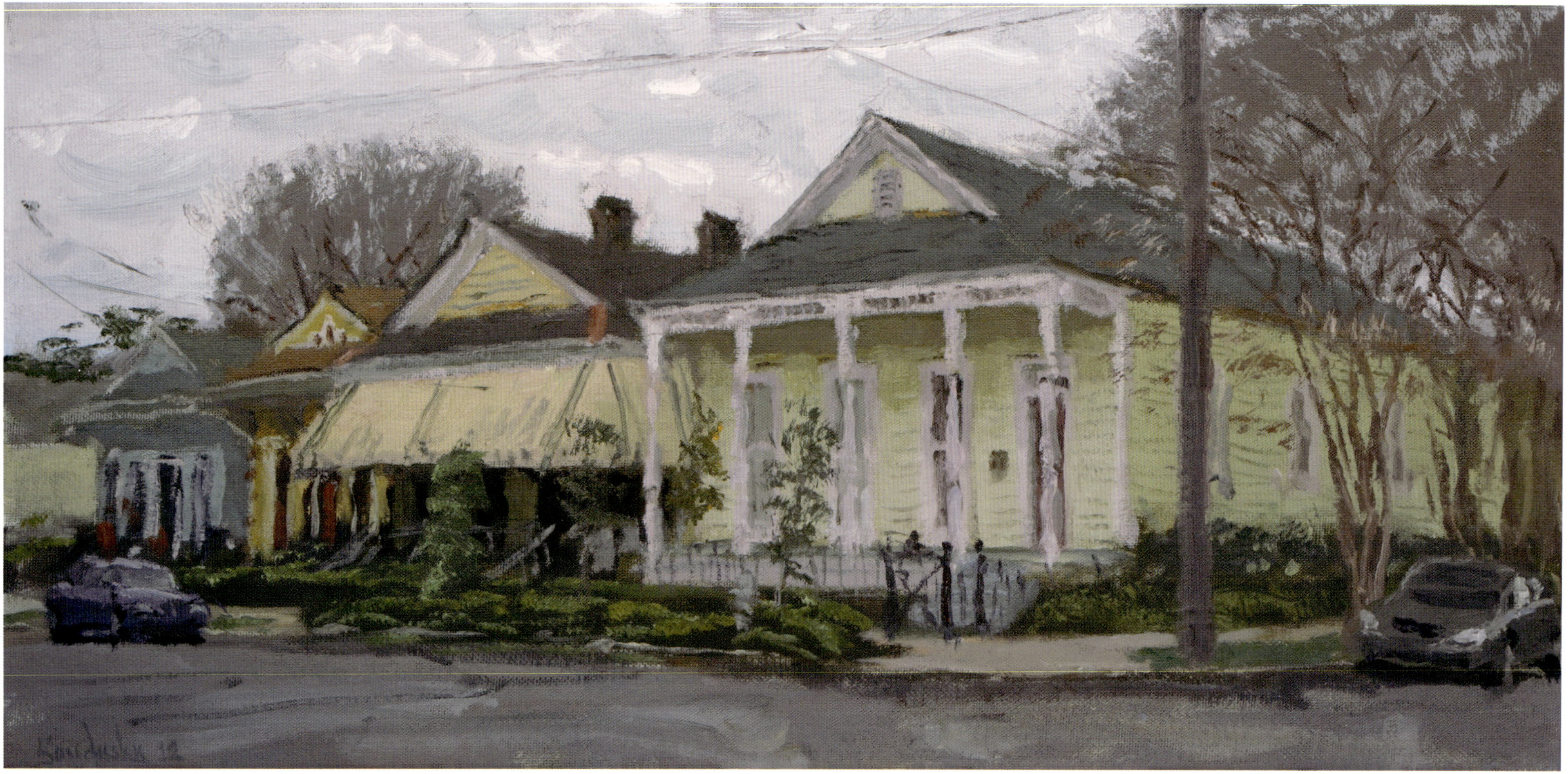

HOUSES AT WEBSTER AND LAUREL STREETS (OVERCAST) 10" X 20"

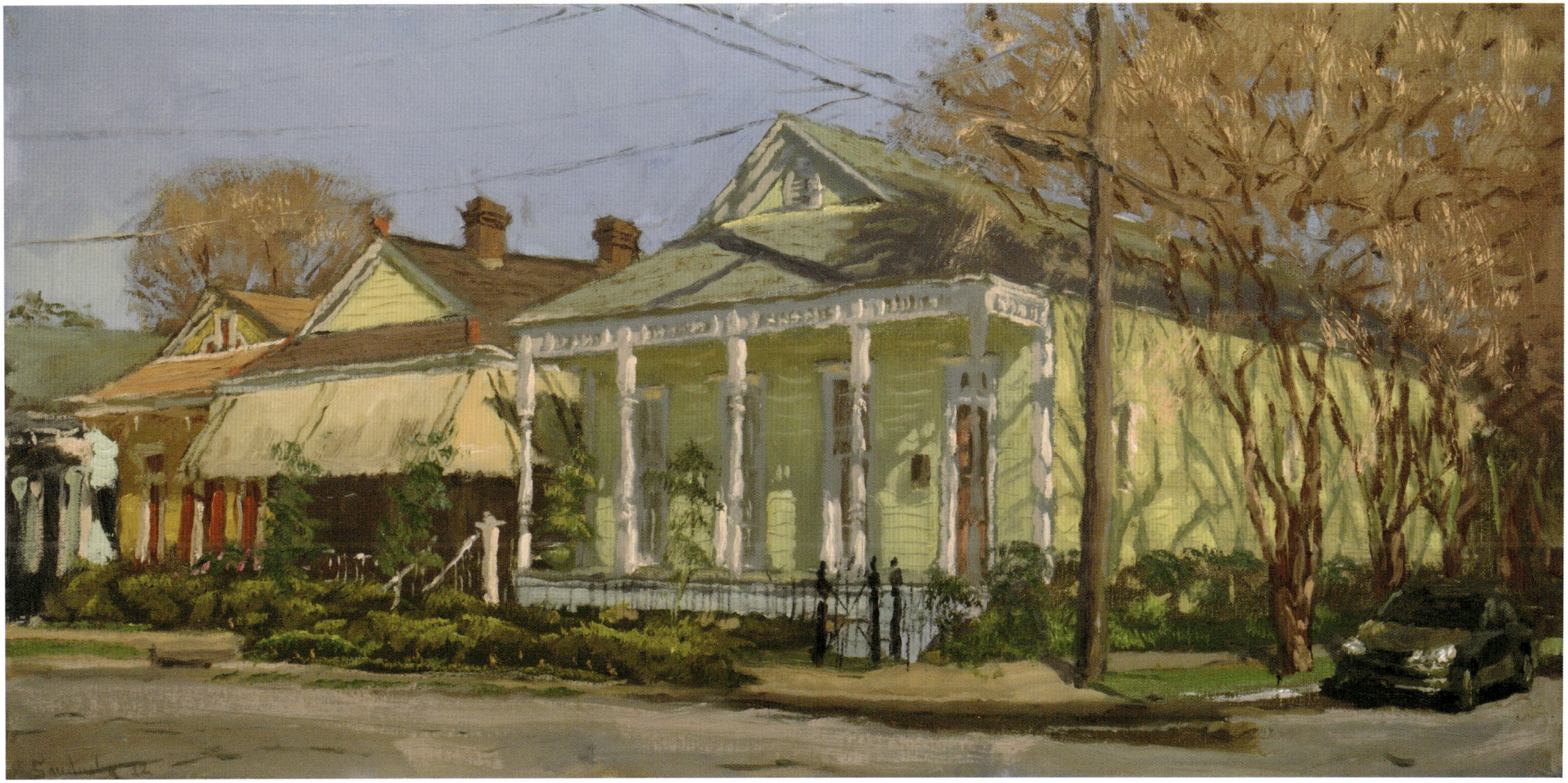

Houses at Webster and Laurel streets (sunny) 15" x 30"

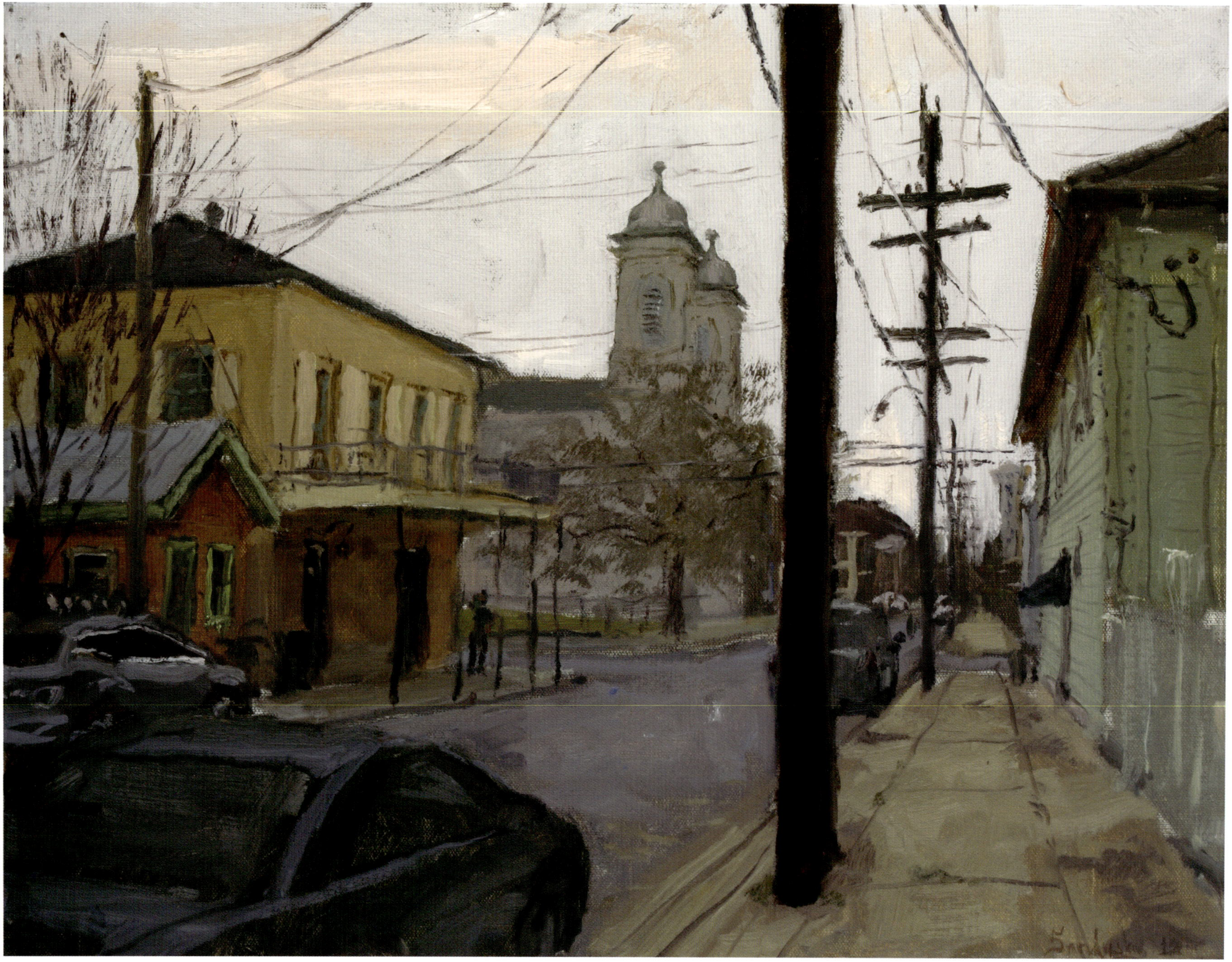

St. Ferdinand Street close to Dauphine Street 16" x 20"

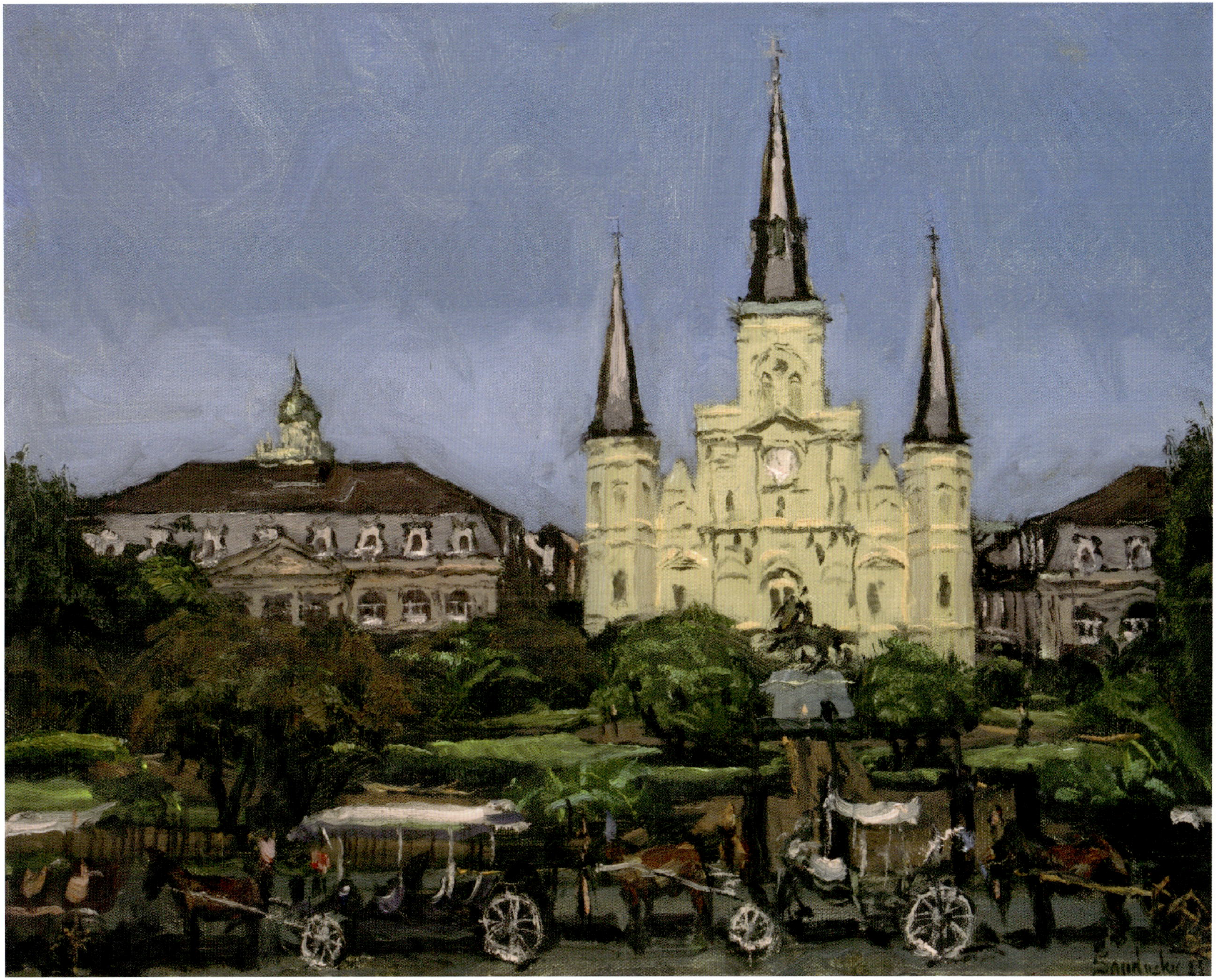

St. Louis Cathedral and Jackson Square 16" x 20"

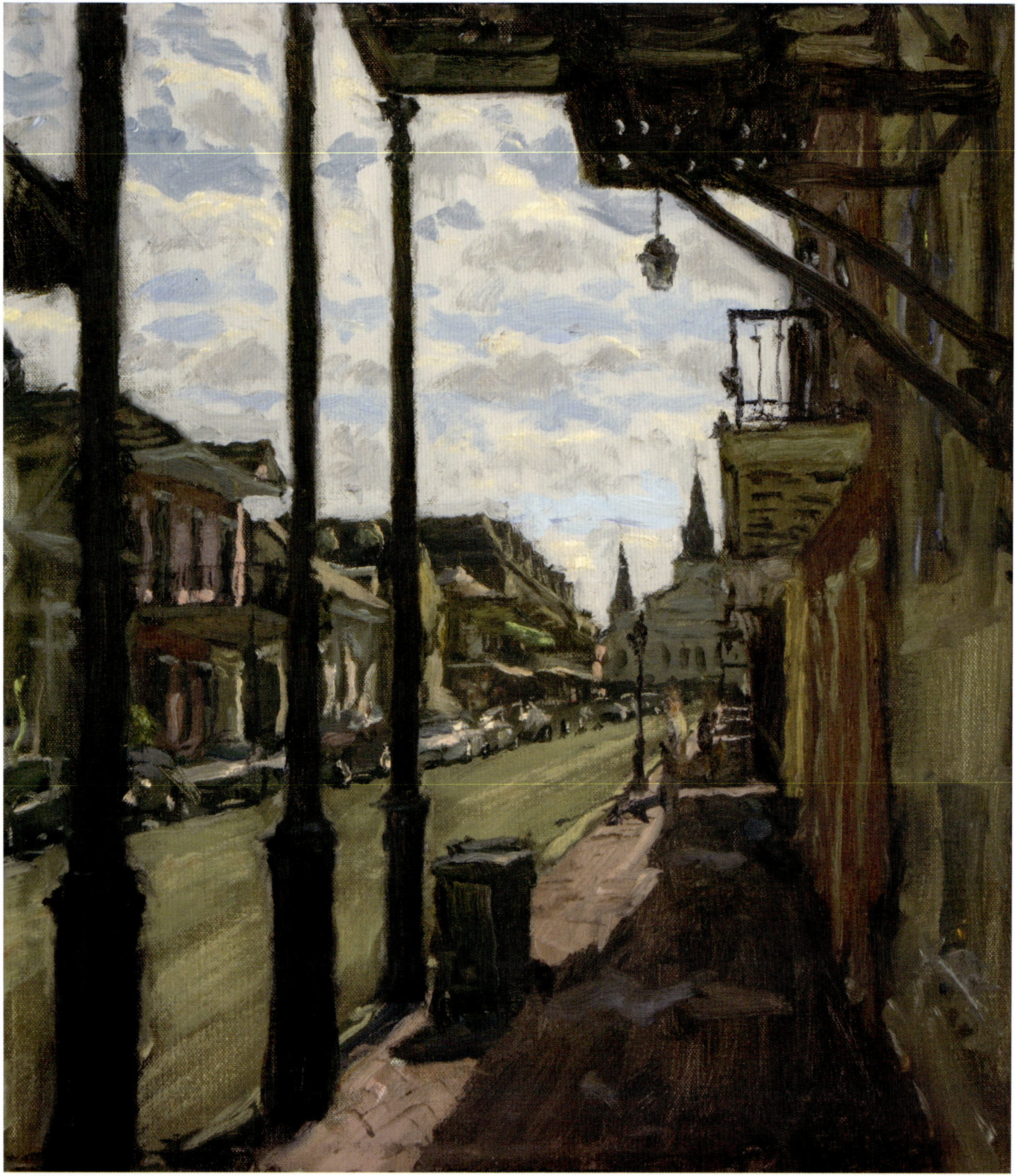

LOOKING DOWN ORLEANS STREET FROM DAUPHINE STREET WITH THE BACK OF ST. LOUIS CATHEDRAL SEEN IN THE DISTANCE 20" X 16"